MW01074157

AGELESS
BRAIN

The Drug-Free Way
to Cut Your Alzheimer's Risk IN HALF
and Stay Healthy FOR LIFE!

AGELESS
BRAIN

FROM THE **EDITORS** OF **Prevention**.
WITH JULIA VANTINE

This book is intended as a reference volume only, not as a medical manual. The information given here is designed to help you make informed decisions about your health. It is not intended as a substitute for any treatment that may have been prescribed by your doctor. If you suspect that you have a medical problem, we urge you to seek competent medical help.

Mention of specific companies, organizations, or authorities in this book does not imply endorsement by the author or publisher, nor does mention of specific companies, organizations, or authorities imply that they endorse this book, its author, or the publisher.

Internet addresses and telephone numbers given in this book were accurate at the time it went to press.

© 2017 by Rodale Inc.

All rights reserved. No part of this publication may be reproduced or transmitted in any form or by any means, electronic or mechanical, including photocopying, recording, or any other information storage and retrieval system, without the written permission of the publisher.

Prevention® is a registered trademark of Rodale Inc.

Printed in the United States of America

Rodale Inc. makes every effort to use acid-free ∞, recycled paper ♻.

Photographs by Mitch Mandel/Rodale Images

Library of Congress Cataloging-in-Publication Data is on file with the publisher.

ISBN 978-1-62336-850-0

2   4   6   8   10   9   7   5   3   1   hardcover

We inspire health, healing, happiness, and love in the world.
Starting with you.

For everyone who worries about their memory
and wants the peace of mind of knowing they are doing all they can.

CONTENTS

PART 1: YOUR AMAZING BRAIN

1

PUT ALZHEIMER'S ON THE RUN! • 3

2

AN AGELESS BRAIN FOR LIFE • 19

3

ARE YOU LIVING A BRAIN-HEALTHY LIFESTYLE? • 41

PART 2: STAY-SHARP BASICS

4

THE 10 COMMANDMENTS OF AN AGELESS BRAIN • 63

PART 3: STAY SHARP!

5

SAVOR BRAIN-BOOSTING FOODS • 99

6

HIT THE WALKING TRAIL OR GYM • 133

7

ADJUST YOUR ATTITUDE • 155

8

REDUCE BRAIN-SHRINKING STRESS • 175

9

PRESERVE YOUR WITS WITH PLAY • 201

10

BRAIN-HEALTHY MEALS • 223

APPENDIX: THE AGELESS BRAIN STRENGTH-TRAINING WORKOUT • 277

ENDNOTES • 299

INDEX • 331

PART 1

YOUR

AMAZING

BRAIN

Put Alzheimer's on the Run!

IF YOU'RE OLD ENOUGH to remember landline telephones (or even party lines), there's a good chance you've walked into a room and couldn't remember why. Or found your misplaced keys in a strange place, like the refrigerator. Or experienced those maddening tip-of-the-tongue situations. These minor episodes of forgetfulness are so common—and often humorous—that they have an affectionate nickname: "senior moments."

Once you hit middle age, it's normal for the brain to backfire every now and again.[1] But if you find these momentary lapses worrisome, you're not alone. A recent survey found that we fear Alzheimer's disease (AD) more than cancer.[2] That's no surprise. Every 66 seconds,[3] an American is diagnosed with this progressive brain disease that robs sufferers of more than memories. Over time, it steals their ability to live independently and erases their very identities. You may even have a friend, parent, or relative who's battling the disease.

There's no denying that Alzheimer's and other age-related dementias are scary. But there's every reason for hope: Recent research offers compelling evidence that you *can* strike a blow against them, and it's as simple as making healthy changes. In 2015, the Alzheimer's Association evaluated more than 150 studies that examined the links between cognitive decline and lifestyle factors such as diet, exercise, and sleep. The association's mind-blowing conclusion: "The public should know what the science concludes: certain healthy behaviors known to be effective for diabetes, cardiovascular disease, and cancer are also good for brain health and for reducing the risk of cognitive decline." That means more greens and grains and less white flour, sugar, and animal fat. More moving, less sitting. More sleep, less stress. More mental challenge, less channel-surfing. You have more control over your brain health than you may have ever thought possible.[4]

So, take heart—then take action. As the search for an Alzheimer's cure continues, this book reveals the simple actions you can take *today* to sharpen your memory and thinking now and in the years to come. It's chock-full of the most effective tips out there, all supported by the most current and credible research, organized into digestible chunks that will be easy for you to read through and understand. And it's never too early, or late, to start incorporating this knowledge into your life. So take a breath. We've assessed and translated the findings of scores of studies so we could bring you the ultimate guide to staving off and fighting Alzheimer's. You're about to get the very latest, science-backed lowdown on how to maintain and sustain your brain.

LEARN THE FACTS, LOSE THE FEAR

There are three primary risk factors for Alzheimer's. The first is age—nearly one in three people over the age of 85 develop it.[5] The other two

Three Weird but True Alzheimer's Triggers

Ninety percent of what is known about Alzheimer's disease has been discovered in the past 15 years[6]—and researchers have come across some surprising potential triggers. To be clear, no study has yet conclusively identified the cause of Alzheimer's disease. However, the three factors below are believed to play a role. Consider this list a heads-up. You'll get the details of the research, plus simple but effective solutions, later in the book.

A long-banned pesticide. Remember the insecticide DDT? The United States hasn't used it for almost 50 years, but it's still in the environment. And higher blood levels of a DDT-breakdown product, called DDE, seemed to raise the risk of developing Alzheimer's.[7]

Common medications. Several prescription and over-the-counter drugs—including a class of medications commonly prescribed to treat ulcers—have been linked to Alzheimer's and other forms of dementia.[8]

Emotional problems. Sadness, loneliness, worry, or boredom can cause confusion and forgetfulness.[9] So can major depression.[10] The good news: Evidence suggests seeking treatment for symptoms of major depression may help protect against dementia.

are a family history of the disease and a handful of extremely rare, hereditary genes[11] (see sidebar on page 14). Although you can't change these factors, consider this: Having the risk factors *does not mean* a person will definitely develop the disease.

Equally important: When it comes to Alzheimer's, there's compelling evidence that prevention is the first and best line of defense. Study after study suggests that healthy lifestyle choices help keep the disease at bay and may prevent or delay the onset of mild cognitive impairment (MCI), the form of memory loss that has been found to increase the risk of developing full-blown Alzheimer's.

For example, consider the findings of one landmark study conducted on over 1,200 older people in Finland. Researchers randomly assigned their participants, who were between 60 and 77 years old, to one of two groups. For 2 years, one group ate a diet of whole, natural foods, exercised at least three times a week, and received 30 to 45 minutes of computer-based brain training a week. (The findings on computerized exercises to promote cognitive health hold promise but are far from conclusive. See page 13 to learn the facts about those online subscription-based programs.) Health conditions associated with a higher risk of dementia, such as diabetes or high blood pressure, were monitored. The control group received health advice, and that's it.[12]

Two years later, the lifestyle group scored 25 percent higher overall on a battery of thinking and memory tests compared to the control group. On some tests, this group's scores were astonishing. For example, compared to the control group, it scored 150 percent higher in mental processing speed (how quickly the brain takes in and responds to information) and 83 percent higher in executive function (the ability to plan, organize, and focus on details).

These findings, and others, can help you move past the fear that surrounds Alzheimer's and other types of dementia. Worry won't help (in fact, research suggests it may increase the risk of Alzheimer's!). Action will. You can use the research findings in the book to design your personal anti-Alzheimer's action plan.

FOUR ALZHEIMER'S MYTHS TO FORGET

Chapter 2 lays out everything you need to know about Alzheimer's and other age-related dementias. For now, it's enough to know that the aging process affects the brain just as it affects other parts of your body. The changes of *cognitive aging*[13] are normal, come on gradually, and vary widely from person to person, but are distinct from Alzheimer's. So let's clear up some common misconceptions.

Fallacy: As we grow older, memory is the most important aspect of a sharp, healthy brain.

Fact: A keen memory is an important part of brain health, but it isn't the only one. Good cognitive health also includes the ability to solve problems, make decisions, and pay focused attention.

Fallacy: Alzheimer's is at the root of all age-related memory problems.

Fact: While Alzheimer's is the most common cause of memory problems, it is just one of many. Diseases that affect the brain, such as Parkinson's disease, strokes, or multiple sclerosis, can also affect memory. But as you'll learn, so can diabetes, thyroid disease, vitamin deficiencies, and some prescription and over-the-counter medications.[14]

Fallacy: Age-related changes in thinking and memory aren't normal.

Fact: Cognitive aging occurs in everyone. What's not normal is *dementia,* characterized by declines in cognitive abilities that affect the ability to perform day-to-day tasks. Alzheimer's is the most common form of dementia. It progressively destroys cognitive function and the mental processes that include thinking, knowing, judging, and reasoning,[15] and it begins well before symptoms like memory loss show up. The hallmark physical characteristics of a brain with Alzheimer's are the progressive accumulation of *plaques* (a protein fragment called

What to Expect from an Ageless Brain

Although it's unlikely you'll reclaim the mental sharpness of your 25-year-old brain, that doesn't mean you're destined to lose your marbles, either. Some cognitive abilities decline with age, some don't.[16]

Memory. The ability to remember events that happened years ago, called remote memory, is relatively preserved in older brains. (That's why you may remember exactly where you were when you heard the news of Elvis Presley's death.) However, the ability to recall information from minutes, hours, or days ago, called recent memory, typically declines. (Short-term memory seems to improve until around age 25, level off for several years, and then drop starting at around age 35.)[17]

Reasoning and problem solving. An older brain typically maintains its time-tested ways of using logic and solving problems. Problems it's never encountered—for example, learning how to send a text on a cell phone—may take longer to figure out.

Processing speed. Aging

beta-amyloid) outside neurons in the brain and *tangles* (twisted strands of a protein called tau) inside neurons. These changes eventually damage and kill neurons. You'll learn more about them in later chapters.

Fallacy: Only children's brains produce new brain cells to help build the *neural circuits* that act as information highways between different areas of the brain.

Fact: Scientists have discovered that the adult brain continually generates new nerve cells, a process known as *neurogenesis*. One of the most active areas of neurogenesis in the brain, the hippocampus, plays a key role in memory and learning.[19]

The bottom line: Your brain ages along with the rest of you. But just

affects the speed with which the brain performs cognitive and motor processes. So while it may take a healthy older brain longer to arrive at a solution or perform a task, it still can.

Attention. Increasing age causes few changes in focused attention, such as the ability to follow a TV show. Harder to preserve, however, is divided attention—say, trying to watch that show and talk on the phone at the same time.

Intelligence. The ability to use knowledge and experience accumulated over a lifetime, called crystalized intelligence, typically doesn't change with age. However, the ability to solve new problems or use logic in new situations (called fluid intelligence) tends to decline.

Language. Verbal abilities such as vocabulary stick around as we age. But as you already may know, tip-of-the-tongue moments are common. (One theory suggests that the links connecting one unit to another in the memory system get wonky as we get older. This deterioration causes "transmission deficits" that make it harder for aging brains to generate words, particularly people's names.)[18]

as it's possible to build stronger muscles at any age, there's plenty you can do to help keep your mind and memory in top shape. It's all here in these pages.

TEACH YOUR OLDER BRAIN NEW TRICKS

Along with a nutritious diet, regular exercise, and sufficient good-quality sleep, an ageless brain needs mental stimulation, which it gets from regular interaction with other people, learning new things and being open to new ideas, and exploring the big, beautiful world. Here's what the research shows.

Why Women Need the Ageless Brain Advantage

An estimated 5.1 million Americans 65 and older have Alzheimer's disease and other types of age-related dementias—and 3.3 million are women. Why do women account for almost two-thirds of all cases?[20]

Researchers don't yet know, but they have some theories. The most common one: Women live longer than men on average, and older age is the greatest risk factor for Alzheimer's. But recent research suggests that this is likely not the whole story.

Women may be genetically vulnerable. Stanford University researchers looked at medical data from over 8,000 older people to see who carried the APOE-e4 gene—which plays a role in an estimated 20 to 25 percent of late-onset Alzheimer's cases—and who went on to develop Alzheimer's. The team also tracked who developed mild cognitive impairment.

Men who carried the gene were a bit more likely to develop Alzheimer's, but women who had it were almost twice as likely to develop mild cognitive impairment (MCI) or Alzheimer's during the study as those who didn't,[21] which suggests an interaction between APOE-e4 and the female sex hormone estrogen.[22]

● ***Being socially active boosts brain function!*** Do you have at least a few people in your life you can talk to, have fun with, and turn to when life gets tough? While there's no need to be (or become) a party animal to sustain your brain, research associates social activities, larger social networks, and social contact with better thinking and memory function and reduced risk for cognitive decline.

On the one hand, estrogen appears to reduce the accumulation of amyloid proteins in the brain, so its sharp decline after menopause might increase women's risk of Alzheimer's. On the other, taking estrogen after menopause has been found to raise women's risk of cognitive problems. It may be that estrogen use in the early years of menopause protects the brain, while taking it later causes harm.[23]

Gender differences in education and career options. A half century ago, compared to men, women had fewer opportunities to pursue higher education and hold jobs that challenged their brains, both of which have been shown to protect against dementia.[24]

Gender differences in heart health. Compared to women in midlife, men in middle age have a higher rate of death from cardiovascular disease. So it may be that men who live beyond age 65 may be in better cardiovascular health, and thus at a lower risk for dementia, than women of the same age.

The bottom line: Although Alzheimer's is an equal-opportunity disease, it's especially critical for women to protect their brain health. Fortunately, this book offers plenty of simple ways to take control—all backed by the latest and best research available.

● *To stay sharp, stay classy!* A high level of schooling consistently is linked to a reduced risk of Alzheimer's. Whether you take up a musical instrument or a second (or third) language or learn more about a subject you've always been interested in, formal education at any age has been found to help reduce risk of cognitive decline and dementia. That's a great reason to sign up for a class at your local college or community center or online.

● *Challenging your brain keeps it youthfully plump!* In one study, researchers asked over 300 middle-aged people how often they played cards or board games or put together puzzles.

Compared to participants who rarely or never broke out the games and puzzles, those who did at least every other day had greater volume in several brain regions known to be damaged by Alzheimer's, including the hippocampus. The game players also got higher scores on cognitive tests.[25]

THE BREAKTHROUGH SCIENCE OF LIVING SHARP

This book clues you in to the simple lifestyle habits associated with keen thinking and memory. These habits are based on five pillars of brain health, and the first letter of each pillar spells out the word SHARP.

Savor Brain-Boosting Foods. Meal by healthy meal, you can protect your brain against Alzheimer's. That's because certain foods contain vitamins, minerals, and other nutrients shown in studies to preserve memory and reduce the risk of dementia. The Mediterranean-DASH Intervention for Neurodegenerative Delay study (or MIND, for short) identified nine foods that should make regular appearances on your plate and five foods to cut back on. Chapter 5 reveals them all, along with how to pick, store, and prepare the all-stars to maximize their brain-healthy benefits and simple ways to turn them into quick, flavor-packed meals.

Hit the Walking Trail or Gym. In one study, exercise was found to slash the risk of Alzheimer's by more than 60 percent. So step right up to one of the best ways to keep your brain nimble—a regular half hour of exercise that raises your heart rate, along with simple muscle-building

The Surprising Truth about "Brain Games"

If you've thought about subscribing to one of those computer-based brain-training programs, consider this: Exactly zero studies have conclusively demonstrated that commercially available brain games prevent Alzheimer's or other types of dementia.[26]

More than 70 neurologists, psychologists, and psychiatrists led by researchers at Stanford University's Center on Longevity and the Berlin Max Planck Institute for Human Development reviewed studies used by the brain-game industry to support its claims. The panel's consensus: Some study findings show promise and merit further study. However, "The consensus of the group is that claims promoting brain games are frequently exaggerated and at times misleading," the panel wrote. "The promise of a magic bullet detracts from the best evidence to date, which is that cognitive health in old age reflects the long-term effects of healthy, engaged lifestyles."

That said, research on computerized brain training continues to evolve. In a study of almost 3,000 older people presented at the 2016 Alzheimer's Association International Conference in Toronto, those who completed 11 or more sessions of computer-based training called speed-of-processing training, had a 48 percent reduced risk of dementia over a 10-year period, compared to a control group.[27] That's a big deal—if these preliminary findings hold up.

moves. If it's been a while since you've been physically active, relax. Chapter 6 offers plenty of fun ways to get moving, from golf to dancing. And if your motivation to work out is in the basement, you'll learn new, science-proven ways to fire it up.

Alzheimer's in Your Family? The Good (Yes, Good!) News

If one or both of your parents was diagnosed with Alzheimer's, you're likely all too aware of the genetic component of this disease. The good news is, genes are far from the only factor that influences your risk.

Rarely, Alzheimer's develops because of mutations to any of three genes—the gene for the amyloid precursor protein (APP) as well as those for the presenilin 1 and presenilin 2 proteins. People with any of these genetic mutations typically develop symptoms before age 65, sometimes as early as age 30. This type of Alzheimer's, familial or early-onset type, affects multiple family members in multiple generations. But it's rare, accounting for less than 1 percent of cases.[28]

Most people with Alzheimer's develop the late-onset type, which develops at age 65 or later. Experts believe that this more common type develops because of multiple factors, including lifestyle and environment. The greatest risk factors

---

Adjust Your Attitude. There's no one in the world exactly like you; your personality is uniquely your own. But get this: Researchers have associated certain personality traits with both an increased or reduced risk of Alzheimer's. Chapter 7 reveals what they are. The good news is, you don't have to change your incredible self to protect your brain. What you *can* do is work to cultivate traits linked to having a sharp, keen mind in older age.

Reduce Brain-Shrinking Stress. Constant worry and stress do more than wreak havoc on your health and drain the joy from your life. They've been shown to shrivel parts of the brain vital to thinking and memory. There's more—losing out on high-quality sleep appears to

are older age, a family history of Alzheimer's, and the apolipoprotein (APOE) e4 gene—APOE-e4, for short.

The APOE-e4 gene is one of three common forms of the APOE gene (the others are APOE-e2 and APOE-e3). All of us inherit a copy of some form of APOE from each of our parents. Those who inherit one copy of the e4 form have a threefold higher risk of developing Alzheimer's compared to those without it, while those who inherit two copies have an eight- to twelvefold higher risk.

Researchers estimate that 40 to 65 percent of people diagnosed with Alzheimer's have one or two copies of the APOE-e4 gene. But carrying the gene does not make getting Alzheimer's a done deal. Some people who carry APOE-e4 never develop Alzheimer's, while some who don't get the disease anyway.

In other words, genes are only part of the story. And while you can't change your genes, you can change your lifestyle. And the time to do it is in midlife, when these chronic conditions typically are diagnosed.

stress the brain, research suggests. Chapter 8 offers simple techniques shown to reduce the assault of chronic worry and tension on your brain. If stress keeps you up at night, the sleep-better tips can help soothe you into the restorative shut-eye an ageless brain thrives on.

Preserve Your Wits with Play. Building an ageless brain isn't work. As you'll discover in Chapter 9, it's more like play. Just as you lift weights to build muscle, you challenge your brain to keep it keen—and there are so many ways to do it, you can forego crossword puzzles if they're not your cup of tea. Simply take up an activity in which you'll learn. How about joining a photography club or signing up for tango lessons? Your brain doesn't care if your photos are fuzzy or you have two left feet. What counts is that you're creating new neural pathways and perhaps new neurons, and following your passions in the process. In the "recipe" for an ageless brain, mental and creative stimulation are incredibly important ingredients.

START TRIMMING YEARS FROM YOUR BRAIN TODAY!

Although you can't stop your brain from aging, there's striking evidence that you *can* slow the rate at which it grows old. What's incredible is that some studies have actually counted up the number of years healthy lifestyle habits can shave off your "brain age." We will share the best with you as the book helps you prepare your brain to thrive—not just in the years ahead, but right now. Here's a sneak peek.

Lose weight, gain a decade of potential brainpower! Being overweight or obese in midlife may age the brain by around 10 years, according to a study of over 500 adults.[29]

Get moving, trim a decade off your brain age! In a study of almost 900 older adults, those who got little or no physical activity experienced a decline equal to 10 more years of aging as compared to those who got moderate physical activity.[30]

Fork up veggies, shear off 5 years! Just two servings of veggies a day averted the equivalent of 5 years of mental aging in people older than 65.[31]

Eat berries, prune 2.5 years! In one study, at least a cup a week of either strawberries or blueberries, which brim with brain-protecting plant chemicals, slowed brain aging by two and a half years.[32]

Sleep tight every night, shave off 2 years! A 14-year study that followed over 15,000 women found that those who got 5 hours of shut-eye a day or less, or 9 hours a day or more, had lower average mental function than those who slept 7 hours.[33] In other words, too little sleep, or too much, was equivalent to 2 years of cognitive aging.

The rest of Part 1 will give you a quick tour of the 3-pound super-organ between your ears and present a detailed quiz to help you gauge how well your lifestyle aligns with the scientific research that links a healthy lifestyle with a reduced risk of cognitive decline.

Part 2, Stay-SHARP Basics, presents the basics of brain health. These "commandments" are your first steps to staving off memory loss and cognitive decline. Nail these, and you're ready to go on to Part 3, Stay SHARP! These chapters present the specifics of how to keep your mind and memory keen with diet, physical activity, attitude, stress reduction, and mental stimulation.

Here's the amazing thing: Just learning this stuff gets your brain percolating. And once you put the research to work and lock down the healthy habits presented in these pages, you'll be on the ageless brain path for the rest of your life.

An Ageless Brain for Life

HOW COMPLEX IS THE brain? Well, one neuroscientist compared its structure to that of the universe. Imagine the 100 billion or more stars of the Milky Way Galaxy. Now, imagine them packed into an area the size of your fists, side by side. That's the size of the average brain, and its "stars" are nerve cells, or neurons.[1]

What an incredible image! Just as amazing: That 3-pound lump of tissue in your skull, its billions of neurons, and the trillions of connections between those cells, called synapses, form the raw material of *you*.

Your brain directs both the functions you don't notice, like heart rate and breathing, and the high-level thinking that allows us to make lifesaving drugs, skyscrapers, and art. Powered by electrochemical activity, its intricate webs of neurons and synapses shape what you love and fear, the decisions you make, and your perceptions of yourself and the world. Your life experiences have in turn shaped your brain—literally altered its genes, molecules, cells, and circuits.

Although the workings of the brain will always be mysterious, science is revealing some of its secrets—including what may keep it keen far into old age. In this chapter, you'll learn about brain regions vital to thinking and memory, how they work, how aging changes them, and which changes are normal and which are not.

As you'll learn, even older brains are pretty sharp, with the ability to compensate for normal changes related to age. In fact, neuroscience now recognizes that "old-dog" brains *do* have the ability to change—and learning new tricks may help keep them in top shape.[2]

A Universe between Your Ears

Okay, so your brain looks like a walnut encased in the "shell" of your skull. But give it some respect—it generates your deepest thoughts and emotions and houses the core of your identity: your memory. Here's a quick tour.

Two of the brain's three main parts help keep you alive and vertical. The hindbrain controls the body's automatic functions, while the midbrain covers reflexes and eye movement. But the biggest, most developed part of your brain—the forebrain, located right behind your forehead—is key to thought and memory.

Most of the forebrain consists of the cerebrum and its grooved, wrinkled coating, the cortex. They're at work when you think, feel, and solve problems, or dream, imagine, and create.[3] Although the cortex—or "gray matter," as researchers call it—is no thicker than a stack of two or three dimes, it's where most of the brain's information processing happens.[4]

Your brain is divided into left and right hemispheres, with each hemisphere divided into lobes.[5]

The *frontal lobes* involve the brain's executive-function abilities that allow you to plan, organize, solve problems, set goals, and multitask. Ever hosted a holiday dinner? This lobe gets a workout as you prep different dishes in the oven and on the stove, bark out a steady stream

THIS IS YOUR BRAIN ON BIRTHDAYS

Aging affects every part of your body, your brain included. For example, as the number of candles on your birthday cake grows, brain regions vital to learning and memory shrink. Changes in blood vessels can limit the flow of oxygen-rich blood to the brain, and changes in hormones and brain chemicals called neurotransmitters affect neurons'

of orders to your helpers, and remember to pick up Grandma at a certain time.

The *parietal lobes* process sensory information that streams in from the outside world, including where you are in space. The taste, aroma, and texture of a good meal make these lobes tingle.

The *occipital lobes* process images from your eyes and connect them with images stored in your memory. They're at work right now, as you read these words.

The *temporal lobes* deal with language, hearing, and social and emotional function. They also house the hippocampus, often called the gateway to memory. A part of your "lizard brain" (see page 28), the hippo-campus plays a key role in learning and memory formation and retrieval. It also helps link memories to the original emotions they generated—the more emotionally charged the memory, the easier it is to recall.[6] Some studies have found that depression and stress shrink the hippocampus, while exercise increases its size.

The brain even has its own security system: a layer of special cells that line the brain's blood vessels. Like a bouncer, the blood-brain barrier keeps out unwanted substances, such as bacteria and toxins, while waving in essential substances like hormones, amino acids, oxygen, water, and sugar (glucose), its main source of fuel.

ability to communicate. There's also a rise in inflammation, one of the body's key responses to injury, infection, or threat.[7] Compared to a young brain, an older one processes nerve impulses more slowly, which slows reaction time and performance.[8]

Why these normal age-related changes occur is still under debate, but scientists have dozens of theories. One suggests that "aging genes" may flip on at a certain point. Others point to a lifetime of accumulated DNA damage or glitches in the aging immune system. One theory suggests that, over time, the brain simply "rusts," like a tool left out in the yard. This unstoppable "rusting," called oxidation, is caused by free radicals, harmful molecules that destroy the fats and proteins neurons need to function normally.[9]

All these changes can slow an older brain's processing time, like when your computer "hangs" or freezes. So when whippersnappers add a string of figures in their heads or memorize a phone number, their young brains are likely to outperform older ones. But in memory and thinking tests, given enough time, healthy people in their seventies and eighties often achieve scores similar to those of younger people.[10]

The best news of all: We now have a wealth of data supporting the idea that it's possible to grow old without losing your mind.[11] The ongoing Religious Orders Study, led by researchers at the Rush University Medical Center in Chicago, has followed the same group of people for decades to examine the older brain's transition from normal function to impairment. Launched in 1993, this one study has generated nearly 200 peer-reviewed papers on a wide range of issues related to aging and Alzheimer's disease (AD).[12] Throughout the book, we'll return to the Religious Orders Study again and again because it has revealed a wealth of knowledge about the older brain, both in sickness and in health.

THE OLDER BRAIN: FULL OF SURPRISES

The participants of the Religious Orders Study—more than 1,000 older nuns, priests, and brothers—have gifted researchers with the opportunity to explore the effects of aging on the brain during their lives and after their deaths.[13] They're 75 to 80 years old, on average, with healthy brains when they enroll. Each year, all undergo tests that generate mountains of data on their memories, intellectual performance, and physical health. Because the participants have agreed to donate their brains to science, the study has conducted more than 500 brain autopsies.

When the study began, researchers thought they'd see a clear link between declines in thinking and memory and the biology of AD, which includes the hallmark buildup of amyloid plaques and neurofibrillary tangles. (Though it's normal to develop some plaques and tangles as we age, people with AD tend to develop far more, and in a predictable pattern, beginning in areas important for memory.)[14] But the autopsies revealed a surprise: Many cognitively spry participants' brains showed those unmistakable signs of AD. In other words, having a brain shot through with neuron-killing plaques and tangles didn't always result in obvious cognitive problems.[15]

When the researchers went back to their data for an explanation, they found more surprises: Certain behaviors seemed to shield the brain from decline. For example, reading, driving, and learning new skills were found to be protective against AD.[16] Ditto for physical activity and frequent social interaction (see page 30).[17] Just as interesting: Negative psychological states like depression[18] and loneliness[19] were related to cognitive decline.

You'll learn more about these studies later in the book. For now, keep this in mind: The Religious Orders Study and long-term, ongoing

The "Forest" in Your Head

Whatever you do—scratch your nose, tell (or laugh at) a joke, fiddle with your phone—is the result of instant-messaging among your brain's 100 billion neurons and their 100 trillion synapses. This dense web has been called a "neuron forest."[20] In this forest, different types of neurons, packed tight, send messages between different regions of the brain, and between the brain and the rest of the nervous system.

The electrical impulses and chemical signals zipping through this forest in your head form the basis of every thought, feeling, and memory you have,[21] and different types of neurons do different jobs. Some are involved with thinking, learning, and memory.[22] Sensory neurons transmit information from your eyes, ears, and other sense organs (including the skin) to the brain. Motor neurons send messages from the central nervous

---

studies of aging suggest that your actions *and* attitudes may help "vaccinate" your brain against decline—or make it more vulnerable. Research spotlights two concepts that may protect the older brain: *plasticity* and *cognitive reserve*.

YOUR PLASTIC FANTASTIC BRAIN

Neuroscientists used to think that our brains were fully developed by our midtwenties. Surprise! The brain continues to change far into adulthood. Neuroscientists use the word *plasticity* to describe how novel experiences and learning new things can form new connections in the brain. More amazing still, some brain regions can grow new neurons, a process called neurogenesis.[25]

system to the body's muscles and glands, stimulating them into action.[23]

Every second, even when you're at rest or asleep, your neurons are gleaning information from your environment and speeding messages along your brain's neuron highways. If a mosquito lands on your arm, sensory neurons in your skin would transmit this intel to your spinal cord and brain at a speed of over 150 miles per hour. Your brain would then use your motor neurons—which travel even faster—to transmit the message back through your spinal cord to your hand. Slap! Later, mosquito.

And that's just one example. If you could enter your neuron forest, you'd see what looks like a winking, glimmering shower of stars.[24] That's what neuronal language looks like—the translation of your moment-to-moment experience into electrochemical signals.

In other words, an older brain may be as moldable as Play-Doh. In a scientific review of 36 studies[26] that examined the effects of learning new skills on the brain, researchers found "consistent evidence" that older brains retain plasticity.[27]

And the things that may increase plasticity in adult brains turn out to be surprisingly common. In one study, researchers taught older adults to juggle. Some mastered the skill, some didn't. But those who did showed increases in gray matter in a region of the brain associated with visual motion processing. In another 5-month study of 40- to 60-year-olds new to golf, just 40 hours of practice increased gray matter.[28] Although exactly how such training may change the brain isn't yet known, it may have worked by stimulating neurogenesis in those regions, or by increasing connections between neurons, the review article said.[29]

The Chemicals of Cognition

Your eyes, ears, and other sensory organs detect what's happening in the world around you. This information—sounds, images, temperature, texture, pressure—is converted to neurotransmitters, chemical signals that allow neurons to communicate with other neurons as well as cells throughout the body.[30]

Research has identified dozens of neurotransmitters. Among the most important:

Glutamine. This chemical makes neurons "excitable." When it's released, the likelihood that neurons will fire goes up. This enhances the electrical flow among neurons that's needed for normal function.[31]

Acetylcholine. Like glutamine, acetylcholine excites neurons. It makes muscles contract and causes glands to secrete hormones.[32] Research has associated AD with less-than-normal amounts of acetylcholine.

Serotonin. This chemical is involved in regulating mood, appetite, and sleep quality, among other functions. People with depression often have lower than normal serotonin levels, research shows.[33]

Dopamine. Often called the "feel-good chemical," dopamine is associated with the brain's attraction to natural rewards, such as food, water, and sex (and to less-than-healthy "rewards," such as nicotine or other drugs of abuse). It's also involved in controlling movement and facilitating the flow of information to the forebrain.[34]

GABA. Short for gamma-aminobutyric acid. Some 20 percent of the brain's *inhibitory* nerve cells produce this neurotransmitter, which binds to receptors on nerve cells nearby and makes them temporarily unable to fire.[35] In other words, GABA quiets cells down. GABA is involved with motor control and vision, among other functions.[36]

That said, there's no scientific proof that the "brain games" advertised on TV can stave off memory loss, dementia, or AD. In fact, a company that made such claims recently settled with the federal government, which charged that its advertising was deceptive.[37] In a bid to form new neuronal connections, simply keep your brain percolating with new challenges. Or consider taking up one of the activities that research has associated with increased plasticity[38]—they're covered in Chapter 9, Preserve Your Wits with Play.

KEEPING BRAINPOWER IN RESERVE

Amazing, but true: Two people can have roughly the same amount of amyloid plaques and tau tangles in their brains. Yet one functions normally, while the other displays the unmistakable signs of Alzheimer's— memory loss that disrupts daily life, changes in personality, and increasing difficulty with common tasks such as getting dressed or paying bills. Why?

Scientists have puzzled over this phenomenon since the 1980s, when researchers from the University of California, San Diego, examined the brains of 137 deceased nursing home residents who'd donated their brains to science. During life, some of the residents had been nearly incapacitated by Alzheimer's; others had experienced far fewer symptoms. Yet when the researchers examined their brains, they were surprised to discover that all of them had a similar degree of plaques and tangles.[39]

Further examination revealed that over their lifetimes, the residents with the fewest symptoms had built ageless brains by amassing what we now refer to as *cognitive reserve.*

Your cognitive reserve is your accumulation of knowledge, habits,

Meet Your "Lizard Brain"

Deep inside the brain lies the seat of our instinct and drive to survive. Called the limbic system, this network of structures makes you fight or flee, eat and have sex, and experience primal emotions, like fear or rage. The limbic system also links scents with memory and emotion, which is why a whiff of fresh-baked cookies or a certain perfume can jolt you back to your childhood. Besides the hippocampus, the limbic system includes:

The amygdala. This small, almond-shaped region evokes such primal emotions as aggression and fear and allows you to process and remember strong emotions.[40]

The thalamus. Located at the top of the brain stem, the thalamus is the size of two unshelled walnuts. It organizes sensory messages to and from the highest levels of the brain, which helps you register such sensations as pain, touch, and temperature.[41]

The hypothalamus. Tucked under the thalamus, this pearl-size structure wakes you up in the morning, maintains body temperature, regulates thirst and appetite, and gets your adrenaline pumping in stressful situations. Like the amygdala, the hypothalamus also plays a role in emotions; it regulates the molecules that make you experience anger, sadness, or exhilaration.[42]

experiences, and memories.[43] It's a lot like a 401(k) account for the brain. With a 401(k), the more money you save over your life, the more money you can withdraw after retirement before you feel financially pinched.

Each word you know, each experience you've had, each snippet of knowledge you've memorized, each skill you've mastered, and each memory you've stored is like a dollar in retirement savings for your brain. The more of a cognitive reserve you amass over your life, the more you can lose before you start to struggle.

PLUMPING UP YOUR COGNITIVE "CUSHION"

You might also think of cognitive reserve as a "cushion" of brain function that kicks in if other areas of your brain begin to sputter.[44] One way to inflate it: learn something new every day. In a study published

---

Want to Grow Your Brain? Drive a Cab in London

Some people can't navigate their way out of a parking lot. Others seem to carry a GPS system in their brains. A now-famous study of London taxi drivers, of all people, shows how adult brains can continue to change and develop over time.

Every cabbie in London must pass "The Knowledge," a test that requires them to memorize a city map that includes 25,000 streets and 20,000 landmarks.[45] The memorization required to ace this test is so epic that it targeted the attention of London neuroscientists.[46]

The researchers were especially keen to study the drivers' hippocampus, that seahorse-shaped brain structure so cen-tral to memory. The hippocampus is particularly important in spatial memory, which helps you recall aspects of the environment and where those aspects are in relation to each other. (When you remember where you put your car keys, you're using spatial memory.)

Brain scans of drivers who'd memorized The Knowledge and passed the test showed that a specific part of the hippocampus—the posterior hippocampus—had grown physically larger, compared to that of people in a control group. The cabbies' monumental feat of memorization had literally reshaped a key region of their brains.[47]

in the journal *Neuropsychology*, researchers had almost 400 middle-age and older adults take college courses for a 4-year period. At the start of the study, they tested their participants' thinking and memory to establish a baseline, and then they retested them each year. Compared to a control group, the back-to-schoolers significantly increased their cognitive capacity.[48]

Frequent social contact also builds that reserve. In another study[49] that drew from the Religious Orders Study data, researchers looked at the brains of almost 90 deceased older people not diagnosed with AD and found the plaques and tangles associated with the disease. After checking their data, the researchers found that their late participants had one thing in common: close bonds with friends and family members. When you mingle at a party, attend a weekly bingo or bridge game, or take daily walks with a friend, your brain gets a workout from the back-and-forth of conversation, sharing experiences with others, and being in a stimulating environment.

These findings don't prove conclusively that cognitive reserve prevents AD. However, they suggest that it may stave off its symptoms. According to one review article, all other things being equal, AD should emerge later in people with higher cognitive reserve.[50] And delaying the disease is the next-best thing to avoiding it altogether.

The earlier you start inflating your "cushion," the better, but it's never too late to start. Enroll in a class. Tackle a foreign language. Take up a musical instrument. Widen your social circle. In short, think of your brain as a puppy—both need human connection and something to chew on.

MCI: NOT NORMAL, NOT DEMENTIA

As you learned in Chapter 1, it's not uncommon for people in middle age and older to experience occasional senior moments. What you may

Memory Issues:
What's Normal, What's Not

Can't always find the word you want? Mix up, or even forget, appointments every now and then? Relax; not all memory lapses spell trouble. However, it's possible to distinguish normal, age-related memory glitches from dementia or AD. While these examples from the Alzheimer Society of Canada aren't a diagnostic tool, they may help you determine whether to breathe easy or call the doctor.[51]

NORMAL	TALK TO YOUR DOCTOR
Being unable to recall the details of a conversation or event of a year ago	Being unable to remember the details of an event or conversation that happened last week
Forgetting things and events every now and again	Becoming more and more forgetful
Occasionally searching for the right word (a "tip-of-the-tongue" moment)	Frequently pausing to find the right word, or using substitute words when the right one won't come to mind
Fretting about your memory when no one else is, including your family	Unconcern about your memory, while friends or relatives worry

not know is that there's a "transition stage" between normal brain aging and dementia. It's called *mild cognitive impairment (MCI)* and it affects an estimated 10 to 20 percent of people over 65.[52] Unlike AD, which causes cognitive declines beyond memory, MCI's hallmark is mild memory loss that doesn't affect the ability to live independently.[53]

The symptoms come on gradually. People who have it may start to forget people's names or appointments—things they used to recall easily—or frequently misplace things.[54] While the memory lapses are mild, family and friends may notice them, and the person who has them may be concerned enough to see a doctor.[55]

People with MCI can go about their usual day without much trouble. More often than not, they are aware of their memory glitches and use "cheats" to compensate. For example, they may hang a large calendar so they can keep track of appointments, or jot reminders on sticky notes and place them where they'll be seen.[56] Although MCI increases the risk of developing dementia, it's not a certainty. Even so, the Alzheimer's Association recommends that people diagnosed with MCI be evaluated every 6 months to determine if their symptoms are better, worse, or unchanged.[57]

The "Fertilizer" for Aging Brains

What do daily walks and frequent hugs have in common? Both increase the level of a protein called brain-derived neurotrophic factor (BDNF). Think of BDNF as a "fertilizer" for neurons—it helps brain cells survive and thrive and helps stimulate development of new neurons.[61]

High BDNF levels may help protect against dementia as well, suggests a study by researchers at Rush University Medical Center in Chicago. The team followed more than 500 participants of the Religious Orders Study and the Rush Memory and Aging Project for an average of 6 years, testing their thinking and memory each year.

After their deaths, researchers measured the BDNF levels in their brains and compared them with their test results. Those with the highest levels of BDNF had a 50 percent slower mental decline than those with the lowest levels. Even those with the most plaques and tangles, but

The good news: Some of the same brain-stimulating activities associated with building cognitive reserve may help with MCI. For example, one study found that a short, daily dose of mindfulness meditation (see page 182) may help delay the progression of MCI to dementia.[58]

DEMENTIA: A DESCRIPTION, NOT A DISEASE

"Dementia" describes the symptoms that result when neurons falter, lose connections with other neurons, and die, resulting in a progressive degeneration of thinking and memory. Unlike people with MCI, those with dementia aren't able to live independently.[59]

Although AD is the most common cause of dementia[60]—it accounts

the highest levels of BDNF, showed slower decline compared to those with the lowest BDNF levels.[62]

The association between BDNF and cognitive decline "suggests that a higher level of BDNF protein may provide a buffer, or reserve, for the brain and protect individuals against the effects of the plaques and tangles that accumulate in the brain as a part of Alzheimer's disease," the study's lead author said.[63]

Need more evidence? Boston University researchers tracked more than 2,000 older adults for up to 10 years. Those with the highest BDNF levels at the beginning of the study developed dementia and AD 50 percent less often compared to those with the lowest levels.[64]

Exercise and social interaction, among other factors, have been found to raise BDNF levels. You'll learn more about BDNF-boosting activities throughout the book.

for 60 to 80 percent of all cases—there are other types, which are described below. They're diagnosed with brain imaging, psychological tests, and neurological exams.[65] Bear in mind that distinguishing one type of dementia from another is tricky. Sometimes, the only way to know for sure is through a brain autopsy.[66] (That's a medical procedure none of us wants to have anytime soon!)

Vascular dementia, the second most common type after AD, causes memory and thinking issues similar to those of AD (which is why brain imaging and other testing is necessary). Its symptoms are caused by conditions that reduce or block bloodflow to the brain, which deprives neurons of the oxygen and nutrients they need. Strong evidence suggests that managing risk factors for vascular dementia, particularly high blood pressure, can significantly reduce the likelihood of developing this type of dementia.[67]

The late comedian Robin Williams may have been afflicted with *dementia with Lewy bodies (DLB),*[68] thought to be the third most common form of dementia. With DLB, abnormal deposits of a protein called alpha-synuclein, or Lewy bodies, invade nerve cells throughout the brain. Many people with Parkinson's disease eventually develop thinking and reasoning problems, leading to *Parkinson's disease dementia (PDD),* and many people with DLB have movement problems like those associated with Parkinson's disease, such as hunched posture and a shuffling walk.[69] As DLB and PDD progress, their symptoms become more and more similar.[70]

Frontotemporal dementia (FTD) involves the degeneration of the frontal and temporal lobes, which play a key role in making decisions and managing behavior, emotion, and language. People with FTD may not have significant memory loss. Instead, they may behave inappropriately or have trouble naming common objects.[71]

Mixed dementia typically combines the plaques and tangles associated with AD with vascular dementia's blood vessel damage. It's not known how many older people diagnosed with a specific type of dementia actually have mixed dementia, but autopsies suggest that this condition may be more common than previously thought.[72]

AD: THE HIJACKED BRAIN

Every 66 seconds, someone in the United States develops AD,[73] the most known—and feared—form of dementia. At the center of this cruel disease are two abnormal proteins that accumulate both within and outside of nerve cells. They typically invade regions of the brain vital to memory and higher cognitive function, destroying and eventually killing neurons.[74]

Plaques are abnormal, chemically "sticky"[75] deposits of the protein fragment beta-amyloid that build up between nerve cells. Plaques may block neuron communication at synapses, as well as activate immune-system cells that trigger inflammation. *Tangles*—twisted strands of a different protein called tau—form inside the neuron. Both disrupt and eventually cut off neurons' ability to communicate.[76]

Researchers suspect that AD's damage to the brain starts a decade or more before symptoms appear, and that it begins in the hippocampus. In this symptom-free, preclinical stage, plaques and tangles build up, affecting the function of healthy neurons. Overwhelmed, they begin to work less efficiently; communication between them sputters and winks out, and eventually they die. As neuron death continues, the damage spreads and affects other parts of the brain. These areas begin to shrink, a process known as atrophy.

No one test can show whether a person has AD. Diagnosing this

Two Easy Ways to Protect Your Noggin

Brain injuries caused by a blow to the head, as from a car crash or a fall, may raise the risk of developing AD years later, evidence suggests.[77] So buckle up when you're in the car.

Older adults who'd had a moderate brain injury (one that knocks you out for more than 30 minutes) more than doubled their risk of AD compared to those who hadn't, research has found. A severe brain injury, one which causes unconsciousness for more than 24 hours, carried nearly five times greater risk.

An injury to the brain may raise AD risk by changing the chemistry of the brain. Although more study is needed, evidence suggests a relationship between brain injury and the development of the disease's plaques and tangles. Fortunately, not all head injuries lead to dementia, and there's no evidence that a single concussion increases risk.

Another way to protect your brain: improve your balance. You may think that you're too young to worry about falls, but they're the most common cause of brain injury. And balance exercises are so simple you can do them as you do your dishes or brush your teeth. To check them out, log on to the National Institutes of Health's Senior Health website, *nihseniorhealth.gov*.

disease requires a thorough medical evaluation, which should include a detailed medical history, thinking and memory tests, and physical and neurological exams, as well as blood tests and brain scans to rule out other possible causes of dementia-like symptoms. Your primary-care doctor may be able to refer you to a specialist trained to diagnose and treat AD and dementia. If not, the Alzheimer's Association chapter in your area can (to find yours, log on to *alz.org*).[78]

People with mild AD, the stage at which the disease is most often diagnosed, have trouble handling money and paying bills and may display changes in personality and behavior. By its last (late) stage, the ability to walk or communicate with words is lost, and round-the-clock care is needed. Medications can help treat symptoms like memory loss and changes in behavior and sleep. Although they can't stop the disease, they can temporarily keep symptoms from getting worse, thereby improving the quality of life for people with AD and their caregivers.[79]

THE AD GENE: READY, TEST, GO?

Your mother or father had late-onset AD. You're concerned that you may develop it, too. Should you get tested for APOE-e4, the gene associated with a raised susceptibility to this form of the disease? The choice is yours—but make it with care.[80, 81]

Most experts are in the "don't get tested unless you have symptoms" camp, for a variety of reasons. The thinking is that whether or not you have a parent with AD, there's nothing you can do if testing reveals that you have the gene. (Of course, if that's the case, there's plenty you can do to help delay onset of the disease.) Further, a positive result becomes part of your medical record, which can affect eligibility for insurance and long-term care. And because a positive result doesn't mean you'll definitely develop AD, why live with a sword dangling above your head?

The main reason that most experts counsel against testing for the gene is that a positive result could trigger major emotional and psychological distress. However, the findings of a study published in the *New England Journal of Medicine* suggest otherwise. People at high risk for developing late-onset AD who received genetic and psychological counseling *before* they received their test results weren't any more depressed or distressed than those who didn't learn their result at all.

Larger studies that follow people for more than a year are needed to examine whether testing has any negative long-term effects, the study said.[82]

Bottom line: If you decide to get tested, seek the services of a trained genetic counselor, who will take you through the pros and cons of testing and help prepare you for the result. Also bear in mind that although you can't change your test results, you *can* change your lifestyle. And the science-backed strategies in this book may make a difference.

If someone in your life has memory loss or AD, it's natural to be concerned about your own brain health. Although the main risk factors for dementia—age and family history—can't be changed, you can take charge of many other risk factors, starting as soon as today. Channel your concern into positive action, and you give yourself the best shot at good brain health for years to come.

How's your diet? Your weight? Do you stay active, shrug off stress, and sleep well? Is your brain on a steady diet of stimulation? Keep reading, to see how your current lifestyle may be affecting your brain health. There's plenty you can do to take control.

DESIGN THE ANTI-ALZHEIMER'S PLAN THAT WORKS FOR YOU!

This book is packed with hundreds of simple actions you can take to help keep your brain keen as you grow older. Many of these strategies can make your life more rewarding and meaningful as they stimulate your brain to make new connections and perhaps even sprout more neurons. The best news of all? You get to design your own personal Ageless Brain plan.

This book gives you all the latest science-backed tactics found to help safeguard thinking and memory. So it's fine to take the Chinese menu approach, selecting tips from each SHARP pillar that most appeal to you. Here's how to create and customize your own anti-Alzheimer's plan, step by simple step.

Begin by turning to the next chapter and taking our Ageless Brain quiz. It'll familiarize you with the SHARP pillars of brain health—diet, physical activity, attitude, stress management, and mental stimulation. Your results will give you an idea of where you're doing great and where you can improve. (Do commit to revamping your diet and/or starting an exercise program if your results indicate these areas need work. A wealth of research links these positive lifestyle habits strongly to brain health.)

Then, read and digest Part 2, Stay-SHARP Basics. Covering topics from blood pressure to weight and beyond, Part 2 explains the very least you should be doing, right now, to nurture and protect your brain.

In Part 3, pick the pillar you'd like to tackle first—S, H, A, R, or P. Then, read and digest that section and choose one or two of its strategies to try each week. Once you've worked all the strategies you've chosen from that section into your life, pick another pillar to focus on. Repeat until you've worked your way through each pillar. Remember—making just a few simple changes can deliver big benefits to your brain! And you can't overdo it.

Consider starting an Ageless Brain notebook in which you keep a weekly record of the strategies you try. Day by day, week by week, you'll be able to track your progress, troubleshoot challenges, and discover which strategies work for you and which don't. Your notebook can also be where you write out your shopping list for the week (don't forget those brain-healthy greens!), track your walks and strength-training workouts, and critique the stress management techniques and attitude adjustments you try. Bonus: Just keeping the notebook can help spark your brain!

3

Are You Living a Brain-Healthy Lifestyle?

EACH DAY, YOU MAKE countless small decisions that chart the course of your day. Do you opt for a doughnut for breakfast or an egg-white-and-spinach wrap? Take time to defuse stress, or deny it and let the pressure build? Head for the couch after dinner, or head out for a brain-clearing walk? Turn in before midnight, or work or worry into the wee hours of the morning?

Cumulatively, small choices like this can have big effects. That's because choices have a way of becoming habits, and habits impact health—for the better, and for the worse. So the question is: Do the small choices you make every day support your brain health, or threaten it? Lower your risk of Alzheimer's, or raise it? That's where this quiz comes in.

The quiz has two parts. Part 1 features simple yes-or-no questions based on variables used in a significant study of Alzheimer's risk factors (more on that to come). Part 2 consists of five sets of multiple-choice questions that address the quality of your diet, how physically active you are, the ways you see yourself and the world around you, the level of psychological stress in your past and present, and the typical amount of stimulation your brain gets each day.

Think of your score as the "you are here" point on the path to an ageless brain, indicating whether to stick to the healthy track you're on, make some course corrections, or change direction completely. The good news is, no matter what your score, you can move closer to the sharp-as-a-tack brain you want. Even better, the quiz will help reveal the areas in your lifestyle that are most in need of change.

Consider photocopying this quiz and taking it twice—now, to gauge your current lifestyle habits, and again in a few months, once you've put the brain-healthy strategies in these pages to work. You may be amazed at how much your score improves, and how much sharper and more energetic you feel.

Part 1

10 QUESTIONS THAT CAN ASSESS YOUR FUTURE BRAIN HEALTH

As you're aware, there's no way to prevent certain risk factors for Alzheimer's, such as age or a family history of the disease. But researchers are zeroing in on ways to identify people at the highest risk for Alzheimer's, in the earliest stage possible. That way, they can work with their doctors to reverse the risk factors they *can* change, perhaps delaying or even preventing the disease.

Researchers at the Mayo Clinic recently developed a scoring system to predict a person's risk of progressing from cognitively normal to mild cognitive impairment, or MCI.[1] Published in the journal *Neurology*, the study followed more than 1,400 people ages 70 and over for almost 5 years. None of the participants had thinking or memory problems when the study began, and their cognitive skills were tested every 15 months. During the study period, almost 30 percent developed MCI, which allowed the team to zero in on factors that predict a person's risk of developing dementia.

Although more research is needed to validate this scoring system, here are some of the variables the researchers used to develop it. Answer questions 1–4 whether you're a woman or a man, and questions 5–10 based on your gender.

1. Have you ever been diagnosed with an alcohol problem?

2. Do you have any self-reported memory concerns?

3. Do you have less than 12 years of education?

4. Do you have heart problems, such as a history of arterial fibrillation?

IF YOU'RE A WOMAN:

5. Do you currently smoke?

6. Have you been diagnosed with diabetes in midlife?

7. Have you been diagnosed with high cholesterol in midlife?

8. Have you been diagnosed with high blood pressure in midlife?

IF YOU'RE A MAN:

9. Have you remained single, or are you widowed?

10. Is your body mass index (BMI) greater than 30 (which indicates obesity)?

SCORING: PART 1

If you answered "yes" to three or more questions, schedule an appointment with your doctor and show him or her your results. Your doctor may give you an on-the-spot cognitive screening or refer you to a specialist for the more extensive testing described in Chapter 2.

Part 2

THE AGELESS BRAIN LIFESTYLE QUIZ

As you progress through each set of questions, give yourself 2 points for each (a) answer, 1 point for each (b) answer, and 0 points for each (c) response. When you're done with Part 2, add up the total number of points in each category.

DO YOU EAT FOR AN AGELESS BRAIN?

There's ever-growing evidence that a healthy diet helps a brain thrive and promotes a youthful mind and memory. This set of questions helps you gauge how well your diet gives your brain the nutrients it needs to stay sharp.

The phrase that best describes your typical diet is:

a. Clean and green. Most of my plate is crowded with veggies, beans, and whole grains, with fruit for dessert and a couple of servings of fish or poultry per week.

b. Well-intentioned. One or more of my daily meals is healthy—plain yogurt and fruit for breakfast, a grilled-chicken salad for lunch. But I'm no stranger to frozen pizzas, drive-thru meals, and other ultra-processed foods.

c. Meat and starch. Most of my meals include red or processed meat (beef, pork, bacon, sausage, all-beef frankfurters, deli ham), potatoes, or processed side dishes (white rice, boxed stuffing, pasta), with the occasional side of canned corn or peas or a piece of fresh fruit.

Think about the whole, natural plant foods you eat in a typical week. How many different varieties do you estimate you eat on a regular basis?

a. Ten or more different kinds a week. I prowl the produce and natural-foods aisles of my supermarket and local farmers' market, constantly looking for a fruit, veggie, grain, or bean I haven't tried.

b. Less than 10, but more than five. My go-to foods include steel-cut oatmeal and brown rice, fruits and veggies in virtually every color, and main-dish bean entrees.

c. Five or less. I'm not a big fan of fresh fruit and vegetables and rarely have time to cook, so I stick to convenience foods I can whip up in a hurry.

Mentally inventory the whole grain products in your bread box, frig, or pantry. How many do you have?

a. Lots—one or more varieties of whole grains, such as quinoa or brown rice; a couple of boxes of 100% whole grain pasta, buckwheat-flour pancake mix.

b. A few—100% whole grain bread and/or ready-to-eat cereal.

c. None—I prefer white rice and products made with white flour.

You hit the drive-thru burger or chicken place or order takeout (pizza, Chinese):

a. Once or twice a month or fewer.

b. Once a week or less.

c. At least once a day.

You probably know that fish is considered "brain food"—but so are dark green leafy vegetables such as spinach, kale, or mustard or collard greens. How often do you eat them?

    a. Almost every day (six times a week).

    b. Two or three times a week.

    c. Once a week or less.

When you reach for a snack, you typically choose something:

    a. All natural, such as apple slices with a tablespoon of natural peanut butter, a dollop of hummus with a few whole-grain crackers, or a handful of nuts and a stick of string cheese.

    b. Sugary sweet but seemingly healthy, such as a container of fruit-on-the-bottom yogurt or a handful of honey-roasted peanuts.

    c. Junky, such as chocolate kisses, gummy worms, or chips.

Whether you sauté veggies or cook fish or poultry, you reach for which of the following?

    a. Extra-virgin olive oil, because it delivers so much flavor for so few artery-clogging bad fats.

    b. Butter, but for health reasons, I stick to less than a tablespoon a day.

    c. Margarine or animal fat, just as my mother (and grandma) did.

If you drink alcohol, how would you describe your drinking habits? (One drink equals one 5-ounce glass of wine, one 12-ounce beer, or one 1.5-ounce "shot" of distilled spirits.)

a. Up to one per day and I'm a woman (for a total of seven or fewer per week), or up to two per day and I'm a man (for a total of 14 or fewer per week).

b. I rarely drink during the week, but on a weekend, I might have four or more drinks within 2 hours (I'm a woman), or five or more drinks in that time period (I'm a man).

c. More than one a day (for a total of eight drinks or more per week) and I'm a woman, and more than two a day (for a total of 15 drinks or more per week) and I'm a man.

MY DIET SCORE

_____(a) _____ (b) _____ (c)

DO YOU SWEAT FOR AN AGELESS BRAIN?

Regular exercise boosts blood circulation, so the brain gets the oxygen and nutrients it needs to function at its best. Further, even standing more than you sit can benefit your noggin. How physically active are you really? This section helps you figure that out.

Which phrase best describes your history of physical activity?

a. Lifelong exerciser. I've been physically active since I was a kid, teen, or young adult—it's just part of who I am.

b. Late bloomer or yo-yo exerciser. I started to exercise in middle age to lose or control my weight or stay healthy. Or I keep starting a workout routine, but fizzle out after a few days, weeks, or months.

c. Yet to start. I've rarely or never been physically active.

How much do you move during the day, whether or not you work outside your home?

> **a.** A lot. I have a physically active job (mail carrier, server, retail worker), or I'm always on the move.

> **b.** So-so. I'm not entirely sedentary—I consciously take the stairs instead of the elevator as often as possible and get out for a brisk walk most days of the week.

> **c.** Not so much. I sit for most or all of the day.

How many times a week do you engage in exercise that gets your heart pumping (cardiovascular exercise), such as brisk walking, bicycling, tennis, or swimming?

> **a.** Five or six days a week, for 30 minutes or more.

> **b.** At least 3 days a week, for at least 30 minutes.

> **c.** One day a week or less, for less than 30 minutes.

How many times a week do you engage in muscle-strengthening exercise (in which you use weight machines, dumbbells, resistance bands, or body-weight exercises)?

> **a.** At least twice a week.

> **b.** Once a week or more infrequently.

> **c.** I don't do muscle-strengthening exercises.

In the coming week, you know you'll be working extra-long hours, or you have a more packed schedule than usual. How will you get your workouts in?

    a. Break my usual 30-minute walk into three 10-minute chunks—one before work, one during lunch, and one before or after dinner.

    b. I'll skip a formal workout or two, but strap on my pedometer and strive to take 10,000 steps a day. It's not hard when I walk during phone calls, take the stairs, and park farther away from store entrances.

    c. I won't. I'll start again (I hope) next week. Or I'm not working out right now.

What's the main thing that makes it difficult for you to engage in physical activity?

    a. Time. I can't fit it into my day.

    b. Motivation. I want to be active, but I can't seem to stick with a routine.

    c. Desire. I'm not interested in being physically active.

Which of the following "downtime" activities sound most like you?

    a. Puttering in the house or garden or engaging in an active hobby. I'm not one to sit still.

    b. Scrapbooking, knitting, or some other relaxing craft or hobby.

    c. Binge-watching old TV shows on Netflix.

With your eyes open, stand on one leg. How many seconds can you keep your balance?

    a. More than 20 seconds.

    b. At least 20 seconds.

    c. A few seconds, at most.

MY PHYSICAL ACTIVITY SCORE

_____(a) _____ (b) _____ (c)

DO YOU HAVE A BRAIN-HEALTHY ATTITUDE?

Research has associated specific personality traits with a rise or reduction in Alzheimer's risk. The good news is, making conscious changes to your thinking and behavior can make a difference. This section helps reveal whether you have an ageless brain mentality, or could use an attitude adjustment.

In general, how often do you interact with other people?

a. Virtually every day! I have a wide circle of friends or a close-knit family, have friends at work, and can strike up a conversation anywhere.

b. On a regular basis. I'm no social butterfly, but there are a few people in my life I can count on when I need them, and I'm there for them, too.

c. Rarely or never. I often feel lonely or isolated.

When you are in a social gathering where you don't know many people, you tend to feel:

a. Relaxed and confident. Strangers are friends I haven't met yet.

b. Shy or unsure at first. But more often than not, I find someone to talk to.

c. Uncomfortable. I generally dislike social situations, especially when I don't know anyone.

Would you describe yourself as an optimist?

    a. Yes, I tend to look on the bright side and feel things will work out.

    b. Sometimes I feel positive, sometimes negative.

    c. Usually I have a negative, "glass-half-empty" outlook.

Would you describe yourself as a diligent, industrious type of person?

    a. Yes. I'm organized, work hard, and plan ahead.

    b. Yes, although sometimes I work harder at things I enjoy, and let things I don't care for slide (even if I know I shouldn't).

    c. Not really. I'd like to develop more self-discipline and follow-through on my plans.

Which word best describes your feelings about getting older?

    a. Positive. Age is just a number, and there's still a lot of world to learn about and explore.

    b. Philosophical. Aging is a natural part of life, and life is what you make it.

    c. Pessimistic. I worry about my health, or that my best years are behind me.

Have you ever been diagnosed with major depression?

    a. No.

    b. No, although I've experienced occasional bouts of the blues.

    c. Yes, I was diagnosed earlier in my life or in recent years.

How often do you worry or feel anxious?

a. Rarely. Some things are out of my hands, and that's okay.

b. Sometimes. I have occasional bouts of worry, but mostly take life a day at a time.

c. A lot. I typically imagine the worst possible outcome to my worries, even if what I fear might happen is unlikely.

Chances are, you've experienced adversity in your life. When setbacks occur, do you generally cope with them in healthy ways and recover quickly?

a. Yes. Although hard times are never easy, long walks to manage stress, the support of friends and family, and/or my faith pull me through.

b. So-so. My support system is there for me, but I tend to struggle with eating healthy and getting regular exercise.

c. No. I typically cope with a crisis in less-than-healthy ways—with food, cigarettes, or alcohol—or suffer in silence.

Do you feel that your life has meaning and purpose?

a. Yes. I feel good about what I've accomplished in the past, and look forward to my future.

b. Yes, but recently I've felt the need for more challenge in my life, or even a shake-up.

c. Not really. I feel adrift, and am starting to wonder if there's something else I'm meant to do with my life.

MY MENTAL ATTITUDE SCORE

_____(a) _____ (b) _____ (c)

HOW MUCH OF A "STRESS BURDEN" DO YOU CARRY?

Like death and taxes, stress is a fact of life. But how it's perceived and managed can change the structure of the brain and impact Alzheimer's risk, studies suggest. Do you cope with stress in ways that help or harm the brain? This section helps answer that question.

Think back over the stress you've experienced in the past year, beyond the day-to-day pressures of life (work, chores, and responsibilities). You would describe these stressors as:

a. Minor—I got a traffic ticket, went on vacation, or hosted a holiday get-together.

b. Moderate—I was promoted or demoted at work, moved to a new house, took on (or foreclosed on) a mortgage.

c. Major life change—I or my spouse retired, lost a job, or started a new job; my relationship or marriage broke up; I, my partner, or a close family member was diagnosed with a serious chronic illness; I experienced the death of my partner or a close family member.

Do you have family or friends who give you emotional support when you need it?

a. Yes. I have a strong support system.

b. I have only a few people I depend on for emotional support, but they're dependable.

c. No. I have no reliable sources of emotional support.

On a scale of 1 to 5, 5 being the most stressful, how stressful do you feel your life is now?

a. A 1 or a 2. I have some stress in my life, but nothing I can't handle with a walk, a girls' night out, or some me time.

b. A 3 or a 4. I have too much to do and not enough time to do it, and the frantic pace is wearing me down.

c. I'm at stress level 5. I'm a caregiver to a spouse or aging parent or have long-standing financial, work, or relationship problems.

Your go-to stress-busters include:

a. More than one proven tension-taming activity such as deep breathing, exercise, meditation, yoga, or tai chi.

b. One of the activities above, or the support of a close friend or family member.

c. None of the above. I can't seem to get a handle on my stress.

How much sleep do you typically get?

a. At least 8 hours a night. Any less, and I can't function.

b. It varies. Sometimes I get 8 hours, sometimes 6, depending on the day (or when I decide to turn off the late show).

c. Six hours or less. I tend to toss and turn, or wake up hours before my alarm goes off.

Are you a raise-the-roof snorer and/or have you been diagnosed with sleep apnea?

a. No. I don't usually snore (according to my partner) and have not been diagnosed with sleep apnea.

b. Yes. I've been diagnosed with this condition, but use a breathing machine at night.

c. Yes. I know I'm a heavy snorer but have never talked to my doctor about sleep apnea.

On most days when you first wake up you feel:

a. Ready to seize the day.

b. Ready to seize the day, *after* I've had my coffee.

c. Like pulling the covers back over my head.

You had the morning from hell—you bickered with your partner, spilled coffee on the rug right before you had to leave for an appointment, and hit every red light on the way there. You arrived late, with a pounding headache. How likely is a meltdown?

> **a.** Not likely. I practiced deep breathing to get back on track.

> **b.** 50/50. I tend to stay cool when disaster strikes, but can fall apart over the trivial things.

> **c.** I'm almost sure to snap at someone or shed tears in the bathroom.

MY "STRESS BURDEN" SCORE

_____(a) _____ (b) _____ (c)

DO YOU CHALLENGE YOUR BRAIN ENOUGH?

Like the tastiest soups, the sharpest minds are kept at a steady simmer. The best way to keep your brain bubbling is to learn new things, be open to new experiences, and rediscover your sense of youthful curiosity. In this section, you'll find out if you give your brain the stimulation it needs to stay keen.

What's your educational background?

> **a.** I graduated college.

> **b.** I didn't attend college but often take adult-education courses because I have an interest in a subject (history, cooking, pottery).

> **c.** I graduated high school and have not pursued further education.

Reading a book or magazine, you come across a word you've never seen before. You:

> **a.** Look it up on the spot.

> **b.** Write it down so I can look it up later.

> **c.** Skip past it and keep reading.

Do you play a musical instrument or are you a music buff?

    a. I play an instrument often and for fun, or regularly attend musical events such as concerts.

    b. I don't play as often (or attend musical events as often) as I used to, and I miss it.

    c. No, music is not one of my interests.

Do you practice a brain-stimulating hobby such as reading, word games, chess, or bridge, or a complex physical activity such as dance lessons, golf, yoga, or tai chi?

    a. Yes, I enjoy at least two of those activities, or others like them.

    b. Yes, I practice at least one of those activities, or others like them.

    c. I prefer hobbies that relax rather than challenge my brain.

Would you consider learning a second language, and using it daily, to keep your mind and memory sharp?

    a. I already know and use a second language—how about a third?

    b. Absolutely. I've always wanted to learn a second language—its brain-boosting benefits are icing on the cake.

    c. No. I don't have the time or the interest.

Think back over the past week. How many hours did you spend watching TV or movies?

    a. An hour a day or less.

    b. Two hours a day or less.

    c. More than 3 hours a day.

How often do you use the Internet?

a. Often. I often use it to research topics that interest me.

b. Sometimes. I often use it to play online computer games, like solitaire, chess, and Scrabble.

c. Rarely or never.

MY MENTAL STIMULATION SCORE

_____(a) _____ (b) _____ (c)

SCORING: PART 2

Fill in the blanks below, so you can see your scores for all five sections in one place.

My diet score: _____ (a) ____ (b) ____ (c)
My physical activity score: _____ (a) ____ (b) ____ (c)
My mental attitude score: _____ (a) ____ (b) ____ (c)
My "stress burden" score: _____ (a) ____ (b) ____ (c)
My mental stimulation score: _____ (a) ____ (b) ____ (c)

A score of fewer than 6 points in any one category suggests room for improvement.

Is diet your weak spot? Turn to Chapter 5, Savor Brain-Boosting Foods.

Could you step up your physical activity? See Chapter 6, Hit the Walking Trail or Gym.

Could you have a more positive mental outlook? You'll find strategies in Chapter 7, Adjust Your Attitude.

Is stress taking its toll on your brain? Chapter 8, Reduce Brain-Shrinking Stress, has solutions.

Does your noodle need a workout? Turn to Chapter 9, Preserve Your Wits with Play.

OVERALL SCORE FOR PART 2

Count up your (a), (b), and (c) answers.

_____(a) _____ (b) _____ (c)

Mostly *a*'s: Congratulations! You live a super-healthy lifestyle, and are well on the way to an ageless brain. Keep up the good work, and get ready to learn healthy-brain strategies you may not know. Even a brainiac like you can learn something new every day, which is great news for your noggin.

It's possible that in a certain category, you ended up with a lower score than you'd hoped. For example, perhaps your score revealed that you could be more physically active, or that you carry more of a stress burden than you realized. No worries. Turn to the suggested chapter for strategies that can shore up that weak spot.

Mostly *b*'s: On the whole, you live a brain-healthy lifestyle, and likely aced one or more categories. Maybe your diet is squeaky-clean, or you're naturally optimistic or a lifelong learner. Or perhaps you've committed to taking control of the stress in your life, and already practice meditation or other science-backed stress-busters.

Now that you've identified your strengths, get ready to build on them. If you scored less than 6 points in one or more categories in Part 2, turn to the appropriate chapters and put their suggestions to work in your life. Before long, you'll develop the habits of a bona fide ageless brainer.

Mostly *c*'s: It's never too late to swap less-than-healthy habits for those that sustain your brain. In fact, making positive lifestyle changes at midlife can benefit thinking and memory, studies show. So don't sweat your score. You're about to embark on a new lifestyle that can help protect your brain and rev up your thinking and memory abilities, and it's easier than you might think. Turn the page to get started!

PART 2

STAY-
SHARP
BASICS

The 10 Commandments of an Ageless Brain

IN YOUR QUEST FOR an ageless brain, where to begin? With the fundamentals, of course. Research links the "commandments" in this section to a reduced risk of dementia, including Alzheimer's disease, and you're in for some surprises.

- Residue from a long-banned pesticide still lurks in the food we eat, and some studies have associated exposure to it to a higher risk of Alzheimer's.

- If you take prescription or over-the-counter medications for heartburn, allergies, or other common conditions, you should know that certain meds have been linked to increased dementia risk, studies show. (Thankfully, there are alternatives to these medications.)

- Do you snore like a chainsaw? Loud, heavy snoring is a symptom of sleep apnea, which studies have found raises the risk of mild cognitive impairment and Alzheimer's. But there's a simple way to counteract this potential mind and memory stealer.

The commandments on weight, high blood pressure, and diabetes include some wakeup calls as well. Even if you think you've heard it all before, what you may not know is that all these conditions, along with heart disease, are linked to increased Alzheimer's risk, beginning in as early as middle age.

So it's amazing, isn't it, that more and more studies link cardiovascular benefits to a sharper, healthier brain? The good news just keeps coming.

This section presents the evidence that backs each commandment, then offers simple ways to put it to work in your life today. Your path to a sharper, keener brain begins right here, right now. Step right up!

Commandment #1: Quench Chronic Inflammation

When illness or infection strikes, the body's immune system snaps into action. One of its basic tools is a process called inflammation, and it comes in two different forms. When you stub your toe, the redness, pain, and swelling of *acute* inflammation mean your body's inflammatory response is working properly. Acute inflammation lasts a few days, then goes away. But when this healing response doesn't shut off and becomes chronic, it starts to threaten your health—and potentially your brain.

Chronic inflammation is the body's misguided immune response to everyday threats—a diet packed with unhealthy added sugars and bad fats, too little sleep, too much stress, and too much body or belly fat. This low-grade "smolder" in the body plays a key role in a wide variety of chronic diseases, such as obesity, heart and blood-vessel disease (also called cardio-vascular disease), type 2 diabetes[1]—and Alzheimer's disease (AD).[2,3]

Along with plaques and tangles, chronic inflammation is a hallmark

STAY-SHARP STRATEGY

PILE YOUR PLATE WITH PLANTS

Nothing wrong with moderate amounts of animal protein, but a healthy, plant-packed diet seems to play a vital role in reducing dementia risk. Further, quite a few plant foods—fruits, veggies, whole grains—appear to quench inflammation in the body.

In a recent study,[4] researchers put 63 people on one of five diets. One diet excluded animal foods (vegan). Two included either eggs and dairy or fish (vegetarian or pesco-vegetarian diets, respectively). One included small amounts of poultry and red meat (semivegetarian). The last diet included both plant and animal foods (nonvegetarian).

Compared to the non- or semivegetarian groups, the vegan or vegetarian groups scored lower on a tool called the Dietary Inflammatory Index (DII), created by investigators at the University of South Carolina to evaluate a person's diet for its potential to increase or reduce inflammation. Foods that other research has associated with reduced dementia risk also popped up in this study. They include garlic, fiber, omega-3 fatty acids (in fish), and the spice turmeric. And if you like poultry and fish, the research-backed MIND diet is right up your alley—see page 108.

of a brain with Alzheimer's. In fact, some research has proposed that it's behind the die-off of brain cells that characterizes the disease, and may happen because a specific type of cell in the brain starts to malfunction. When these cells—called microglia—falter, inflammation in the brain runs amok.[5]

The key players in the central nervous system's immune response, microglia help manage inflammation, munch invaders like bacteria and viruses, and eat cellular "trash," including clusters of amyloid protein (the material that plaques are made of). But with AD, microglia may turn against healthy brain tissue, causing neuron-destroying inflammation. The plaques in brain regions related to the disease are packed with microglia gone rogue.[6]

Beyond the possible role of microglia, a substance called C-reactive protein (CRP) also may play a role in the development of dementia. This substance is made by the liver and sent into the bloodstream, and its presence in the blood is a telltale sign of chronic inflammation.

You may have heard that a high CRP level often is associated with increased heart-disease risk. However, research has linked high CRP levels with both plaques and tangles in brains with Alzheimer's.[7] In a study of 1,050 men that spanned more than two decades, men with the highest blood levels of CRP were three times more likely to have dementia 25 years later, compared to those with the lowest.[8]

PUTTING THE RESEARCH TO WORK

Extra pounds, a junky diet, and a stressed-out, no-sleep lifestyle all increase chronic inflammation, research shows.[9] Cool it with a healthy, whole-foods diet and these other science-tested inflammation fighters.

Sleep tight every night. A scientific review of 72 studies associated insomnia and other sleep disturbances with increased levels of CRP and interleukin-6,[10] another marker of bodywide inflammation.[11] For surprising solutions for sleeplessness, see page 197.

Take a daily walk break. While chronic inflammation typically increases with age, regular exercise, even walking, can help reduce it. In one study of over 4,000 men and women, those who engaged in moderate exercise 2.5 hours a week lowered their markers of inflammation by over 10 percent, regardless of their weight.[12] That works out to about 20 minutes a day!

Just say om. When you do mindfulness meditation, you tune in to your thoughts, feelings, and body sensations in a nonjudgmental way. In a recent study of stressed-out adults, 4 months of this simple technique reduced blood levels of interleukin-6. The technique resulted in brain changes that improved the ability to manage stress. Those changes, in turn, reduced inflammation.[13]

Baby your brain. The daily low-dose aspirin found to help keep heart disease at bay may also protect your brain. In a study of older women at high risk for cardiovascular disease, 75 to 160 milligrams of aspirin a day was found to slow decline in memory and thinking skills (but not AD) over a 5-year period.[14] Although it's not clear exactly how aspirin may protect the brain, multiple studies have linked its use— along with other nonsteroidal anti-inflammatory drugs—to a lowered risk of Alzheimer's. Note: Consult your doctor before you take any type of aspirin, especially if you're at risk for gastrointestinal bleeding or hemorrhagic stroke.

Kick the cigarettes. Smoking is a prime cause of chronic inflammation. But in one study, women who quit showed significantly reduced blood levels of CRP, interleukin-6, and tumor necrosis factor, another marker of inflammation, in just weeks.[15] For more on smoking's link to AD—and quit tips—see page 94.

Commandment #2:
Lose the Weight and Whittle Your Waist

If you live a relaxed-fit lifestyle, you're far from alone. Nearly 70 percent of Americans have too much body fat, national health studies show. That statistic is based on a measure of weight classification called body mass index (BMI). A BMI at or above 25 is considered overweight; a BMI at or above 30, obese.[16]

Based on a ratio of height to weight, BMI isn't a precise measure of body fat. Still, researchers consider it a useful estimate. BMI is also a good gauge of risk for a slew of diseases linked to excess body fat, such as high blood pressure, cardiovascular disease, type 2 diabetes, and breathing problems. As BMI rises, so does risk.[17]

However, BMI doesn't account for one crucial factor: excess belly fat (or as experts call it, abdominal obesity). When you carry extra fat around your middle, not only do the odds of the diseases just listed go up. You may also put your thinking and memory in harm's way.

Excess abdominal fat's damaging effects on the brain may begin years before the signs of dementia appear.[18] In a study that spanned 36 years, researchers measured the abdominal fat of almost 6,500 people no older than 45. Decades later, those with the highest amount of belly fat earlier in their lives were nearly three times more likely to develop dementia in their seventies, compared to those with the lowest amount.[19]

What makes belly fat so vicious? Its proximity to vital organs may be a factor. Packed deep in your abdomen, and wrapped around your liver, pancreas, and intestines, abdominal fat acts similarly to a gland and stirs up metabolic mayhem. It pumps out chemicals that ignite harmful, bodywide inflammation and fatty acids and hormones that lead to

TREAT THIS MEMORY-STEALING SYNDROME

Has your doctor expressed concern about your blood sugar, blood pressure, or cholesterol?

If this sounds familiar, you may have metabolic syndrome, a cluster of separate risk factors that together spell trouble. Compared to people without this condition, those with it have three times the risk of heart attack and ischemic stroke, and five times the risk of type 2 diabetes.[20]

Metabolic syndrome may mess with memory, too. In a study of over 7,000 men and women 65 and older, people with the condition were 20 percent more likely to show intellectual decline on cognitive tests, compared to those without it. The study also associated higher triglycerides and low HDL cholesterol with poorer memory scores, and linked type 2 diabetes to poorer word fluency scores.

If you have three of the five risk factors below, you may have metabolic syndrome. (Taking medications to treat any of these conditions doesn't negate the risk factor.[21])

1. A large waistline (over 35 inches if you're a woman and over 40 inches if you're a man)

2. Blood pressure of 130/85 mmHg or higher

3. Fasting blood sugar of 100 mg/dl or higher

4. Triglycerides of 150 mg/dl or higher

5. HDL cholesterol of less than 50 mg/dl for women and less than 40 mg/dl for men

The good news? Your doctor can treat metabolic syndrome with the healthy strategies in this book to help protect against its brain-harming potential.

rises in LDL cholesterol, triglycerides, blood sugar, and blood pressure.[22] In fact, excess belly fat is one of the cluster of symptoms that make up metabolic syndrome (see page 69).

Even if you don't have a big belly, having an outsized BMI at midlife may increase Alzheimer's risk. Researchers followed nearly 1,400 people for 14 years, using data from a national aging study to track how the participants' cognitive abilities changed over time.[23, 24]

What they found: A higher BMI at age 50 correlated with an earlier onset of AD. Specifically, for each unit increase in BMI at 50, the disease set in an average of 7 months earlier. In other words, a 50-year-old with a BMI of 30 could experience the onset of AD more than a year earlier than someone with a BMI of 28. The study also found that those with a higher BMI in middle age had more amyloid deposits in an area of the brain called the precuneus, which often shows early signs of Alzheimer's-related changes.[25]

But there's no need to let extra pounds steal your brainpower. Lose even 5 to 10 percent of your current weight, and studies suggest that you'll reap better health and a sharper brain.

PUTTING THE RESEARCH TO WORK

You lose both body and belly fat the same way—move more, and eat the right foods in the right amounts. See page 104 for the three superstar diets with science-proven benefits: weight loss, reduced risk of chronic disease, and lowered risk of dementia. Consider these two bonus belly-fat busters, too.

Say so long to soda. Sip water instead, and you're likely to see your stomach flatten a bit. In a study published in the *Journal of Nutrition*, soda-sippers had 10 percent more abdominal fat than those who didn't.[26]

Dust off your pedometer. Or invest in one. Then aim to take 10,000 steps a day. People who were moderately active lowered their rate of abdominal fat accumulation by 7 percent, compared with those who moved less, a study published in *Obesity* found.[27]

As you lose excess fat all over your body, you'll lose it around your waist, too. Your target: a waist circumference of less than 35 inches for women, and 40 inches or less for men. That's the cutoff point for heart disease and type 2 diabetes risk, per the National Heart, Lung, and Blood Institute. To get an accurate measurement, stand tall and place your tape measure just above your hipbones. Breathe out, and then take your measurement.

Commandment #3: Keep Blood Pressure in Check

If you have high blood pressure, as one in three adults in the United States do, you likely already know that you're at higher risk for stroke and heart attack.[28] But did you know that runaway blood pressure may threaten your thinking and memory?

Uncontrolled hypertension, or high blood pressure, is a key risk factor for cardiovascular disease. It's also the single strongest predictor of brain health, according to the American Stroke Association.[29] Now, research links it to memory loss,[30] vascular dementia (caused by conditions that block or reduce bloodflow to the brain[31]), and Alzheimer's.[32] Indeed, high blood pressure doubles the risk of developing the disease.[33] Studies that followed participants for decades, tracking both their blood pressure and cognitive health, have found that those who went on to develop dementia had a history of high blood pressure decades earlier.[34]

Here's the connection: High blood pressure can lead to changes in

Safeguard Your Brain against Stroke

Having a stroke more than doubles the risk of developing dementia, and symptoms come on FAST.

- Face drooping
- Arm numbness
- Speech difficulty
- Time to call 911[35]

There are two main types of stroke, and in each case, high blood pressure is a prime culprit. In an ischemic stroke, a blood clot blocks a vessel that carries blood to the brain. Most strokes are of this type.[36] With the less common hemorrhagic stroke, an artery in the brain leaks blood or breaks open, and the leaked blood exerts pressure that damages brain cells.[37]

Similar to a stroke is a transient ischemic attack (TIA), or ministroke, which temporarily blocks bloodflow to a portion of the brain.[38] Symptoms of a TIA are like that of a full-blown stroke, but the attack typically lasts less than 5 minutes[39] and causes no permanent damage to brain cells. But a TIA isn't an event to brush off. It's a warning sign that a full-blown stroke may be about to strike. So if you experience the symptoms above, get a sudden, severe headache, or develop sudden vision problems, call 911 right away.

An easy way to reduce your risk of stroke: put one foot in front of the other. Women who walked 2 hours a week cut their stroke risk by 30 percent, a 12-year study of nearly 40,000 women found. Those who walked briskly saw their risk fall by 37 percent.[40] Those 2½ hours work out to just 20 minutes a day. Such a simple change can make a dramatic difference in your future brain health.

the brain like those caused by a stroke. These changes may not cause symptoms, which is why they're dubbed "silent strokes." Studies also have found that high blood pressure may also injure the small arteries that nourish white matter, the cells that relay information from one region of the brain to another.[41]

The connection doesn't stop there. With each 10 mmHg rise in systolic pressure, the risk of ischemic stroke increases 28 percent; hemorrhagic stroke, 38 percent.[42] The cumulative impact of multiple strokes—including those "silent" strokes—is a common cause of vascular dementia. Again, high blood pressure is the culprit. By contrast, every 10 mmHg reduction in systolic blood pressure reduces stroke risk by 27 percent, a systematic review of over 100 studies found.[43]

If all this doesn't make you sit up and take notice, consider this: Recent studies link high blood pressure, especially in midlife, to an increased risk for dementia later in life.

In one study, the brains of people in their forties showed subtle changes associated with higher levels of "arterial stiffness," the earliest sign of systolic high blood pressure. Typically, this "top number" rises with age, as vessels stiffen and gunk up with plaque.[44] The changes the researchers saw were found in both white matter and gray matter, the outer layer of the brain.[45]

In the second study, researchers measured the blood pressure of almost 400 men and women between the ages of 50 and 60, and then tested their intellectual performance 30 years later. Those who'd had high blood pressure in middle age scored more poorly on tests of attention and executive function.[46]

The bottom line: To protect your future brain, get a handle on your blood pressure now.

The foundation of any healthy-pressure plan: a clean, green diet. The blood pressure diet DASH (short for Dietary Approaches to Stop Hypertension) pushes whole foods like veggies and fruits, whole grains, low-fat dairy foods, and fish, and skimps on red meat, harmful fats, sweets, and sugary drinks. Just 2 weeks on DASH can reduce blood pressure, studies show.[47]

A healthy diet also can help shed the extra pounds that burden brain health. In an analysis of 25 clinical trials, an 11-pound weight loss shaved 4.4 points off systolic blood pressure and 3.6 points from diastolic pressure.[48] And if you drink alcohol, do so in moderation—one drink a day for women, two a day for men. More than that can send high blood pressure higher, and heavy drinking raises stroke risk.[49]

Get a move on, too. Cardiovascular exercise helps reduce blood pressure by making arteries more pliable, so blood can flow through them more freely. It also gets your heart pumping, which boosts the flow of oxygen-rich blood to your brain.[50] Regular bouts of "cardio" have also been shown to elevate mood—and HDL levels—as they lower LDL cholesterol and high blood pressure. See Chapter 6 for more on exercise's brain benefits and recommendations on how long and how often to exercise. (Before you start, get your doctor's okay.)[51]

If these lifestyle changes don't reduce your blood pressure, medication may be the next step.[52] Fortunately, evidence shows that treatment with antihypertensive medications may help stave off dementia.

In one study, researchers divided almost 3,000 people with high blood pressure into two groups. One group received blood-pressure medications; a control group did not. Compared to the control group, those taking the hypertensive medications slashed their risk of both AD and vascular dementia by an incredible 55 percent.[53]

In a more recent study of over 2,000 healthy older people with no thinking or memory problems, certain drugs commonly used to treat high blood pressure, including diuretics and ACE inhibitors, were found to reduce Alzheimer's risk by 40 to 50 percent over a 6-year period. (In this study, calcium channel blockers were not associated with reduced risk.[54]) Researchers weren't sure how antihypertensive meds reduced AD risk. It may be that, because high blood pressure is a known risk factor for memory problems, lower blood pressure alone may be a memory-saver.

Commandment #4: Safeguard Your Cardiovascular Health

"Waxy buildup" isn't limited to kitchen floors. Cardiovascular disease is driven by a lifetime of unhealthy habits and a process with an ugly name: atherosclerosis.

In this silent process, a slick mixture of fat and cholesterol in the blood,[55] called plaque, builds up on arteries' inside walls.[56] This waxy buildup, along with chronic inflammation caused by unhealthy habits like smoking, a sedentary lifestyle, and a steady diet of processed junk, thickens the walls of the vessels. The result: hard, stiff arteries.[57] This can reduce bloodflow to the heart and other organs—including the brain—and lead to heart attack and stroke.

Atherosclerosis is also a risk factor for dementia. High levels of LDL cholesterol have been linked to Alzheimer's disease and found to raise the risk for vascular dementia.[58] High *total* cholesterol, defined as

STAY-SHARP STRATEGY

CUT OFF ALZHEIMER'S AT THE NECK

Worldwide, most AD cases stem from nine lifestyle-driven conditions, according to a scientific review that examined hundreds of studies and nearly 100 conditions that potentially affect Alzheimer's risk.[59] Along with the usual suspects, such as obesity, smoking, and type 2 diabetes, the review identified one condition you may not know about, but should: carotid artery disease.

This condition starts with the buildup of plaque inside the carotid arteries that run along the sides of your neck, which makes it hard for blood to reach your brain. It's already known that carotid artery disease increases the risk of stroke,[60] which itself is linked to an increased risk of AD.

The good news: The healthy lifestyle habits in these pages can help stave off the condition. If you're diagnosed with it, follow your doctor's treatment plan, which may include medication. It'll reduce your risk of stroke and perhaps the memory and thinking issues that can develop poststroke.[61]

240 milligrams per deciliter of blood (mg/dl) or higher, also may increase dementia risk. In a study of almost 10,000 men and women, high cholesterol in midlife was found to spike AD risk 30 years later by 66 percent! Borderline high cholesterol (200 to 239 mg/dl) in midlife raised risk for later vascular dementia by 52 percent.[62, 63]

All in all, cardiovascular disease appears to be murder on the brain. In fact, a scientific review that examined the link between cardiovascular risk factors and Alzheimer's found "abundant and converging evidence" that they—and cardiovascular disease itself—play a key role in this brain devastator.[64] Consider some of the findings from this review.

- Peripheral artery disease (PAD), which ups risk of heart attack and stroke, is strongly associated with AD. While PAD typically reduces bloodflow in the legs, arteries that transport blood from your heart to other organs can be affected.

- People with atrial fibrillation (AF), an abnormally fast, irregular heartbeat caused by a number of conditions including heart disease and high blood pressure, are at an increased risk of AD.

- Studies have associated heart failure, a condition in which the heart can't supply the body's cells with all the blood they need, with cognitive impairment and AD.

The good news: Every heart-healthy action you take may benefit your brain, too.

PUTTING THE RESEARCH TO WORK

A heart-healthy lifestyle is a twofer—it protects your heart and throws in a healthier brain for free. As you now know, weight loss, regular exercise, and quitting smoking improve the risk factors that can, over time, undercut your thinking and memory. Beyond those healthy changes, follow these general heart-smart guidelines, and turn to the pages indicated for more information.

Eat for two—heart and brain. A diet low in bad fats and rich in whole foods benefits them both. Research associates three specific diets—the MIND diet,[65] the Mediterranean diet,[66] and the blood pressure-lowering DASH diet[67]—with a reduced risk of AD. Their common bond: more whole foods and less added sugars and artery-clogging saturated and trans fats.[68] In one study, replacing 5 percent of calories from saturated fats with the same amount of polyunsaturated fats (such as those found in walnuts and sunflower seeds or their oils) or monounsaturated fats (such as olive oil or avocado) lowered heart disease risk by 25 percent and 15 percent, respectively.[69] For more about these diets and their brain benefits, see Chapter 5.

Keep your LDL and HDL in the healthy range. In general, aim for LDL cholesterol below 100 mg/dl and HDL cholesterol at 60 mg/dl or higher.[70] Here's a brain-centric reason to improve those numbers. In a study of 74 older adults published in the journal *Neurology,* higher fasting LDL cholesterol levels and lower HDL cholesterol levels were associated with more accumulation of amyloid plaque in the brain.[71] According to the study, unhealthy cholesterol levels may be behind the higher levels of amyloid known to contribute to Alzheimer's, in the same way that they promote heart disease.[72] So get your cholesterol tested each year, more often if you're at high risk for heart disease.

Squelch chronic stress. When you're swamped by stress, healthy habits tend to fall by the wayside. What's more, stress causes hormonal and chemical changes in the body that may raise the risk for AD, research suggests.[73] For more on the link between stress and dementia, and ways to control stress so it doesn't control you, see Chapter 8.

Commandment #5: Prevent or Manage Type 2 Diabetes

An estimated 29 million Americans have full-blown diabetes,[74] fueled by obesity and less-than-healthy lifestyle habits. Why are people who have this chronic disease twice as likely to develop Alzheimer's disease as those who don't?[75] Although research hasn't quite connected all the dots, evidence of a link between type 2 and AD—as well as vascular dementia—continues to mount.

- A primary driver of type 2 diabetes, insulin resistance happens when the normal amount of insulin made by the pancreas isn't enough to get glucose into the body's cells. (In other words, cells "resist" insulin's action). In a study of middle-aged men and women with a family history of AD, insulin resistance was associated with poorer performance on memory tests.[76]

● In a study of almost 1,500 older adults with an average age of 80, the brains of people diagnosed with diabetes in midlife were in worse shape than those of people who developed diabetes later in life. Compared to the brains of nondiabetics, the brains and hippocampi of those with diabetes in middle age were an average of

---

Alzheimer's Disease: Could It Be "Type 3 Diabetes"?

If you've ever heard AD referred to as "type 3 diabetes," you may wonder why. It's because some research proposes that, like type 2 diabetes, AD is a metabolic disease that afflicts the brain.[77]

Like any other cell, brain cells are fueled by glucose, and insulin tells them to take it from the bloodstream. Insulin also is known to affect various aspects of thinking and memory.[78]

According to the "type 3" theory, brain cells can develop insulin resistance, just like other cells in the body. Brain insulin resistance can lead to the damaging buildup of amyloid proteins and neuron death characteristic of the disease.[79]

Evidence of the insulin resistance/AD link continues to mount.[80] One recent study concluded that in the disease, brain insulin resistance starts even before cognitive problems begin, and contributes to that decline beyond other known causes.[81] While more research is needed, this study adds to the evidence that AD just might be a distinct form of type 2 diabetes—"type 3."

---

3 percent smaller and 4 percent smaller, respectively. (As you may remember, the hippocampus is the brain region key to short- and long-term memory.) The study also found that, compared to people without diabetes, those who developed it at midlife were twice as likely to have mild cognitive impairment (MCI).[82]

● Women with type 2 diabetes—but not men—had a nearly 20 percent higher risk of developing vascular dementia, a scientific review of 14 studies found.[83]

The connection between vascular dementia and type 2 diabetes is clear. The blood-vessel damage that leads to the complications of type 2 diabetes, such as heart and kidney disease, eye problems, and nerve damage,[84] can likewise damage vessels that feed the brain.[85] Although diabetes' association with AD is less straightforward, both diseases share common cardiovascular risk factors such as high blood pressure, impaired circulation, and obesity.[86] Type 2 diabetes also promotes the chronic inflammation that may damage or kill brain cells[87] and raises the risk of having a stroke.

If you've been diagnosed with type 2 diabetes, the disease may already be affecting your brainpower. In a study of men and women with type 2, researchers measured bloodflow to different areas of participants' brains and gave them a battery of cognitive tests to evaluate their ability to think and remember over time. After 2 years, their intellectual performance had slipped. The declines most affected their executive function, which involves the ability to plan, organize, prioritize, pay attention, and start tasks.[88]

PUTTING THE RESEARCH TO WORK

An estimated 86 million US adults have *prediabetes,* or elevated blood sugar levels that aren't yet high enough for a type 2 diabetes diagnosis.[89]

The good news is, those healthy changes can head off type 2 at the pass, according to the Diabetes Prevention Program (DPP), a study of more than 3,000 people at high risk for the disease.

The people in the DPP's lifestyle change group, who lost 15 pounds, on average, in the study's first year, reduced their risk of diabetes by

STAY-SHARP STRATEGY

PACK YOUR DIET WITH FIBER

How might a fiber-rich diet help keep your brain keen? By keeping your blood sugar on an even keel. A fiber-rich diet encourages the growth and activity of gut microbes associated with good metabolic health. And a gut packed with such "friendly" intestinal bacteria may help to keep blood sugar steady, according to research presented at the 2015 annual meeting of the Endocrine Society.[90] And rock-steady blood sugar may mean a sharper brain down the road.

As strange as it may seem, fiber's gut-friendly effects stem from the fact that it can't be digested. Prebiotics are specific types of fiber that pass through your small intestine intact and enter your colon. There, they become food for the beneficial beasties that call your colon home. With names like inulin and fructo-oligosaccharides, prebiotics occur naturally in many plant foods, including blueberries, whole grains, spinach, onions, and garlic.

There's an easy way for you to help prebiotics make your gut a hospitable host to different strains of friendly bacteria. That's to team prebiotic foods with probiotics—foods that contain live bacterial cultures, like yogurt, fermented sauerkraut, and raw apple cider vinegar. Savoring prebiotic and probiotic foods is a tasty way to help steady blood sugar and shore up your gut health.

58 percent over 3 years. Age was no barrier to success, but participants ages 60 and older who made healthy lifestyle changes reduced their risk by a staggering 71 percent![91]

And if you snore loudly at night, tell your doctor. It's a symptom of a condition called sleep apnea, which left untreated can raise the risk of type 2 diabetes and other chronic diseases.[92] Studies have also linked sleep apnea with a higher risk of developing MCI and Alzheimer's.[93] For more information on sleep apnea, see page 84.

If you've already been diagnosed with type 2 diabetes, don't fret. There's still plenty you can do to protect your brain health. Follow your doctor's lifestyle recommendations, take your medications as directed, and keep tabs on your blood sugar levels. Every healthy choice makes a difference!

Commandment #6: Brush Up on Your Brain Health

Hopefully, your gums are a dentist's dream, pink and firm. But if they bleed when you brush or floss, dial your dentist today. An emerging body of evidence associates dental health with mental health, and suggests that gum disease may raise the risk of MCI and dementia later in life.[94]

The mild form of gum disease, gingivitis, takes hold when the bacteria-packed film on your teeth, called plaque, hardens and can't be brushed away. This bacteria infects and inflames gums, making them redden, swell, and bleed. Untreated gingivitis can lead to periodontitis. In this severe form of gum disease, the gums pull away from the teeth, and the exposed "pockets" fill with bacteria and become infected. The end game of untreated periodontitis: tooth loss.

And if you lose teeth, memory may follow. One study of older men found that for each tooth lost per decade, the risk of a poor showing on cognitive tests rose 9 to 12 percent.[95] So what's the connection between poor oral health and dementia? One possible explanation: The bacteria that wreak havoc on chronically infected gums may do the same to the brain.[96]

In a study published in the *Journal of Alzheimer's Disease*,[97] researchers examined brain samples donated from 20 people; 10 had dementia, 10 didn't. The researchers found signs of *Porphyromonas gingivalis*—a bacterium that instigates periodontitis—in four brain samples that showed Alzheimer's, but none in the samples that didn't.

These bacteria enter the bloodstream when we chew or even do healthy things like brush our teeth or undergo dental procedures, the study said. In people with good oral health, this isn't a problem. Trouble arises with serious gum disease, however.[98] "We are working on the theory that when the brain is repeatedly exposed to bacteria and/or their debris from our gums, subsequent immune responses may lead to nerve cell death and possibly memory loss," stated study researcher Sim K. Singhrao, PhD.[99]

Even infrequent brushing—a prime cause of gum disease—may affect memory. A study that followed over 5,000 older adults for 18 years found that those who reported brushing their teeth less than once a day were up to 65 percent more likely to get hit with dementia than those who used their toothbrushes three times daily.[100] This study, too, suggested tooth-loosening bacteria as a potential cause.

The take-home message? Take care of your teeth. If the evidence pans out, it may help you brush your way to better brain health.

PUTTING THE RESEARCH TO WORK

Even if you pride yourself on your brush-and-floss game, gum disease is tough to avoid; 47 percent of Americans 30 and over, and 70 percent of those 65 and over, have some form of it.[101] To keep it under control, brush twice a day for 2 minutes at a time and floss at least once a day.

Also, see a dentist at least once a year for a cleaning and checkup. Don't let fear keep you out of the chair. If your gums are pulling away from your teeth, or if you have a foul taste in your mouth that mouthwash or mints can't mask, make a dental appointment today. Treatment for gum disease, which includes deep cleaning and bacteria-controlling medications,[102] can save your teeth and maybe even protect your brain.

Commandment #7:
Take Steps to Snore No More

Raise-the-rafters snoring is no mere annoyance. Especially if the snoring is accompanied by gasps, snorts, or long pauses between breaths. These are symptoms of sleep apnea—a condition characterized by disrupted breathing and sleep and linked to an increased risk of cognitive impairment.[103] Older women with sleep apnea were about twice as likely to develop dementia within a 5-year period as those without the condition, a study published in the *Journal of the American Medical Association (JAMA)* found.[104]

In another study published in *Neurology*,[105] researchers analyzed the medical data of almost 2,500 middle-aged and older people. Some participants had mild MCI or AD; others were cognitively healthy. People with sleep-disordered breathing, or SDB, were diagnosed with MCI a decade earlier, on average, than those without the condition. Specifically, when researchers examined only people who developed MCI or AD during the study, those with nighttime breathing trouble developed MCI at age 73, on average; those without it, at an average age of 84. Further, those with SDB developed AD at an average age of 83, while people without it developed the disease a significant 5 years later, at an average age of 88.[106]

It's not yet clear how sleep apnea may lead to problems with memory and thinking, but studies suggest that sleep apnea can starve the brain of oxygen, which may cause cognitive abilities to wane over time.[107] In the *JAMA* study, women who experienced frequent episodes of low oxygen, or spent most of their sleep time in an oxygen-deprived state, were more likely to develop cognitive impairment.[108]

Another theory suggests that not getting deep sleep hinders the removal of amyloid proteins from the brain. These waste proteins build up between brain cells during the day, when nerves are active, and are cleared out during deep sleep.[109] So in people who experience frequent nighttime awakenings, like those with SDB, this "brain waste" may accumulate, potentially contributing to plaque formation.

The good news: The *Neurology* study also compared participants with untreated SDB to those getting treatment for it and found that people who treated their nighttime breathing problems with a continuous positive airway pressure (CPAP) machine were diagnosed with MCI a decade later than those whose breathing trouble went untreated—at age 82, compared to age 72.[110] Small enough to set on a nightstand, a CPAP machine delivers a constant stream of air through a mask worn during sleep. It helps keep the airway open, prevent snoring, and allow deep sleep without frequent nighttime wakeups.

PUTTING THE RESEARCH TO WORK

If you're a heavy snorer, or suspect that you may have sleep-disordered breathing, CPAP treatment can put you on the path to deep, brain-restoring sleep.[111] These tips can get you started.

Get the ball rolling. Because CPAP machines require a prescription, schedule a doctor's appointment to discuss snoring or breathing concerns. You'll likely be referred to a sleep specialist, who will order a study to measure your brain activity, heart rate, and other data overnight, as you sleep. If you're diagnosed with sleep apnea, you may take another test to determine the optimal air-pressure setting for your CPAP machine.[112]

Most insurance policies cover CPAP units. Typically, a technician comes to your home to set it up and adjust its settings to your prescription.[113]

"Break in" your mask. Yours may cover just your nose, or both your nose and mouth. Regardless, donning it at bedtime likely will feel strange at first. Consider wearing it for short periods during your downtime, perhaps as you watch TV or read, so it feels more natural when you turn in.[114]

Make any needed adjustments. CPAP units and masks are like shoes—you have to find the right "fit." It's common to try a few combinations until you hit upon the right one for you. Your doctor, sleep specialist, or home equipment provider can help.

Keep it clean. A clean machine works better and helps prevent sinus or nasal infections. Following the cleaning instructions that come with your machine, clean your mask, tubing, and headgear once a week, at the same day and time so you won't forget.[115]

Commandment #8: Minimize Your Exposure to Pesticides

Might an insecticide banned in the United States 40 years ago impact dementia risk today? Could prolonged, on-the-job exposure to pesticides raise the risk of Alzheimer's disease later in life? Possibly, studies suggest.

For decades, the United States used DDT (dichlorodiphenyltrichloroethane) to kill pests that damaged crops and mosquitos that spread deadly diseases like malaria. But the Environmental Protection Agency banned its use in 1972 after learning this toxic chemical lingered in the environment and threatened wildlife.[116]

Decades later, DDT is still found in US soil and water, and potentially may remain in the environment for hundreds of years.[117] Moreover, some countries still use this toxic chemical, both legally and illegally. That means we're exposed to it—and to DDE, the chemical compound left when DDT breaks down. The EPA has classified both chemicals as human carcinogens,[118] and their detrimental health effects may extend to the brain.

Rutgers University researchers tested blood samples from 86 people with late-onset AD, and a control group of 79 people without the disease. The blood levels of DDT and DDE in 74 of the Alzheimer's patients were four times higher than those in the control group.[119] It may be that this exposure plays a role in AD, possibly by promoting the growth of amyloid proteins.[120] The study also found that people with the most severe late-onset AD had both the APOE-e4 gene *and* high blood levels of DDE. This suggests that this chemical may interact with genes, perhaps increasing their susceptibility to the disease.[121]

Our main exposure to DDT likely comes from eating fruits, vegetables, and grains imported from countries that still use DDT, or fish from contaminated waterways.[122] This chemical can stay in the body for up to 10 years and is found in up to 80 percent of blood samples collected from the Centers for Disease Control and Prevention (CDC) for its ongoing health and nutrition survey.[123]

If you work with or around pesticides, as agricultural workers,

STAY-SHARP STRATEGY

CONSIDER GOING ORGANIC

The fruits and veggies in your supermarket produce aisle are the building blocks of a brain-healthy diet. The downside: If they're grown using conventional methods, which use synthetic chemicals, they're likely to harbor pesticide residues. Such residues were found on nearly 75 percent of the produce samples tested by the USDA in 2014, according to the nonprofit Environmental Working Group (EWG).[124]

But don't stop eating them! Simply offer your brain some pesticide protection by swapping conventionally grown produce for organically grown varieties.[125]

Local produce, which ideally is grown within 100 miles of where you're buying it, often is organic. You'll find it at seasonal farmers' markets, roadside stands, or the "locally grown" section of your supermarket produce aisle. But bear in mind that "local" doesn't always mean "organic." Getting organic certification can be expensive, and small farmers may not be able to afford the cost. However,

groundskeepers, pet groomers, and fumigators do,[128] take note: A study published in the journal *Neurology* associated on-the-job exposure to these toxic chemicals with a higher risk of AD later.[129] (By the way, "pesticides" also include toxic chemicals that kill weeds, fungi, and rodents.)

This study zeroed in on 3,000 men and women 65 years old or older who lived in a region where many worked as farmers or had other jobs that exposed them to pesticides. Researchers asked their participants if they'd ever been around these chemicals at work and, if they had, which kinds and for how long. Almost 600 participants said their jobs exposed

many local farmers use organic methods anyway. Their "certification" is their reputation with their customers, which is why it pays to "know your farmer." To make sure you're buying local and organic, ask the farmers behind the table or stand, or the workers in the produce aisle.[126]

If local fruits and veggies are also organic, jackpot! When you mostly eat produce that's in season in your area, it's typically in your hands within a day of harvesting. That means it's at the peak of its flavor and nutrient content.[127] Out of season, you'll find organically grown frozen fruits and veggies in your supermarket's freezer section.

Even if you can't go totally organic, you can be aware of the fruits and veggies with the most pesticide residues, and shop accordingly. The EWG's annual "Dirty Dozen" and "Clean 15" lists single out both fruits and veggies with the highest amounts and lowest amounts of residues, respectively. You can check out the list each year at *ewg.org*.

them to pesticides—mostly to organophosphate and organochlorine, known to affect levels of acetylcholine. (As you may recall from Chapter 2, the brains of people with Alzheimer's have reduced levels of this key neurotransmitter.)

The researchers assessed their participants' abilities to think and remember, and reassessed them 3, 7, and 10 years later. After the researchers factored in age, sex, and the APOE-e4 gene, the risk for AD was 53 percent higher among people who'd had exposure to pesticides compared to those who had no exposure.

Each year, more than 2 billion pounds of pesticides are applied to crops, not to mention homes, parks, schools, and forests.[130] Yikes! Fortunately, these simple tips can help minimize your exposure.

TO HELP REDUCE PESTICIDE EXPOSURE FROM FOOD

- Eat a wide variety of fruits and veggies, organically grown if possible. This reduces the potential of increased exposure to a single type of pesticide.[131]

- Wash produce under running water and dry it with a paper towel or clean cloth.

- Toss out the outer layer of lettuce or other leafy vegetables.

- Trim fat and skin from meat, poultry, and fish. This is where pesticide residue accumulates.

- If possible, buy produce grown without pesticides from your local farmers' market. Speak to the farmers who grew it about what pest-control methods they use.

TO MINIMIZE EXPOSURE AT HOME AND AT WORK

To control household pests like ants or mice, or grow a healthy lawn or garden, with no or minimal toxic chemicals, consider using an approach called integrated pest management (IPM).[132] The goal of this health- and environment-friendly method is to prevent pests in the first place, so chemicals aren't needed to get rid of them. This means using simple strategies that include eliminating their sources of food or shelter and sealing cracks and crevices that allow them access.[133] Here's a super-simple IPM tip: If you feed pets outdoors, remove their food promptly after they've eaten, so their chow doesn't attract pests like insects, mice, or rabbits. Also, keep mulch, branches, and vegetation away from the foundation of your home—all can serve as an entryway to pests like ants and even termites. The cooperative extension service in your state can give you more information on IPM techniques.

If you choose to use pesticides, follow the directions and precautions on the label carefully—and these tips, too.

- Before you start, remove pets, toys, and food dishes from the area.

- Protect yourself with goggles, gloves, a dust mask, or long sleeves.[134] Pesticide labels will recommend the appropriate protective apparel.

- Mix pesticides outdoors or in a well-ventilated area. And mix only the amount of pesticide you need, so you won't have to store or dispose of any extra.

- Never use spray pesticides when it's windy. Even on a still day, close your home's windows and doors.

- If you work with pesticides, wear the Personal Protective Equipment (PPE) assigned to you. Keep it clean and check it for holes and rips regularly. Also, remove your shoes before entering your house, shower immediately, and wash work clothes separately from the family laundry. If possible, line-dry work clothes. Sunlight breaks down many pesticides and line-drying can help keep residues from collecting in the dryer.[135]

Commandment #9: Mind Your Medications

In your quest for an ageless brain, don't overlook your medicine chest. In recent years, several classes of prescription and over-the-counter medications—used to treat common conditions like heartburn, overactive bladder, and sleeplessness—have been linked to a higher risk of dementia. Consider talking to your doctor about the medications below.

PROTON PUMP INHIBITORS (PPIs)

Used to treat several types of ulcers and gastroesophageal reflux disease (GERD), PPIs work by reducing the stomach's production of acid. Common PPIs include omeprazole (Prilosec), esomeprazole (Nexium), and lansoprazole (Prevacid).[136]

In a 7-year study, researchers in Germany followed almost 74,000 people ages 75 or older who were dementia-free at the start of the study. Nearly 3,000 used PPIs "regularly" (which the researchers defined as at least one PPI medication in each quarter of an 18-month period).

The researchers also factored in age, gender, certain health conditions such as type 2 diabetes, stroke, heart disease, and other medications taken. After crunching the data, the researchers found that regular PPI use heightened women's dementia risk by 42 percent and men's by 52 percent, compared with nonusers.[137]

PPIs appear to affect levels of beta-amyloid and tau, the proteins associated with AD's hallmark plaques and tangles, the study said.[138]

ANTICHOLINERGIC (ANTISPASMODIC) MEDICATIONS

Used to treat such conditions as overactive bladder, muscle spasms, and breathing problems, this class of drugs blocks the action of acetylcholine. Drugs in this class include the over-the-counter drug diphenhydramine (Benadryl), tricyclic antidepressants like doxepin (Sinequan), antihistamines like chlorpheniramine (Chlor-Trimeton), and, for over-active bladder, oxybutynin (Ditropan).[139]

Some research has associated the use of anticholinergic medications at higher doses, or for longer periods of time, with a higher risk of dementia. In one study led by the University of Washington School of Pharmacy in Seattle, researchers tracked outcomes for 3,434 older people over a 7-year period. Those who took at least 10 milligrams of Sinequan a day, 4 milligrams of Chlor-Trimeton a day, or 5 milligrams of Ditropan a day for more than 3 years were at greater risk for dementia.[140] The cumulative effects of long-term, high-dose use might cause brain changes similar to those observed with Alzheimer's, the study said.[141]

BENZODIAZEPINES (BZDs)

Medications in this class of drugs, commonly prescribed to treat sleep-lessness and anxiety, include diazepam (Valium), alprazolam (Xanax), and lorazepam (Ativan).[142] In a study published by the journal *BMJ*, people who'd taken a BZD for 3 to 6 months, or more than 6 months, raised the risk of AD by 32 percent and 84 percent, respectively. Those who took a long-acting BZD like Valium were at greater risk for the disease than those on a short-acting one like Xanax, Ativan, and tri-azolam (Halcion). (Those who used BZDs 3 months or less had a simi-lar risk of dementia as those who'd never used them.)

The participants could have been using BZDs to manage anxiety and sleep problems, which are common symptoms of early Alzheimer's, the researchers noted. In that case, BZD use "might be an early marker of a condition associated with an increased risk of dementia and not the cause," the study said. In other words, by the time the participants were taking BZDs, they may have already developed AD.

If you have been prescribed any of these medications, *don't stop taking them, or any prescription drug, without your doctor's knowledge.* (For example, abruptly stopping BZDs could lead to potentially serious withdrawal symptoms.[143]) Also bear in mind that each study finding showed only an association between each class of medications and dementia, not a cause-and-effect link.

What you can do: Ask your doctor if an alternative medication may be right for you. According to the lead researcher on the University of Washington study, a possible alternative to Sinequan for depression might be a selective serotonin reuptake inhibitor (SSRI) such as citalopram (Celexa) or fluoxetine (Prozac). An alternative to Chlor-Trimeton for allergies might be an antihistamine such as loratadine (Claritin).[144]

If you've been prescribed PPIs or take over-the-counter forms, ask your doctor whether, in your case, they're truly necessary. In some (not all) cases, lifestyle changes may reduce or eliminate their need.[145]

Commandment #10: Stub Out the Butts

"Those things will kill ya!" If you're a smoker, you've likely heard that line before. But it's a sure bet no one's ever lectured you on smoking's devastating effects on the brain.[146]

The evidence is clear: Smoking is a significant risk factor for AD, a scientific analysis of 43 studies that examined the link between smoking and the disease found.[147] In fact, a recent study estimated that nearly 11 percent of Alzheimer's cases in the United States, and 14 percent of cases worldwide, may be attributable to smoking.[148]

Smoking harms the brain in multiple ways.[149] It gunks up blood vessels with plaque, restricting bloodflow in the brain and driving up the risk of vascular dementia. Cigarette smoke contains toxic chemicals that drive neuron-killing oxidative stress and inflammation. Smoking also raises levels of the amino acid homocysteine in the blood. Although the body produces homocysteine naturally, abnormally high levels can damage artery linings and increase the tendency of blood to clot, and have been linked to brain shrinkage and dementia.[150]

Smoking may also thin the cortex, the outer layer of the brain involved in memory, language, and perception.[151] When researchers gave over 500 older people (average age 73) brain scans, they found that both current and former smokers had a thinner cortex compared to those who had never smoked.

Simple aging causes the cortex to thin, the study noted. However, smoking appears to accelerate that process, and thinning of the cortex is associated with declines in thinking and memory.

Heavy smokers, with multiple-pack-a-day habits, may more than double their risk of dementia decades down the road. A Finnish study that tracked more than 20,000 people over a 14-year period came to a stunning finding: Smoking more than two packs a day in middle age raised the risk of all types of dementia, including AD, by over *100 percent*.[152]

After all those troubling findings, here's one to make you breathe easier: Quitting now can help stave off dementia later. In the Finnish study, former smokers, as well as those who puffed fewer than 10 cigarettes a day, had a dementia risk similar to people who didn't smoke at all.[153] That's the same conclusion reached by the World Alzheimer Report 2014.[154] So as hard as it is to quit, you now have another compelling reason to try, try again.

Ready to set a quit date and reap the brain benefits of a smoke-free life? Whether this is your first quit attempt or one of many, these tips can help increase the odds of success.

Don't sweat your quit method. Considering the nicotine patch? The prescription medication varenicline (Chantix)? A combination of patch and lozenge? All appear to be equally effective, according to a study published in *JAMA*.[155] Compared to the patch, however, varenicline caused more side effects such as vivid dreams, insomnia, and nausea—something to consider.

Consider white-knuckling it. Which quit approach works better—stopping all at once, commonly known as "cold turkey," or tapering off gradually in the weeks before Quit Day? To find out, researchers randomly assigned almost 700 smokers to one of two groups. The first was instructed to quit abruptly on a certain day; the other, to cut back over a 2-week period and then quit completely.[156] At the end of 6 months, 22 percent of the cold-turkey group was still off the cigs, compared to 15.5 percent of the "quit gradually" group. Their conclusion: As painful as it might seem, cold turkey is the more effective quit method.

Get smoke-free via text. If you're determined to quit smoking, you need all the motivation you can get—and that help can be a text away. Consider signing up to receive texts that keep your will strong, such as the service offered by *smokefree.gov*. In a scientific review of five studies, quit "interventions" that smokers received via text—which included motivational messages and practical quit tips—almost doubled the odds of quitting.[157] Nine percent of participants who received these messages were smoke-free after 6 months, compared to 5 percent of those who didn't.

PART 3

STAY SHARP!

Savor Brain-Boosting Foods

A HEALTHY BRAIN LIKES the same foods a healthy body craves—those packaged by nature. That means veggies and fruits, beans and whole grains, and nuts and seeds. In fact, the case for eating a plant-heavy diet "is all but incontrovertible," a recent article published in the *Annual Review of Public Health* declared.[1]

If that describes your diet, great! Meal by healthy meal, you're outwitting the chronic diseases traced to the sugar-laced, fat-packed, sodium-heavy Western diet, like type 2 diabetes, high blood pressure, and heart disease, along with obesity. You're also bucking an unhealthy trend: Processed foods now make up 70 percent of all calories in the average American's diet, a recent study found.[2]

If *that* sounds more familiar, there's still time to hit the brakes. Make a diet detour now, and you'll speed away from disease and toward a sharper brain.

The much-studied Mediterranean and DASH diets swap lots of red meat, added sugars, and refined grains for whole, minimally processed foods. The health benefits are huge—weight loss, healthier blood cholesterol and blood sugar levels, lower blood pressure. But the big news is that these heart-healthy diets protect the brain against Alzheimer's disease (AD) as well.[3, 4]

Time and again, studies show, when people eat a plant-based diet, their risk of thinking and memory problems in older age goes down.[5] As we delve into the Mediterranean and DASH diets, you'll see how the incredible findings about these two closely related approaches ultimately led to the recent creation of the breakthrough MIND diet, developed by researchers at Rush University Medical Center in Chicago. Based on the foundation of the Mediterranean and DASH diets, the new MIND diet takes you even closer to an ageless brain by linking specific food groups, most of them plants, to a reduced risk of AD. Eating more of those groups, and less of others, slashed risk by more than half, the study found.[6]

Don't let the phrase "plant-based" scare you. It doesn't mean *no* meat, and it sure doesn't mean no flavor. A balanced plant-based diet can deliver the variety your taste buds crave, and the protein and nutrients your brain and body need, via both meat and plant products.

So first, digest the evidence that links plant-based diets to a sharper mind and memory, which is presented in the next few sections through the wealth of research on the Mediterranean and DASH diets. Then, dig into the profiles of the newer MIND diet's nine brain-friendly foods (page 109), which include simple ways to turn them into quick, flavor-packed meals. Buckle up—you're in for a tasty ride.

BRAIN PROTECTION BY THE PLATEFUL

Follow the traditional Mediterranean-style diet, and you eat hearty and well. Think naturally sweet plain Greek yogurt topped with nuts and berries for breakfast. A lunch of hearty bean soup, whole grain bread dipped in olive oil and herbs, and fruit for dessert. For dinner, grilled fish with a side of sautéed greens over wild rice. Add a glass of red wine to wash it down with, if you want it.

Women who stuck to a Mediterranean-style diet in their middle years were found to be physically *and* cognitively healthier in their older age, a Harvard study found.[7] After reviewing data on the diets of almost 11,000 women in their late fifties and early sixties, the researchers tracked them for 15 years to see how well their bodies and brains aged. Those who consistently ate Mediterranean-style were up to 46 percent more likely to live past age 70 with no chronic illnesses and no major problems with thinking or memory. In another recent study of almost 2,000 older Americans that spanned 14 years, those who followed a strict Mediterranean diet during that period had a 32 to 40 percent lower incidence of AD compared with those who didn't.[8]

The DASH diet is a Mediterranean-style plan designed to lower high blood pressure and emphasizes low-fat dairy products and low sodium over olive oil and wine. However, both diets were shown to preserve cognition in older age, according to a study of almost 4,000 people ages 65 and over. Those who stuck closest to either diet did best on cognitive tests administered over an 11-year period, the researchers found. In fact, compared to those who strayed furthest from these plans, those who followed them most closely scored as if they were 3 years younger! Three plant foods in this study—nuts, whole grains, and legumes—were specifically linked to sharper, healthier brains.[9] These whole foods also made the MIND diet's all-star list, as you'll see in a moment.

See the cheat sheet on page 104 to help you distinguish this trio of brain-*tastic* eating plans. While they're all healthy, this chapter focuses on the MIND diet, which is a bit simpler to follow.

- Unless noted, all servings are daily servings.
- The DASH plan features a range of servings, based on total daily calories consumed. Eat fewer servings if you consume fewer calories (say, 1,200 calories a day), and more servings if you consume more calories (1,600 to 2,000 a day).
- On the MIND diet, what you don't eat is just as key as what you do eat—the chart on page 104 tells you what to limit.

PLANTS: THEY HAVE WHAT BRAINS CRAVE

Here's what a plant-based diet offers your brain that a steady diet of soda, convenience foods, and takeout can't. Keep in mind that different plant foods contain different nutrients, so eat 'em all, from amaranth

Protein and Your Brain

Your brain needs glucose for fuel. But to build cells, make neurotransmitters, and repair damage, it requires proteins. The proteins you eat don't enter your brain; the blood-brain barrier prevents that.[10] So your brain makes its own with the substances that do cross that barrier—amino acids.

The building blocks of proteins, amino acids connect like beads on a string. When you eat protein in, say, plant foods (meat too), your intestinal tract and liver digest it, breaking its strings of amino acids into single amino acids that circulate in your blood. Like glucose, these solitary amino acids can make it into the brain, where they're assembled into the proteins it needs.

Even though protein is a key nutrient for brain and body, you need less than you might think. (If you eat the traditional meat-

(a type of whole grain) to zucchini, to make sure you cover the bases below.

Fiber. Ditch the fiber cookies and drinks—you don't need them when you pile your plate with whole foods. A fiber-rich diet has been found to promote friendly bacteria in the gut (it's considered a pre-biotic), protect heart health, steady blood sugar, and cut stroke risk, among other benefits.[11]

Women need 20 to 25 grams of fiber daily, and men 30 to 38 grams a day. If you're a woman and eat three meals and two snacks a day, shoot for 5 grams each time you eat. You can get that amount in a large apple or a cup of turnip greens, and nearly that amount in a cup of oatmeal (4 grams) or 3 cups of air-popped popcorn (3.6 grams).

Vitamins and minerals. Plant foods are rich in nutrients such as

(continued on page 106)

heavy Western diet, you're likely getting double the protein your body requires!) For the average adult, the Recommended Dietary Allowance (RDA) for protein is 0.8 gram per kilogram of body weight—and you can get it from plant foods as well as meat.[12]

To find out how much protein you need, multiply your body weight in pounds by 0.36. The answer is your recommended protein intake in grams. For example, if you weigh 150 pounds, you should consume 54 grams of protein (150 x 0.36). You easily can get that amount in a day by eating, for example, 3 ounces of chicken breast (28 grams of protein), a serving of Greek yogurt (18 grams), and 2 tablespoons of peanut butter (14 grams). Don't forget beans, nuts, and quinoa—all are good sources of protein.

FOOD/FOOD GROUP	DASH DIET	
Grains	4–8 servings, mostly whole grains[13]	
Veggies	3–5 servings[15]	
Fruits	3–5 servings[17]	
Dairy	2–3 servings; opt for low-fat or fat-free products[19]	
Animal protein (fish, poultry, red meat)	3–6 servings or less; opt for lean cuts of red meat[21]	
Nuts, seeds, legumes	Weekly: 3–4 servings[23]	
Fats and oils	1–3 servings[25]	
Sweets	Weekly: 3–5 servings or less[27]	
Maximum sodium limit	2,300 milligrams a day (1,500 if your doctor recommends it)[29]	
Alcohol	Not applicable	

MEDITERRANEAN DIET	MIND DIET
Whole grains: 3–6 servings[14]	Whole grains: at least 3 servings
3 servings[16]	Green leafy veggies: at least 6 servings a week Other veggies: at least 1 serving a day
3 servings[18]	Berries: at least 2 servings a week
Weekly: 3 servings of dairy or eggs. Choose 1 percent or fat-free milk, yogurt, or cottage cheese. Egg whites can be eaten any-time.[20]	Not applicable
Weekly: 3 servings of fish; 3 servings of poultry; no more than 1 serving of red meat[22]	Weekly: at least 1 serving of fish; at least 2 servings of poultry; red meat less than 4 times per week
Weekly: 3 servings of nuts and 3 servings of beans or legumes[24]	Weekly: at least 3 servings of beans; at least 5 servings of nuts
1 tablespoon olive oil a day; no more than 4 per day[26]	Use olive oil as your primary fat. Limit butter or margarine to 1 tablespoon per day and cheese to 1 serving per week.
No recommended servings; enjoy occasionally, as a treat or celebration[28]	Weekly: less than 5 servings
Not applicable	Not applicable
Optional: one 5-ounce glass of wine a day. No beer or hard liquor. If you don't currently drink, don't start.[30]	Optional: Alcohol or wine in moderation: up to one drink per day for women, two for men. If you don't currently drink, don't start.

the B vitamin folate, which helps lower blood levels of homocysteine, and the mineral magnesium, which relaxes arteries and enhances bloodflow—always a plus for brain health. Vitamins A, C, and E are powerful antioxidants, which help protect neurons from inflammation and a damaging process called oxidative stress (see sidebar on the opposite page).

Greens are particularly rich in vitamin K, best known for helping blood to clot. However, research suggests that this vitamin may also play a role in protecting cognitive health. A study published in the journal *Neurobiology of Aging* found that older people with the highest levels of vitamin K in their blood showed memory improvements.[31]

Phytonutrients. These compounds help protect plants from threats like insects and fungi. Researchers have identified dozens of phytonutrients, and all offer unique health benefits. A few examples: carotenoids, found in orange and yellow veggies, and lutein, found in leafy greens, have been found to promote both heart and brain health. Grains contain phenolic acids, which help cells fight off oxidative damage.[32] Flavonoids, the pigments that give plants their crayonlike hues, including the anthocyanidins in berries, have been shown to improve blood vessel health.

Good fats. Like creamy avocado and crunchy nuts? You're in luck. Those foods, along with olive oil, nuts and seeds and their butters, and fatty fish, are rich in monounsaturated and polyunsaturated fats, found to help lower cholesterol and the risk of heart disease and stroke.

What a plant-based diet contains *less* of: saturated and trans fats. Saturated fats are found in red meat such as beef and pork and full-fat dairy products such as whole milk, cheese, and butter, while trans

The Five Colors That "Rust-Proof" Your Brain

Ironic but true: Breathing is a dangerous business. On the one hand, your cells need oxygen to perform vital functions. On the other, every breath you take causes free radicals to form. These harmful molecules mess with the body's fats and proteins, and even the DNA inside cells. The chemical "storm" inside your body they cause is called oxidative stress.[33]

The same process that causes iron to rust or a banana to turn brown, oxidative stress is thought to be an underlying trigger of normal aging and of a slew of chronic diseases from heart disease to Alzheimer's disease (AD). Environmental factors such as poor diet, excessive exposure to the sun's ultraviolet rays, cigarette smoke, and pollution can accelerate oxidative stress.[34]

Your body produces substances to fight the "stress storm," but can't repair all the damage it causes. That's where plant foods come in. They're rich in antioxidant nutrients like vitamins E, C, and A, which help fight free-radical damage and protect cells.

Further, many phytonutrients in plant foods have powerful antioxidant effects. For example, flavonoids such as those that produce the red of tomatoes or the purple of eggplant are thought to suppress inflammation, protect neurons against injury and enhance their function, and induce neurogenesis.[35]

The more colorful the veggie or fruit, the more health-promoting phytonutrients it packs. So to really "taste the rainbow," dress up your plate with the five brightest hues in the produce aisle—red and purple berries, ruby-red beets, emerald-hued greens, sunny yellow peppers and squash, and deep orange sweet potatoes and pumpkin.

fats lurk in fried foods and processed foods made with partially hydrogenated oils. Because they tend to raise levels of LDL cholesterol, these unhealthy fats encourage the production of beta-amyloid plaques in the brain. In a study published in the journal *Neurology*, people who ate the most saturated fat had triple the risk of developing AD.[36]

FOOD FOR THOUGHT: THE MIND DIET

Lose 7 pounds, and you celebrate. How does losing 7½ years from your cognitive age sound? The MIND diet appears to deliver, according to a study[37] published in *Alzheimer's & Dementia*. This finding is on top of an earlier study by the same researchers, which found that the MIND diet may reduce the risk of getting AD, period.[38]

Based on years of research on foods known to benefit (and harm) thinking and memory, the MIND diet combines the best of the Mediterranean and DASH diets, locking in the parts of each associated with dementia protection. Although the MIND diet couldn't have a better name, it's short for the Mediterranean-DASH Intervention for Neurodegenerative Delay.

The team followed over 900 men and women ages 58 to 98 for an average of 4½ years, assessing their diets with detailed food questionnaires and testing their cognitive function annually. They scored participants' diets by how closely they matched recommendations for the Mediterranean, DASH, or MIND eating patterns.

The DASH diet reduced AD risk by 39 percent, the MIND diet by 53 percent, and the Mediterranean diet by 54 percent. But hold on—when participants followed the diets moderately well, rather than to the letter, only the MIND diet returned significant results. It reduced AD risk by 53 percent in those who followed it to the letter, and by 35 percent in those who followed it reasonably well.

What this means is that strict adherence to the DASH and Mediterranean diets may reduce AD risk—but so might *moderate* adherence to the MIND diet. Good to know when you splurge on the occasional chocolate-chip cookie.

What makes the MIND diet a standout? For one thing, it's low in those unhealthy trans and saturated fats. For another, it's loaded with specific nutrients and phytonutrients shown to slow cognitive decline, lower risk of AD, and reduce oxidative stress and inflammation.[39] It's worth noting that in the study, those with the highest MIND diet scores ate cheese and fried or fast food less than once a week, red meat less than four times a week, and desserts, pastries, or sweets less than five times a week. They also used less than a tablespoon of butter or margarine a day, and used olive oil as their main source of fat. Translation: It's not enough to eat the brain-friendly groups. To help reduce AD risk, it's necessary to limit these less-healthy groups as well.

PUTTING THE RESEARCH TO WORK

The rest of this chapter covers nine food groups that the MIND diet study linked to cognitive health. Pair these "all-stars" with one veggie serving of your choice every day, and you're on your way to Brainytown.

1. WHOLE GRAINS

Daily servings to aim for: at least 3

One serving equals: ½ cup cooked whole grain, 100% whole grain pasta, or 100% whole grain hot cereal; 1 slice 100% whole grain bread; 1 cup 100% whole grain ready-to-eat cereal

Two Ways to Tell "Faux Grains" from Whole Grains

When you shop for whole grain products like breads, cereals, or crackers, don't be misled by marketing buzzwords like "stone ground" or "multigrain." Follow these strategies, and you'll zero in on products that really, truly are made with whole grains.[40]

Look beyond the stamp. If a product has the Whole Grain Stamp from the Whole Grains Council, be leery. When Harvard researchers evaluated the nutritional content of over 500 whole grain products, they discovered an unpleasant surprise: Products with the stamp contained more calories and sugar than those without it.[41]

Don't panic—products with

What makes brown rice, oatmeal, and popcorn (yes, popcorn!) "brain food"? The same thing that research links to lower rates of heart disease, type 2 diabetes, and reduced body fat: fiber and ample amounts of vitamins, minerals, and phytonutrients.[43]

Whole grains sit atop the MIND diet's brain-friendly food groups because they contain every nutrient-rich part of the grain: the flaky *bran* that surrounds the kernel, the *germ* that sprouts into a new plant, and the main part of the kernel, the *endosperm*.[44] Those first two parts, particularly the bran, hold the lion's share of fiber, magnesium, B vitamins, the antioxidant vitamin E, and phytonutrients such as phenolic acids.[45]

Unfortunately, most of the grains the average American eats are refined, meaning that the bran and germ were removed during the milling process. Without them, grains' fiber and nutrients take a nosedive, and a quarter of their protein is stripped away.

this stamp may well be good sources of whole grains. But it's smart to read labels and ingredient lists very closely. Honest-to-goodness whole grain products list one of the following ingredients first.[42]

- 100% whole wheat flour
- Whole wheat, oats, or rye
- Whole grain barley or corn
- Brown rice, buckwheat, bulgur
- Millet, oatmeal, popcorn
- Quinoa, rolled oats

Distinguish between "fiber" and "whole grains." Another reason to check the ingredients list first: Some products add fiber, like bran, yet contain little (if any) whole grains.

Your body and brain know when they're being fed nutrient-poor refined grains.

In a British study, middle-aged people who ate the least whole grains, and the most red and processed meat and fried food, experienced higher inflammation levels and faster cognitive decline over a 6-year period. Moreover, whole grains were most strongly linked to healthy anti-inflammatory markers.[46]

Another study published in the *American Journal of Clinical Nutrition* linked whole grains—along with nuts and legumes—to better thinking and memory, and said that these foods "may be core neuroprotective foods common to various healthy plant-centered diets around the globe."[47]

As a bonus, several whole grains are especially rich in protein, which makes them standouts in a plant-based diet.

(continued on page 116)

10 WHOLE GRAINS AT A GLANCE

WHOLE GRAIN	FIBER PER SERVING (GRAMS)	FLAVOR AND TEXTURE	COOK TIME (MINUTES)	
Popcorn (air-popped)	3.6 (3 cups, popped, or slightly less than 2 table-spoons unpopped)	Dust with cinnamon, and it's sweet; shake on chili powder and a squeeze of lime or 1 tablespoon Parmesan cheese, and it's savory	3–5	
Bulgur wheat (wheat kernels that are boiled, dried, and cracked)	2.9	Mild, fluffy	10	
Barley (whole, hulled, or hull-less)	2.8	Nutty, chewy	50–60	
Whole wheat kernels ("wheat berries")	2.0	Mild (white wheat); stronger (red wheat); chewy texture	45–60	
Oats* (rolled or steel-cut)	1.7	Sweet and slightly chewy	30	

*Oats can be contaminated with wheat during growing or processing. Companies that offer uncontaminated oats include Bob's Red Mill and Avena Foods. Ask your doctor if these brands are acceptable for you.

BONUS POINTS	GOOD FOR	GOOD TO KNOW
Good source of poly-phenols	A 100 percent whole grain "anytime" snack	Gluten-free; you can pick up an air popper for less than $20 at big-box stores
Fiber powerhouse	Side dishes, pilafs, or the Middle Eastern cold salad tabbouleh, flavored with fresh chopped mint and lemon juice	Often called "Middle Eastern pasta" because of its versatility
Its cholesterol-busting powers may outdo oat bran's	Soups, stews, cold salads, breads	Avoid "pearled" barley—it's not tech-nically a whole grain
Most US studies of "whole grains" include whole wheat, (i.e., whole wheat flour), which contains all three parts of the grain	Enjoy as a hot cereal; chill and use in a cold salad (great with white beans and a vinaigrette); add to soups	Just ¼ cup uncooked packs 6 grams of protein
Contains cholesterol-lowering beta glucans and the antioxidant avenanthramides, found to help protect blood vessels from LDL cholesterol damage	Don't care for oat-meal? Replace bread crumbs with rolled oats in turkey meat-loaf or add ¼ cup to pancake batter	Gluten-free

(continued)

10 WHOLE GRAINS AT A GLANCE (CONT.)

WHOLE GRAIN	FIBER PER SERVING (GRAMS)	FLAVOR AND TEXTURE	COOK TIME (MINUTES)	
Buckwheat groats	1.6	Light in flavor and texture	15	
Quinoa	1.1	Mild, once the tiny seeds are rinsed; fluffy texture	15	
Amaranth	1.1	Peppery, fluffy	20	
Wild rice	1.0	Nutty, chewy	45–50	
Brown rice	0.6	Mild, chewy	45–50	

BONUS POINTS	GOOD FOR	GOOD TO KNOW
Contains the antioxidant rutin, shown to improve circulation and prevent LDL cholesterol from blocking blood vessels	Cold salads; stuffings; grind into flour to make hearty buckwheat pancakes	Gluten-free; for richer flavor, toast groats in a saucepan over medium-high heat for 3 to 4 minutes before cooking
Protein-rich (4 grams per ½ cup serving); rich in flavonoids and brain-boosting omega-3 fats	A tasty substitute for oatmeal; use in cold salads, or as a replacement for brown rice	Gluten-free; rinse several times in a fine-mesh strainer before cooking to remove its bitter coating
Protein-rich (almost 5 grams per ½ cup); contains phytosterols, found to help lower cholesterol	Pop like popcorn on your stove top; mix the crunchy puffs with nuts and no-sugar-added dried fruit for a healthy trail mix	Gluten-free; to "test-drive" the grain, add a tablespoon to a pot of brown rice and cook them together
Compared to brown rice, contains more brain-friendly vitamin E, folate, and zinc	Use in place of white rice in casseroles, soups, and pilafs	Gluten-free; "cut" with less costly brown rice
Lower in fiber than wild rice, but nutrient-dense	Use in place of white rice in any dish	Gluten-free; make rice pudding with leftovers (sweeten with cinnamon, vanilla extract, and berries)

If you're a whole grain newbie, the chart on page 112 tells you everything you need to know about the most common (and tasty) varieties.[48, 49] They're listed in order of their fiber content per serving and found in most large supermarkets, along with the flours made from them.

Although you'll find some familiar favorites, stray outside of your culinary comfort zone and taste-test a few you've never tried. With the wide variety of flavors and textures, you're sure to find several that appeal.

No need to let long cook times chain you to your stove top, either. Prep a large quantity at one time, then refrigerate or freeze. Keep uncooked grains you will use regularly in a cool, dry place. (Glass jars will keep out critters like weevils.) Store uncooked grains used less often in the freezer—they'll keep longer.

2. GREEN LEAFY VEGETABLES

Weekly servings to aim for: 6

One serving equals: 1 cup cooked, 2 cups raw

How'd you like to regain the memory and brainpower you enjoyed a decade ago? It might be worth your while to fold spinach into your breakfast omelet and fork up kale or collards for dinner: Leafy greens are true brain food, studies show.[50]

Leafy greens are packed with nutrients found to hold off cognitive decline, such as the carotenoids lutein and beta-carotene, folate, and vitamin K.[51] In a study published in *The FASEB Journal*, which covers experimental biology, researchers examined the diets and cognitive abilities of over 950 older people for an average of 5 years. Compared to those who ate no greens, those who munched one or two servings a day demonstrated the thinking abilities and memory of a person 11 years younger.[52] Bumping up greens intake could be a simple way to hold off AD and dementia, according to the study's lead researcher.[53]

These studies are far from the only ones to zero in on the brain benefits of leafy greens. Previous research has associated at least two servings a day with slower cognitive decline; the strongest benefits accrued with six or more servings a week.[54] The darker the green, the higher its nutrient and phytonutrient content, which is an excellent reason to swap pale iceberg lettuce for baby spinach, Swiss chard, or kale.

The 10 Healthiest Greens You Can Chomp

A recent study ranked almost 50 types of veggies and fruits and dubbed those with the most nutrients per calorie as "powerhouses." Leafy greens took every top-10 spot.[55]

Tuck a few leaves of spicy watercress in a sandwich, or toss a handful of chopped parsley (yes, the garnish) into your salad for a fresh, bright flavor. Stud your stir-fries with chunks of Chinese cabbage, and sauté the others with chopped garlic and a drizzle of olive oil.

Watercress

Chinese cabbage

Chard

Beet greens

Spinach

Chicory greens

Leaf lettuce

Parsley

Romaine lettuce

Collard greens

From spring to fall, splurge on locally grown greens at seasonal farmers' markets, if possible. It's likely they were harvested that day, at the peak of their nutrients, and grown without pesticides. (Ask to be sure.) When they're out of season, keep a few bags of the frozen variety in your freezer. They're as nutritious as fresh, and you'll always have a brain-boosting staple on hand.

Coffee: Perks for the Brain?

If you're a coffee lover, you've likely cheered the research that links moderate consumption to a reduced risk of heart disease and type 2 diabetes, and even a longer life. But your brain may get health perks from regular jolts of joe, too.[56]

In a Finnish study of over 1,400 people, those who drank three to five 8-ounce cups of coffee a day in their forties and fifties were up to 70 percent less likely to have Alzheimer's Disease (AD) 21 years later.[57] And in a study published in the *Journal of Alzheimer's Disease (JAD)*, researchers tested the blood levels of caffeine in older people with mild cognitive impairment (MCI). Two to 4 years later, those whose blood contained caffeine amounts equivalent to about three cups of coffee were significantly less likely to have progressed to dementia, compared to those with low blood levels of caffeine.[58]

Researchers suspect that caffeine doesn't act alone. For example, coffee is rich in phytonutrients called polyphenols, also found in red wine and chocolate. According to some studies, coffee's high antioxidant activity may help protect neurons from oxidative damage.[59] The jury's still out on whether decaf coffee and tea have the same health benefits as the caffeinated variety, however. On the one hand, the decaffeination process destroys some of tea's phytonutrients. On the other, a

If you prefer mild flavors, choose spinach, red leaf and romaine lettuces, bok choy, and cabbage. Kale; mustard, beet, turnip, and collard greens; and broccoli rabe offer stronger flavors—spicy and peppery to pleasantly bitter. To tame them, add them to soups and stews, or sauté or roast them.

Even if you buy bagged, prewashed greens for convenience, it's smart to wash them yourself. Fill your sink with lukewarm water—it removes grit faster than cool—and swish them around. Drain and pat them dry

major study linked consumption of both caffeinated and decaffeinated coffee with increased longevity.[60]

Although black or green tea contains significantly less caffeine than coffee, it *is* high in polyphenols, and at least one study has linked tea consumption with cognitive benefits. Older women who drank more than three cups of coffee or an equivalent amount of tea scored better on memory and cognitive tests, compared to those who drank one cup or less of either, a study published in the journal *Neurology* found.[61]

Three to five 8-ounce cups of coffee a day contain about 400 milligrams of caffeine, the daily cap recommended by the USDA. Don't add lots of cream and sugar, especially if you drink more than a cup a day. You might even give black coffee a try—you'll reap all of the health benefits, with none of the sugar or fat. Besides, high-quality coffee can be surprisingly tasty taken "neat." Needless to say, skip whipped-cream coffee drinks and caffeinated soft drinks or "energy" drinks, which contain unhealthy amounts of sugar and fat.

One more thing: Take your last sip of coffee or caffeinated tea way before bed—at least 6 hours. A caffeine buzz can make you toss and turn, and some studies have associated disturbed sleep to a higher risk of cognitive decline and AD.[62]

with paper towels, or give them a whirl in your salad spinner. Wrap washed, dried greens in damp paper towels, place in a plastic bag, and pop them into the crisper. If you keep the paper towels damp, they should keep for a week.[63]

In general, it's best to lightly steam or sauté greens, rather than boil them, so their nutrients don't leach into the water.[64] To preserve the fat-soluble carotenoids in kale, roast it. It's simple: Toss one bunch of roughly chopped kale with a tablespoon of extra-virgin olive oil and chopped garlic to taste and spread it on a rimmed baking sheet. (It's okay if the kale overlaps—it'll shrink.) Bake for 15 to 20 minutes at 375°F. You can roast broccoli rabe or other strong-flavored greens, too.

No matter which greens you choose, don't cook them in aluminum pots and pans. This metal reacts to sulfur compounds in the greens, resulting in a funky taste and appearance.

3. NUTS

Weekly servings to aim for: 5

One serving equals: a small handful (1.5 ounces) of nuts or 2 tablespoons of nut butter

Thank goodness we've moved on from that dreadful low-fat mania of 20 years ago! We now know that nuts and seeds are tiny nutritional gems. They're packed with fiber, protein, minerals, and free-radical-busting vitamin E, and their fat is mainly the heart-healthy monounsaturated kind. Studies confirm that people who enjoy regular, sensible portions have lower rates of heart disease, stroke, and type 2 diabetes[65] *and* less belly fat, to boot.[66] Seeds have the same nutritional pedigree, so keep on crunching.

Regular consumption of nuts and seeds appears to delay cognitive aging, too. In one study, researchers tracked the diets of over 2,600 adults for 5 years. Regular cognitive testing revealed that, compared to those who ate the least nuts, those who ate the most had the intellectual powers of people 5 to 8 years younger![67]

English walnuts may be particularly brain-friendly. In a study published in the *Journal of Nutrition,* people who ate about 2 ounces a day for 6 weeks significantly improved their verbal reasoning skills—that is, solving problems with words and language—compared to those who didn't.[68] Another study linked eating walnuts as part of a Mediterranean diet to better memory and brain function.[69]

Walnuts are especially rich in brain-friendly fats. These include omega-3 fats, the same heart-healthy type found in oily fish, and alpha linoleic acid (ALA), important for a healthy brain throughout life. They're also high in polyphenols, which play a vital role in reducing inflammation and oxidative stress in the aging brain, according to a scientific review of the evidence linking walnut consumption to brain health.[70]

STAY-SHARP TIPS

As satisfying as nuts and nut butters are, stick to the recommended daily serving so you won't gain weight. Select healthy options, too. For example, choose raw or dry roasted nuts over those roasted in oil or smothered in sugar, and avoid candy-studded trail mixes. The nut butter you choose should have two ingredients—nuts and (maybe) salt—and no added sugar.

Certainly, savor your daily serving of nuts as a snack, or spread it across your whole grain breakfast toast. But lend their intense flavor to other foods, too. Stir chopped walnuts into yogurt, sprinkle slivered almonds in your salad or stir-fry, and use creamy almond or sunflower butters as a base for tasty dips or sauces. Don't forget about seeds—teeny flax and chia seeds boost your smoothie's nutrition, sunflower seeds add crunch to a salad, and sesame seeds enhance the flavor of Asian dishes.

Shelled nuts and seeds can go bad when exposed to air, so store them in the fridge. They'll keep for up to a month (or in the freezer for up to a year). Store nut butters and nut oils in the fridge, too.

4. BERRIES

Weekly servings to aim for: 2
One serving equals: ½ cup (no added sugar)

What's whole grain cereal or plain, whole milk yogurt or a salad without a handful of berries? Good things come in small packages, and blueberries, strawberries, blackberries, raspberries, and even cranberries are nature's way of proving it. Every serving is rich in fiber, and the phytonutrients that give berries their jewel-like colors pack a powerful antioxidant punch.

Some of berries' brain-boosting effects appear to come from anthocyanins, and blueberries and strawberries are particularly good sources. In a study published in the *Annals of Neurology,* researchers tracked the eating habits of just over 16,000 women in their fifties and sixties. In their seventies, the participants underwent a battery of thinking and memory tests.

The team found that those who ate at least a cup of blueberries or strawberries a week (or more) had slower rates of cognitive decline than those who didn't. In fact, that amount of berries seemed to delay brain aging by 2½ years! The study also linked higher consumption of both anthocyanins and total flavonoids to slower cognitive aging.[71]

Berries may also improve neurons' ability to communicate, according to a scientific paper published in the *Journal of Agricultural Food Chemistry.* How? By revving up signaling between neurons, which helps quench damaging inflammation and protect cognitive function.[72]

As tasty as berries are, conventionally grown varieties commonly are treated with pesticides. That's a good reason to buy organically grown berries. If that's not possible, wash supermarket berries before you eat them. No need for a store-bought vegetable wash. Just put the berries in a colander and run water over them, or use the sprayer, for a full minute. The water's force washes away the residues.

Strawberries should be fragrant and red from top to tip. Keep them in the fridge, and don't rinse or remove their green caps until you're ready to use them. Blueberries should be plump, smooth-skinned, and free of mold. Don't worry if they have a silvery coating. This natural "bloom" helps protect their skins. To preserve it, don't wash blueberries until you're ready to eat them. Just pop them in the fridge, in their clamshell box (it allows air to circulate).

Frozen berries are just as antioxidant-rich. A University of California, Davis, study compared nutrients like vitamin C and beta-carotene in frozen and fresh blueberries and strawberries, among other types of produce, and found no significant differences.[73] Just make sure the brand you buy contains no added sugars, or freeze them up yourself in the summer when berries are available at lower prices and in large abundance at your local farmers' market or produce stand.

If you enjoy dried cranberries, bear in mind that they're calorie dense and commonly sweetened with sugar (they're lip-puckeringly sour without it). Stick to a tablespoon, stirred into yogurt or tossed in a salad.

5. BEANS

Weekly servings to aim for: at least 3

One serving equals: ½ cup cooked

Your body needs protein to thrive. But if you follow the typical Western diet, you consume far more of it than you need, and mostly from meat. That's where beans come in. Simmered in soups, mashed into dips and spreads, tossed into salads, or served over whole grains as a hearty main meal, beans and other plant foods can provide all the protein the body needs—and they're MIND diet all-stars, too.

Beans are brain boosters because they're good sources of nutrients that promote the health of the heart and blood vessels, like fiber, folate, magnesium, and potassium, without the bad fats and cholesterol that can harm them. In a study published in the *Journal of the American College of Nutrition,* when overweight people ate two servings of beans and four servings of whole grains a day in place of foods high in refined carbs, their blood pressure, triglycerides, weight, and waist circumference all went down.[74] In another, people who ate slightly less than 1 cup of beans a day for 10 weeks saw their blood pressure fall significantly.[75] And lower intakes of legumes and vegetables were associated with cognitive decline in a study of 5,000 older people, published in the *Journal of Nutrition, Health, and Aging.*[76]

Like all plant foods, beans brim with phytonutrients.[77] In fact, when it comes to antioxidant power per serving, small red beans, red kidney beans, and pinto beans are right up there with blueberries.[78] Black beans, too—scientific testing has found that they contain a mother lode of anthocyanins.[79]

STAY-SHARP TIPS

All beans are nutrient powerhouses, and canned beans are as nutritious as dried. So eat a wide variety, from black beans in Tex-Mex dishes and burritos to chickpeas tossed with olive oil and lemon juice and fresh herbs. When you're in the mood for vegetarian chili or Southern-style black-eyed peas, use your slow cooker, and walk away as the beans simmer into savory goodness. Also, beans and whole grains "dance" well together—think beans served over a bed of brown rice or quinoa, or combined in a cold salad with chopped veggies.

Lentils aren't commonly canned, perhaps because they cook up so fast, in 25 minutes or less. They make delicious soups, cold salads, and *dals,* a traditional Indian dish of spicy lentils served over rice. Lentils come in a variety of colors—brown, green, red, yellow—and are particularly rich in protein. Just a half cup, cooked, provides 9 grams. (Chickpeas are a close second, with 7.3 grams of protein.)

Canned beans commonly are loaded with sodium you don't need. So rinse them before you use them, or buy sodium-free brands and use the nutritious liquid in your recipe. If you *do* cook beans from scratch, let them sit in their cooking water for an hour after they're done. They'll reabsorb some of the nutrients that have leached into the liquid.

6. OLIVE OIL

Use as a primary source of fat, in place of butter or other fats

A drizzle (or two) a day—over salads, fish, cooked veggies—keeps disease away. You likely already know about this fragrant, flavorful oil's connection to reduced rates of heart disease, high blood pressure, stroke, and high blood cholesterol and triglyceride levels.[80] But did you know that olive oil also helps keep brains keen, far into old age?

AD is less common in Mediterranean countries, where people consume olive oil as their main source of fat, studies show.[81] In a study of older Italians published in *Neurology,* the likelihood of cognitive decline fell one-third in those who consumed the most olive oil—about 3 tablespoons a day, on average.[82]

Olive oil also appears to protect two particular types of memory:

Olive Oil: What's in a Name?

There's olive oil, and then there's good olive oil. Your brain and taste buds deserve the best, so buy the highest quality you can afford.

Pass these by: olive oil, light olive oil, and olive pomace oil, which are processed with either heat or chemicals. While such processing squeezes more oil out of olives, it ruins the oil's flavor and reduces its content of flavonols and polyphenols.

Snap up: extra-virgin olive oil, the variety used in many studies. This type is "cold pressed," meaning that it's not treated with heat or chemicals. Its color and flavor depend on the variety of olives used and where they were grown; the oil may be yellow or green, and its flavor peppery or fruity. Whatever the flavor, it's delicious. While you can cook with the extra-virgin variety, heating it can destroy its healthful substances, so it's best to use this top-shelf variety cold. Drizzle it over salads, raw or cooked veggies, or fish.

Virgin olive oil isn't refined, either, so its phytonutrients are intact. While it lacks the perfect flavor of the extra-virgin variety, it's great for grilling, sautéing, roasting, or frying.[83]

visual memory, the kind you use when you recall the time on your watch the last time you checked it, and verbal memory, which allows you to recall words and abstract ideas. In a study conducted in France, researchers tracked the olive-oil consumption of almost 7,000 older adults. Roughly 22 percent of participants used no olive oil; the rest used moderate or large amounts. During the 4 years the study ran, intensive users were 17 percent less likely to experience a decline in visual memory compared to nonusers, and 15 percent less likely to show declines in verbal fluency.[84]

It's thought that olive oil's high amounts of heart-healthy monoun-saturated fats help protect blood vessels in the brain.[85] But extra-virgin olive oil also is rich in those inflammation-fighting, free-radical-fighting polyphenols, and recent research has zeroed in on one called oleocanthal. In studies with mice, oleocanthal caused levels of proteins and enzymes that break down beta-amyloid and move it out of the brain to rise significantly.[86] Although clinical studies are needed to find out if this substance has the same effects in *our* brains, drizzle away—olive oil's other health benefits are well established.

STAY-SHARP TIPS

The MIND diet doesn't set a daily quota for olive oil; just use it in place of other oils and butter, and splurge on the extra-virgin variety.

Beyond salads and marinades for fish and poultry, there are more uses for olive oil than you think.[87]

- To bring out the sweetness of veggies like broccoli, asparagus, carrots, and cauliflower (most veggies, really), chop, toss in olive oil, and roast at 425°F until they're just tender. Or drizzle olive oil over microwaved vegetables just before you eat them.

- Scramble eggs and cook omelets in olive oil instead of butter.

- To make a tasty spread or dip that combines two MIND diet all-stars, pull out your food processor. Add a can of drained, rinsed white beans, along with a drizzle of olive oil and chopped garlic and herbs, salt, and pepper to taste. Process and enjoy on whole grain bread or crackers.

- Olive oil tastes great on air-popped popcorn. Place popped corn in a paper bag, add a drizzle of olive oil and a tablespoon of Par-mesan cheese, and give the bag a shake.

To get the most from extra-virgin olive oil, it's got to be fresh. Buy a bottle in a size you know you'll use up in a month or two. Also, check the date the oil was bottled; it should be no more than 18 months old. Store the bottle in a cool, dark place, so light, heat, and oxygen won't turn it rancid or affect its flavor and phytonutrients. If your oil comes in a clear bottle, cover it with foil to protect it from light.

7. POULTRY

Weekly servings to aim for: 2 or more

One serving equals: 3 ounces

If you're surprised to find chicken and turkey on the MIND diet list, don't be. Compared to red meat like beef, pork, and lamb, poultry is a good source of lean protein with relatively low levels of saturated fat.

Poultry is also rich in the B vitamin choline, needed to make the neurotransmitter acetylcholine. As you may recall from Part 1, low levels of acetylcholine are linked to AD. In a study of almost 1,400 people ages 36 to 83, those who consumed the most choline-rich foods fared better in tests of executive function and verbal learning, among other cognitive tests. They also were less likely to show areas of "white-matter hyperintensity" in the brain, MRI scans showed. Those areas, thought to be a sign of blood vessel disease in the brain, may raise the risk of AD.[88]

STAY-SHARP TIPS

These tips can help you get the most from your poultry servings.

Consider pasture-raised poultry. Organic, pasture-raised chickens aren't confined to cages—they spend a good part of their days foraging outdoors. In a study published in the *Journal of Cleaner Production*, researchers compared the meat of chickens raised indoors with that of those raised organically (some outdoor time, organic feed) and *extra* organically or "organic plus" (lots of time outside, organic feed). Compared to conventionally raised chickens, "organic" birds had more healthful omega-3 fatty acids in their breast meat. So did "organic plus" chickens—but their meat *also* contained more antioxidants, and their fat had less oxidative damage.[89]

You can find organic chicken in supermarkets. To find pasture-raised poultry in your area, log on to *eatwild.com*, which features a directory of local farmers that supply it. Even better, look for the "Certified Humane" label, created in 2016 by the nonprofit organization Humane Farm Animal Care. It has a stricter definition of "pasture raised" and "free range" than the USDA. For more information on these distinctions—developed with the humane treatment of poultry and other animals in mind—log on to the HFAC's website, *certifiedhumane.org*.

Cook (and order) clean. Bake, grill, roast, or sauté poultry, rather than fry it, and remove the skin and visible fat before cooking.

Be safe. Wrap refrigerated poultry in two layers of plastic, so it won't drip onto other foods. Immediately wash your hands with hot soapy water every time you handle raw poultry, and before you handle other foods. Do the same with work surfaces, cutting boards, and utensils. Use a food thermometer to ensure that chicken reaches an internal temperature of 165°F when cooking.

8. FISH

Weekly servings to aim for: 1

One serving equals: 3 to 4 ounces

From a juicy salmon steak to tiny, silvery sardines, fish does a brain good—all fish, but especially the oily, fatty varieties, which are rich in omega-3 fatty acids, mainly DHA and EPA. Evidence suggests that if your diet lacks these fats—shown to reduce disease-promoting, body-wide inflammation as well as help protect the heart—your future brain health may pay the price.

In a study published in *Neurology,* researchers gave almost 1,600 older people MRI brain scans and cognitive tests, and also measured the levels of omega-3 fats in their blood. Compared to those with the highest blood levels of omega-3 fats, those with the lowest levels had smaller brain volumes, with the shrinkage equaling about 2 years of brain aging! Their scores on tests of visual memory and executive function, including problem solving and multitasking, were lower, too.[90]

The good news: Just one serving of fish a week may stave off cognitive decline and dementia,[91] and DHA appears to be one key to fish's protective effects. In a study published in the *Archives of Neurology,* people with the highest levels of DHA at the start of the study were 47 percent less likely to get dementia *during* the study, compared to those with the lowest. They were also 39 percent less likely to develop AD. [92]

Perhaps you're concerned about the mercury levels in fish. After all, seafood is a main source of this toxic element, thought to damage neurons and contribute to thinking and memory problems. But there's more encouraging news to report: Mercury levels in fish don't appear to raise dementia risk, according to a recent study published in *JAMA.*[93]

Researchers studied the link between seafood consumption, dementia, and mercury levels in the brains of almost 300 older people after they'd passed on. They wanted to find out if two things—either eating fish or brain mercury levels—were related to signs of dementia in the brain, like plaques, tangles, and Lewy bodies.

Fish-eaters' brains *did* contain more mercury, the study found. Even so, the brains of those who'd reported a seafood meal at least once a week were *less* likely to show brain changes associated with AD. Overall, their brains had a 47 percent lower chance of being diagnosed with the disease.[94]

Compared to mild-tasting "white" fish like cod or flounder, those with darker flesh and more total fat, like herring, salmon, mackerel, and bluefish, contain the highest levels of omega-3 fats.[95] That said, eat the fish you like and prepare or order it in healthful ways, just as you do chicken. That means baked, broiled, poached, or grilled, rather than deep-fried.

If you're a fan of canned tuna, consider searching out "troll- or pole-caught" albacore tuna caught in western US and Canadian waters. Fish caught by these methods have lower levels of mercury than tuna caught in other areas of the world, because they're typically younger and mercury has had less time to build in their systems. American Tuna (*americantuna.com*), Wild Planet, and Ocean Naturals brands are other healthy, sustainable options, per the environmental organization Greenpeace.[96]

Try canned sardines as well; they're tiny but mighty omega-3 powerhouses that add flavor to salads, whole grain pasta, and (of course) pizza. Sardines are caught in the wild, so choose any brand packed in healthy olive oil.

Selecting healthy seafood can be a breeze—just log on to the Monterey Bay Aquarium's "Super Green" list (*seafoodwatch.org*).[97] Fish on the list contain the highest levels of omega-3s and the least amount of mercury.

9. OPTIONAL: ALCOHOL/WINE

Daily servings to aim for (if you already imbibe): up to one drink a day for women, two for men (no more!)

One serving equals: One drink is a 12-ounce beer, a 5-ounce glass of wine, or one shot (1.5 ounces) of 80-proof spirits.

If you look forward to your nightly cocktail or glass of wine, toast this news: A daily drink appears to protect the aging brain.

Moderate drinkers enjoy a lower incidence of type 2 diabetes and cardiovascular disease,[98] studies show. A daily drink has also been found to raise good HDL cholesterol[99] and lower blood levels of inflammatory markers like IL-6 and CRP.[100] Those health benefits appear to benefit the brain as well. In a scientific review of 143 studies that looked at alcohol intake and cognitive risk, moderate drinkers were 23 percent less likely to develop thinking and memory problems.[101]

In that study, wine was particularly protective. It also came out on top in a study published in the *Journal of Epidemiology,* which followed the health of over 1,400 Swedish women for over 30 years. Those who drank wine only were nearly 70 percent less likely to develop dementia.[102]

Red wine is loaded with resveratrol, an antioxidant found to reduce inflammation and oxidative damage and make it harder for beta-amyloid to form in the brain.[103] Other antioxidants in red wine dilate blood vessels and promote bloodflow. (Compared to red wine, the white variety contains few antioxidants, because it doesn't contain grapes' antioxidant-rich skins.)

Don't drink? Don't start just to protect your brain health. If you do, remember that it's moderate drinking that's been found to be protective. Whether you're into Merlot or martinis, "moderate" means no more than one drink a day for women, and two for men. Also bear in mind that heavy drinking—more than three drinks a day—has been found to accelerate the onset of AD by 2 or 3 years.[104]

6

Hit the Walking Trail or Gym

WHETHER YOU WALK, SWIM, pump iron, or dance like no one's watching, exercise is the Swiss army knife of health tools. Strengthens your heart, lungs, muscles, and bones? Check. Melts excess belly fat, offering protection from chronic diseases like diabetes? Check. Builds an ageless brain? Absolutely.[1, 2]

Regular sweat sessions increase bloodflow to the brain and keep regions vital to thinking and memory youthfully plump. And did you know a protein in your brain acts as a kind of neuron "fertilizer"? Amazing and true—and physical activity boosts its levels.

In other words, exercise is the older brain's best friend. In a study that followed people for 31 years, midlife exercise slashed the risk of dementia, including Alzheimer's, by up to 66 percent![3] But you won't wait decades for its brain-boosting benefits to kick in. As little as 8 weeks of cardiovascular exercise or cardio—the kind that gets your heart pumping—improved memory, attention, and processing speed, an analysis of 29 studies found.[4] The good news is, brisk walking counts.

Even so, the brain needs more than cardio to stay nimble. Enter strength training, which does double duty. As it helps build or maintain the muscle that keeps you mobile and independent, it fends off declines in memory and thinking. And that's even if you don't achieve a Ms. America physique.

If you're a hard-core lounge-arounder, getting active can help you feel better now as you protect your future mind and memory. Alzheimer's is linked to depression,[5] poor sleep,[6] and stress[7]—the very things that regular exercise melts away. So it's no exaggeration that getting active can change your life, and brain, for the better.

This section presents the evidence that links regular exercise to a sharper brain and offers simple ways to put the findings to work in your life. If you haven't been physically active in a while (or ever), we've got your back—you have plenty of options, and most feel more like fun than work. And if your motivation to work out is in the basement, you'll learn new, science-proven ways to fire it up.

So get ready to slip on your walking shoes, challenge your muscles, and treat your brain to the ultimate "youth serum." It's never too late to get active, and it takes surprisingly little sweat to benefit brain health. Here's how the exercise magic happens.

FIT HEART, SHARP BRAIN

Each time you break a sweat, bloodflow increases throughout your body, including in your brain. Better circulation means that more oxygen and glucose make it to your brain, while wastes that can dull thinking and memory are quickly whisked away.

Researchers at the University of Kentucky wanted to know if being physically fit improves bloodflow to the brain's key thinking and memory centers in particular, thereby offering protection against dementia. To find out, they gave 30 people, average age 64, treadmill tests to assess their fitness levels. A few weeks later, the team gave everyone MRI brain scans.

Those with higher fitness levels had better bloodflow to brain regions where Alzheimer's plaques and tangles typically show up first, the researchers found. That's significant—it means their brains were getting the oxygen and nourishment they needed. The study noted that arteries stiffen with age, and cardio may help arteries that carry blood to the brain stay supple.[8, 9]

Cardio also sharpens executive function, that all-important ability to plan, organize, and pay attention. A review of 18 studies, conducted on people ages 55 to 80, found that those who engaged in regular bouts of heart-pumping activity performed four times better on thinking and memory tests than nonexercisers. Interestingly, the review also found that teaming cardio with strength training was more beneficial than cardio alone.[10]

The great thing about cardio is that there are so many choices, you're bound to find at least one you absolutely love. Country line dancing? Yes. Golf? Go for it, if you lose the cart and carry your clubs. Want to stick with brisk walking? That's fine, too. The best type of exercise is the type you'll do. If you're shopping for the right cardio workout for you, page 141 lists 15 calorie-burning, brain-boosting options.

SWEAT SESSIONS "FERTILIZE" BRAIN CELLS

One amazing brain perk of physical activity: It stimulates the production of a neuron "fertilizer" that helps sprout new brain cells, form new connections between neurons, and protect the connections your brain

Launch a Sweat Offensive against "Type 3 Diabetes"

As you learned in Part 2, research associates insulin resistance, a key first step toward type 2 diabetes, with poorer performance on memory tests.[11] Sitting on your duff is a shortcut to insulin resistance, but getting active can help you make a U-turn.

When you exercise, your muscles empty their reserves of glucose. To "refuel," they not only become more sensitive to insulin's effects, they start to absorb glucose on their own, without insulin's help.[12] Just one more reason to walk that trail, lift those dumbbells, or step onto the dance floor.

already has. In other words, what natural fertilizers like compost or manure do for your veggies or roses, exercise does for your brain.

In the mid-1990s, research led by Carl W. Cotman, PhD, at the University of California-Irvine revealed that exercise triggers the brain's production of brain-derived neurotrophic factor, or BDNF.[13] This protein protects brain cells against injury and promotes plasticity in the connections, or synapses, between nerve cells, where cells "talk" to each other. As you may recall, *plasticity* is the brain's lifelong ability to grow and develop, and healthy connections are key to learning and memory.[14] Anything that promotes synapse plasticity benefits the older brain, and exercise is a BDNF bonanza.

Autopsies on brains with Alzheimer's suggest a link between BDNF and the disease.[15] Conversely, higher BDNF levels appear to offer protection.[16] In one study, researchers examined the brains of over 500 people (average age, 81) after they passed away to compare the rate of their cognitive decline with their brains' levels of BDNF. The participants had been followed for an average of 6 years and given tests to evaluate their cognitive skills every year.

Compared to people with the lowest BDNF levels, the rate of cognitive decline was about 50 percent slower in those with the highest levels, the exams showed. Also, the effect of plaques and tangles on cognitive decline was less pronounced in brains with more BDNF.[17] In other words, although those destructive proteins were present, they didn't significantly affect thinking and memory.

The brain's levels of BDNF wane as we grow older,[18] which is one reason brain function declines with age. But exercise, especially the aerobic kind, is thought to counteract these age-related drops in BDNF and restore young levels of this protein in older brains.[19]

A PLUMP BRAIN IS A SHARP BRAIN

A plump belly isn't healthy. But a plump *brain* is a different story, especially as you grow older. Although normal aging causes the brain to shrink, this loss of volume speeds up with Alzheimer's.[20] The shriveling is most pronounced in the hippocampus and cortex, the wrinkly gray "rind" that coats the outer layer of the brain.[21]

Regular exercise helps keep these vital regions youthfully beefy. In one study,[22] researchers had almost 60 people, average age 66, walk briskly for 60 minutes three times a week. Six months later, their brains showed significant increases in both gray and white matter compared to those of a control group that performed a stretching routine. Gray matter regulates most of your brain's information processing,

STAY-SHARP STRATEGY

UP YOUR WORKOUT, FIRE UP YOUR BRAIN

If you already walk most days, that's great—provided your heart rate is elevated, your brain reaps the bennies. But to maximize exercise's positive effects on the brain, consider switching up your workout. Better yet, tackle a new one. Remember, that 3-pound wad of Play-Doh in your skull is reshaped by new experiences, and exercise promotes that plasticity.[23] If you already have a fitness routine you enjoy, carry on! But small tweaks to a favorite routine can amp up its benefit to your brain. Here are a few ideas to try.

If you walk for fitness:

- Challenge your brain (and heart) with intervals, which is when you alternate short bursts of fast walking (say, 30 to 45 seconds) with longer recovery periods (60 seconds). Doing intervals is like sprinting to catch a bus, then slowing down once it stops for you.

- Try a new route that challenges your brain. You might pick a path with lots of rocks to negotiate, or that requires you to pay attention to trail markers. Just stay within your skill and fitness levels.

while white matter connects different brain regions so they can communicate.[25]

In another study led by the University of Pittsburgh, researchers had people between the ages of 55 and 80—sedentary when the study began—start to walk 40 minutes, three times a week. One year later, MRI brain scans revealed that the hippocampus had increased in size by 2 percent.

- If you play a sport that requires skill and coordination like golf or tennis, sign up for lessons. Even if you've been playing for years, you'll give your brain a workout and improve your swing to boot.

If you're looking for a new workout:

- Consider an activity that requires mastering complex moves. You might try that fencing course offered at the local college, or sign up for a dance class. Any type of dancing will do, but if you like to tango, you're in luck. People in their sixties and beyond who practiced its sultry moves twice a week reaped cognitive gains in 10 weeks, researchers at McGill University in Montreal found. They also improved their balance, helping to head off falls.[24]

- Join a walking or hiking club, or train for one of those fun "color runs" with a friend or family member. Exercising with others treats your brain to another plasticity booster: social contact.

If that doesn't sound like much, consider this: In people over 50, the hippocampus shrinks 1 to 2 percent a year,[26] threatening mind and memory. So that 40-minute walk, three times a week, effectively reversed 1 to 2 years of expected, age-related shrinkage! The walkers also did better on a memory test, compared to their results at the start of the study—an improvement the study associated with the increased size of the hippocampus.[27]

15 Workouts That Slash AD Risk in Half

Walking's wonderful, but it's not the only fitness game in town. Dance. Dig and hoe your garden. Hike. Ride your bike. All these activities—and more—pump up brain volume and dial down Alzheimer's disease (AD) risk, according to a study published in the *Journal of Alzheimer's Disease* (JAD).[28, 29] The best part: You'd do most of them for fun.

A team led by researchers at the University of California, Los Angeles, studied 5 years of data generated by almost 900 older people. The participants, who were 78 years old, on average, had MRI brain scans and periodic evaluations of their thinking abilities and memory. To assess how many calories they burned each week in physical activity, they also completed a scientific questionnaire designed to evaluate how often they engaged in the 15 recreational activities on the opposite page.

The brain scans revealed that participants in the top 25 percent of activity levels had significantly more neuron-rich gray

Regular exercise also has been shown to plump the cortex, which is vital to higher-level thinking ability. Researchers at the University of Maryland School of Public Health had people ages 61 to 88—some with mild cognitive impairment (MCI), some without—walk 30 minutes, four times a week. Three months later, everyone had improved his or her fitness by 8 percent, on average. That's impressive enough, but those who made the most fitness gains reaped the most cortex growth, regardless of whether they had MCI. In fact, compared to those without the condition, those who had it showed greater improvements in two brain regions that degenerate especially fast in Alzheimer's: the left insula and superior temporal gyrus.[30, 31] That's a solid reason to lace up your walking shoes.

matter in their frontal, temporal, and parietal lobes—areas associated with memory, learning, and complex thinking—compared to their less-active peers. Even better, the most active subjects were 50 percent less likely to have developed cognitive memory impairments or AD.

The "menu" of activities from the study follows. If you already do an activity on the list, consider mixing it up with others, if that's possible. Your brain doesn't like ruts any more than your muscles do, and switching among walking, water aerobics, and dance can help keep it percolating.

Walking

Hiking

Bicycling

Dancing

Golfing

Swimming

Gardening

Mowing

Raking

Tennis

Aerobics

Jogging

Racquetball

Calisthenics

Riding an exercise cycle

PUTTING THE RESEARCH TO WORK

So how much exercise do you need, and what kinds? The National Institutes of Health's recommendations for physical activity begin below.[32] If you're age 65 or over or have heart disease, diabetes, or another chronic health issue, ask your doctor to green-light these guidelines or suggest a safe and effective routine for you.

Cardio: 150 minutes a week. That's a half-hour walk, bike ride, dance class, or garden session 5 days a week. You can do any of the 15 activities above or take up something completely different like bellydancing or hula-hooping (see page 151). What matters is that the activity raises your heart rate, so your brain gets bathed in oxygen- and nutrient-rich blood.

If you jog or engage in other vigorous exercise, such as singles tennis or swimming laps, the recommendation falls to 75 minutes a week. Feel free to do both moderate and vigorous activity. If you walk some days and swim laps some days, great! As mentioned, you'll work your brain right along with your muscles.

Strength training: twice a week. You can work all your major muscle groups—legs, hips, back, chest, abs, shoulders, and arms—in two quick bouts per week. You've got options here, too, which include dumbbells, resistance bands, the weight machines at the gym (or the one in your home), or your own body weight. Read on for how to get started simply and safely.

Optional but recommended: balance exercises. They're simple, take 1 or 2 minutes, and act like a vaccination against age-related falls. You'll find two on page 151.

If you haven't been active in a while or have never engaged in formal exercise, that's totally okay. Start small—say, with a 10-minute walk—and build from there, adding strength training as your fitness improves and with your doctor's approval. Stick with it, giving yourself props for your resolve. Before long, you'll be fitter and stronger than you thought possible!

WALKING: STEP AWAY FROM ALZHEIMER'S

As you may have noticed, most studies that examine the link between exercise and brain health involve walking. There's a reason for that—it's the simplest, most convenient form of exercise there is! And the

STAY-SHARP STRATEGY

BUILD MORE ACTIVITY INTO YOUR DAY

Dancing in your seat, folding laundry—every little move you make helps fortify your brain against Alzheimer's disease (AD). Researchers at Rush University Medical Center in Chicago had more than 700 people—average age 82, with no signs of AD—wear a device on their wrist (called an ActiGraph) that measured their each and every movement, no matter how small, 24 hours a day for 10 days. After that 10-day test, the researchers tracked their participants for 4 years, and periodically evaluated them for symptoms of dementia. Those who'd moved least in that 10-day period were more than twice as likely to have developed AD compared to those who'd moved most.[33]

The take-home message: Keep those tail feathers shaking throughout the day. Wash dishes by hand rather than pile them in the dishwasher. Park and go into the bank rather than drive up to the window. Stand and pace each time you make or get a telephone call.

Another way to move more: cook from scratch! Think about waiting in line at the drive-thru. How much do you move? Now, consider how you bustle between your island, sink, and stove as you prepare dinner. Whip up meals that feature MIND diet all-stars, and you benefit your brain even more.

findings couldn't be clearer: Keeping your mind and memory sharp is as easy as putting one foot in front of the other.[34]

One of the best things about walking: It takes surprisingly little to benefit your brain. In a study of almost 19,000 older women, 90 minutes of walking per week significantly improved thinking and memory

SET THE RIGHT PACE

To reap the brain benefits of walking, set a brisk pace—3 miles per hour if you're just getting started, increasing your speed as your fitness level increases.[35] That's good to know if you use a treadmill or elliptical trainer. But if you walk outdoors, how brisk is "brisk"?

Exercise intensity is determined by your maximum heart rate, which is 220 minus your age. For example, if you're 65 years old, your maximum heart rate is 155 beats per minute (220 - 65 = 155). The low end of your target heart rate, which is 50 to 85 percent of your maximum heart rate, is 78 beats per minute; the high end, 132 beats per minute. Most studies define moderate exercise as 50 to 70 percent of maximum heart rate; vigorous exercise, as 70 to 85 percent.

A heart monitor automatically keeps you within your target heart rate for moderate or vigorous intensity. Just set its alarm limits around your target heart range, and it will prompt you to speed up or slow down. But you don't need this gadget. An alternative, low-tech option, called the "talk test," uses your ability to talk as you exercise to gauge your exercise intensity.

When you walk at a moderate intensity, you can talk, but not sing. You're working at a high intensity if you can't say more than a word or two without taking a breath. Use the test as a prompt to increase or reduce your effort. A good rule of thumb: If you can belt out a show tune as you walk, pick up the pace.

abilities.[36] That works out to 15 minutes a day! University of Pittsburgh researchers got a similar finding. When they tracked the physical activity of almost 300 people, average age 78, for 13 years, they found that those who walked at least 6 miles a week—about three-quarters of a mile a day—had larger brains than those who'd walked the least. They also cut their risk of Alzheimer's in half.[37]

This small amount of walking can boost brainpower fast. In a 12-week study led by the University of Texas at Dallas, sedentary people between the ages of 57 and 75 walked on a treadmill or rode a stationary bike for 1 hour, three times a week. At the start and end of the study, and midway through, the team measured memory and bloodflow in the brain at rest. Within 6 weeks, the exercisers showed increased bloodflow to the hippocampus and the anterior cingulate cortex, a brain region linked to better cognitive function in older age. By the end of the study, two aspects of memory—immediate and delayed memory—had improved as well.[38] Immediate memory allows you to hold information briefly, while delayed memory allows you to recall events from the past.

Like a little black dress, walking is versatile. Pair it with your favorite tunes, and you'll look forward to indoor sweat sessions on a treadmill or another cardio machine. Pick a gorgeous setting—say, a path along a river or a trail in a state or local park—and walks become an oasis in a day crammed with deadlines, chores, and responsibilities. Circling the neighborhood or the track at the local high school with your partner or a friend is an opportunity to bond.

STAY-SHARP TIPS

Believe it or not, there's a difference between plain old walking and walking for fitness. In the latter, there's actual technique involved—but it's easy to master. Following are seven ways to walk faster and outsmart soreness, from the American Council on Exercise.[39]

No need to tackle these tips all at once. Take them one at a time, in the order they're presented. Focus on that tip as you start your walk, and check every 15 minutes or so to make sure you're maintaining proper form. After a week, move to the next tip. Before long, you'll be putting them all together and walking like a pro.

Straighten up and walk tall. Imagine that you're Pinocchio, and you're being pulled up by a string attached to the top of your head. When you walk tall, you walk faster.

Keep your head and eyes up. As that imaginary string pulls up your spine, you'll walk taller automatically, and avoid stress on your neck and low back to boot.

Lift your chest and keep your abs tight. Engaging these muscles takes pressure off your back.

Bend your arms at the elbows. Keep your arms at waist level, and your hands in loose fists. This gets your arms swinging, which helps increase your speed and keeps blood from pooling in your hands so they won't swell, tingle, or go numb.

Relax your shoulders. When they're not bunched up around your ears, your arms swing freely, which helps prevent tension in your neck and upper back.

Heed your heels and toes. When you step forward, land gently on your heel and push off powerfully and evenly from your toes. This heel-to-toe motion will carry you farther and faster.

Take measured steps. Giant strides won't help you walk faster. In fact, they'll slow you down. An ideal stride length feels natural and allows you to push off powerfully with your toes.[40]

STRENGTH TRAINING: BUILD MUSCLE, GAIN BRAINPOWER

Strength training isn't just for whippersnappers with six-pack abs. Older bodies (and minds) thrive on it. Less than an hour a week builds or maintains the muscle and bone necessary to walk, drive, get dressed and out of bed, and generally live independently as you age. It also lowers blood sugar and boosts your energy and mood (you're likely to feel like Wonder Woman!). But the rewards of resistance exercise go beyond even these benefits.

Researchers at the University of British Columbia randomly assigned more than 150 women in their sixties and seventies to one of three groups. Two groups worked out with dumbbells and weight machines, either once or twice a week. A third (the control group) did a toning and balance routine. One year later, both groups of iron-pumpers scored higher on several aspects of executive function compared to the control group. For example, they had better selective attention,[41] which allows you to focus on one thing and block out distractions. (You use selective attention when you can read a book as your spouse watches a shoot-'em-up movie in the same room.)

In another study, researchers had men over 65 follow a strength-training routine for 6 months. Three times a week, they performed exercises like chest presses, leg presses, and abdominal crunches. One group lifted at a moderate intensity—50 percent of the most weight they could lift one time (called a one-repetition maximum). The other group lifted at a high intensity—80 percent of their one-repetition maximum. A control group performed a stretching routine.

Before the study, and again at the end, the team tested participants' concentration skills and short- and long-term memory. Both strength-training groups improved their scores on the cognitive tests and increased their levels of IGF-1, a growth factor that promotes the survival of neurons. They also reported a better quality of life. The stretchers showed none of these benefits.[42]

Strength training may benefit the brain by increasing bloodflow or boosting levels of IGF-1, research suggests.[43] Another explanation: Lifting

Exercise May Be "Medicine" for Memory Problems and AD

If someone you care about has been diagnosed with mild cognitive impairment (MCI) or Alzheimer's disease (AD), pass on this preliminary research presented at the 2015 Alzheimer's Association International Conference in Toronto.[44]

Researchers at Wake Forest School of Medicine assigned their 65 participants with MCI, ages 55 to 89, to either cardiovascular exercise (usually walking on a treadmill) or stretching. Both groups exercised 45 to 60 minutes, four times a week. At the start of the 6-month study, and again at the end, the team tested the participants' verbal memory and decision-making abilities, analyzed their blood and spinal fluid, and did MRI brain scans.

weights makes you feel amazing. Studies of older adults have linked a better mood to better thinking ability, and in one study, older people who performed strength training three times a week reported brighter moods 6 months later.[45]

STAY-SHARP TIPS

Whether you're new to weight training or staging a comeback, all you need to begin is confidence—and one of the two Ageless Brain total-body workouts, designed by Marjorie Nolan, MS, RD, author of *The Belly Fat Fix* (see Appendix). If 75-year-olds can lift weights, so can you! Start slow, be consistent, and you'll progress faster than you think.

To avoid soreness and allow your muscles to recover, space workouts at least 1 day apart.

If you plan to join a gym, most will pair you with a trainer to show you the ropes. Likely, you'll start on the weight machines, which are simple and safe for beginners. Typically, trainers suggest an upper- and

Six months later, the cardio group's scans showed a significant increase in bloodflow to brain regions involved in memory and information processing. Their executive function improved as well, possibly because they worked at a higher intensity than the stretching group. Further, the cardio group's spinal fluid showed a significant reduction in tau proteins, the raw material of plaques and tangles.

In another study reported at the conference, researchers from Denmark had people with mild to moderate Alzheimer's walk at either a moderate or vigorous pace for an hour, three times a week. After 4 months, they showed significantly less anxiety, irritability, and depression, the researchers said. Those who exercised the most, and hardest, also improved their mental speed and attention.

lower-body workout, then take you through each exercise, setting the appropriate amount of weight at each machine.

Wherever you choose to work out, assume the correct body position for each exercise and lift and lower weights in a slow, controlled fashion. Good form helps prevent injury. That said, strike a balance between being safe and progressively gaining strength. In other words, don't lift too much weight—or too little. The right amount of weight is the amount you can lift 10 times, and no more. When you can do 10 repetitions easily, try "graduating" to the next-heaviest weight.[46]

NEED MOTIVATION TO MOVE? FOUR SCIENCE-TESTED WAYS TO SPARK IT

Work out with a buddy. Choose activities you enjoy. Pack your gym bag the night before, and place it by the door. These old chestnuts do increase exercise motivation, so do the following tips, which come

The 20-Second Brain-Health Check

How's your balance? A simple do-it-yourself test can tell you in a minute or less. And how well you do may reflect the health of your brain—and your risk of stroke, a Japanese study found.[47]

Researchers asked almost 1,400 people, average age 67 and apparently healthy, to stand on one leg for 1 minute with their eyes open. (They got two tries, and the team used each participant's best time.) The researchers then gave their participants MRIs to examine the small blood vessels in their brains.

Being unable to stand on one leg for more than 20 seconds was linked to damage to the brain's small blood vessels, like tiny bleeds or ministrokes. This condition, called cerebral small vessel disease (SVD), can lead to a major stroke, and high blood pressure is the major risk factor.[48] Just as alarming, not making it to 20 seconds was associated with lower scores on thinking and memory tests.

Try standing on one leg, eyes open, right now. If you can't reach that 20-second threshold, you may be at increased risk for stroke and cognitive decline. Of course, only a doctor can tell for sure, so if you're concerned about your results, make an appointment.

straight from the pages of the latest studies. Try one or more to help ignite your "gymthusiasm."

Remember an amazing workout. Where you were, what you were doing, and above all, how *good* you felt. Positive memories may spark inspired sweat sessions. Study participants who recalled a good memory about exercise both increased their motivation to work out and exercised more over the next week, compared to those who didn't.[52] Laminate that photo of you participating in a charity walk or dance-a-thon. Then, attach it to your workout bag or the door to your

Even if you pass the test, it's smart to work on your balance. When you're sure-footed, you avoid falls, which can cause the brain injuries thought to increase Alzheimer's risk. Balance exercises are so simple it's not fair to call them exercises. Here are two to try throughout the day.

Pretend you're a stork. Stand on one leg as you brush your teeth or do the dishes. Once you can do it with your eyes open, try it with your eyes closed to increase the challenge.

Walk heel to toe. Raise your arms to your sides at shoulder height and focus on a spot ahead of you. Take 20 steps forward, placing your heel just in front of the toe of your other foot. If you feel wobbly, do this move near a wall, so you can reach out and steady yourself if you need to.[49]

You might also consider enrolling in a tai chi class.[50] You'll improve your balance as you reduce your stress. A study of tai chi practitioners in their late sixties, published in the *British Journal of Sports Medicine*, found that on measures of stability, most scored around the 90th percentile of the American Fitness Standards.[51]

home gym, or wear it around your neck as you walk (put it under your top if you like). Or pack a new playlist with the tunes you sweated to when you exercised regularly and were in the best shape of your life.

Try something completely different. Do something you enjoy—but an *uncommon* workout may pump you up even more, a study of over 100 women found.[53] Researchers had inactive women perform either a 30-minute treadmill walk or a workout a kid would love: hula-hooping. (The participants used a hoop that weighed 2 to 5 pounds to increase intensity.) Compared to walkers, hoopers reported more positive feelings and less negativity, and said they were more likely to work out in the next month.

It sounds like a blast—but is hooping exercise? The researchers noted that the activity's been shown to raise heart rate and burn calories at a rate like other forms of moderate exercise, walking included.

To give fitness hooping a whirl, check out fitness hoops ($25 and up) at sporting-goods stores or online retailers such as Amazon. (You'll even find fitness hooping exercise DVDs.) Or try another unconventional activity, such as ballet, Pilates, or Frisbee golf.

Treat yourself to an mp3 player. Listening to music as you exercise distracts from fatigue, elevates mood, and makes sweat sessions feel less difficult. But did you know that popping in those earplugs *before* a workout, as well as during, can amp you up? So powerful is the music/motivation link that a scientific review of its effects—written by the foremost experts on music and exercise—described it as "a type of legal performance-enhancing drug."[54] Consider buying an mp3 player, found in the electronics section of some big-box stores or online. Most are less than $30. If you don't know how to get tunes on the gadget, have a tech-savvy friend or one of your kids show you how (yet another exercise for your brain!) or check out a pre-created playlist on your favorite music streaming service.

Connect exercise with your "big picture." People with a purpose in life tend to exercise more, a study published in the *Journal of Health Psychology* found.[55] University of Colorado researchers asked over 100 people about their levels of optimism and purpose. Then, for 3 days, they had these folks wear devices designed to measure physical-activity levels. Those with a strong sense of purpose were more physically active.

Think about what gives *your* life purpose and meaning. Family?

Strong faith? A certain passion, such as animal rescue or some other volunteer project? Whatever it may be, connect it to why it's important that you get active and stay that way. Linked to a big-picture purpose, exercise may be easier to stick to. You'll come to see that physical activity doesn't complicate your life—it makes life better.

This section began with the brain benefits of exercise and ends with the importance of attitude. How perfect! Next, you'll learn about attributes linked to a lower risk of memory issues and Alzheimer's—things like a positive outlook on life, a close social circle, and interest in other people and the wider world. All these and more can lead you to new people, places, and things—and when you expand your world, your brain takes notice. If you feel stuck in a rut or tend to be serious (or even a bit curmudgeonly), this section will open your eyes to how profoundly attitude can affect mind and memory.

7

Adjust Your Attitude

"ARE YOU A CONTROL Freak?" "How Much of a People-Pleaser Are You?" "How Open-Minded Are You?" At some point in your life, it's likely that you've taken at least one personality quiz in a magazine or online. While they can be fun, let's be honest—the results typically aren't a surprise. By this stage of your life, you know whether you're warm or reserved, laid back or a worrier, a sunny optimist or a glass-half-empty type.

Your personality *traits* are the relatively stable patterns of thoughts, feelings, and behaviors that distinguish you from everyone else.[1] But did you know that certain traits have been found to affect brain health decades down the road?

Here's the good news. Although personality remains mostly fixed throughout your life, it isn't set in stone, especially if you work on changing the ways you think and behave. In fact, some studies show that personality evolves over the years—and the changes tend to be for the better.[2] For example, one study of more than 130,000 people ages

21 to 60, published in the *Journal of Personality and Social Psychology*, found that positive personality traits like conscientiousness (the tendency to plan ahead, delay gratification, and work toward goals) increased with age, while negative traits like neuroticism—psychologist-speak for a tendency to experience distress and anxiety—decreased.[3, 4]

In other words, a personality upgrade is a perk and privilege of aging—we tend to become warmer, calmer, and more responsible and confident as we grow older. What's more, some studies suggest that when you lead a satisfying and meaningful life, positive personality changes may speed up.[5]

You can't remake your personality from scratch. (And why would you want to? You're amazing!) But you *can* become more aware of personality traits found to either protect or undermine cognitive health, build up healthy traits, and manage those linked to cognitive decline.

The first thing to understand: Although your personality is as unique as your fingerprint, the wonder of you boils down to a blend of five basic traits.

THE PERSONALITY/ALZHEIMER'S CONNECTION

Most psychologists agree that all personality traits—laziness, creativity, friendliness, stubbornness, take your pick—fit into five broad domains. These domains—often called the Big Five[6]—spell out the word OCEAN. The "Big Five" are:

1. **O**penness to experience. If you're strong in this domain, you tend to be intellectually curious, imaginative, and insightful; you like to try new things and have wide interests.
2. **C**onscientiousness. People strong in this domain tend to be organized, plan ahead, and work steadily to achieve goals.[7]

3. **E**xtraversion. If you're strong in extraversion, you tend to be active and talkative, enjoy socializing, and typically have a positive outlook on life.

4. **A**greeableness. People with a high level of agreeableness are typically friendly and good-natured, courteous, sympathetic, kind, and affectionate.

5. **N**euroticism. Neuroticism describes a tendency to experience distress and anxiety, and to find it difficult to manage stress and control impulses.[8]

You might think of the Big Five as the main ingredients in the recipe for what makes you, you. Your "recipe" might be ample amounts of conscientiousness and agreeableness and an average amount of extraversion, with dashes of openness and neuroticism. One thing's for sure, though—everyone's recipe is different.

A Swedish study of more than 500 older people[9] is a striking example of how personality potentially impacts Alzheimer's disease (AD) risk. Low neuroticism teamed with high extroversion was the personality combo associated with the lowest dementia risk. In other words, calm, outgoing, relaxed people were the least likely to develop AD— they slashed their risk by an impressive 50 percent. But in good news for introverts, those who were *not* outgoing but were still calm and relaxed *also* slashed their Alzheimer's risk in half, compared to those participants who were both isolated and prone to distress.

PUTTING THE RESEARCH TO WORK

Now that you're familiar with the Big Five, it's time to dig into the research that associates these traits, or traits related to them, with Alzheimer's risk.

As you read, bear in mind that although you can't change your personality significantly, you *can* work to change less-than-healthy thoughts and behaviors to help your ageless brain stay sharp. This section's practical strategies can help get you started. To maximize their benefits, team them with other strategies in this book, such as a healthy diet, regular exercise, and meditation.

Attitude Adjustment #1: Get or Stay Connected

The comfort with which you interact with others is a facet of extraversion. Whether we bond as a family, sip coffee with a friend, chat over the fence with a neighbor, or volunteer in the community, humans thrive in the company of others. Multiple studies link regular social interaction to a host of health perks, from reduced susceptibility to colds[10] to greater longevity.

Regular coffee dates and bingo nights may even help keep your brain sharp.[11] Harvard researchers examined data collected from almost 17,000 older people who were given a simple memory test—their ability to recall a list of words. People who were married, active in volunteer groups, and in regular contact with family, friends, and neighbors had slower declines in memory compared to less social folks. In fact, declines in the biggest social butterflies were about half those of the least-social participants.[12]

Social give-and-take isn't just for older brains, either. Researchers at the University of California, Los Angeles, examined data collected from almost 5,000 people ages 35 to 85. Regardless of their age, those with more social support performed better on tests of executive function and memory.[13]

On the other hand, social isolation appears to put older people's thinking and memory at risk. (Socially isolated people typically live alone, have a shaky social network or none at all, or participate in few activities with others.) In one study, researchers had 800 people, average age 81, fill out a questionnaire in which they rated their response to statements like, "I miss having people around" and "I miss having a really good friend." A score of 5 suggested a high incidence of loneliness. The participants filled out the questionnaire each year for 4 years, and during that time, 76 developed Alzheimer's.

When the team evaluated the loneliness scores of those with the disease, it found that risk was more than double for those with high scores (3.2) compared with low scores (1.4). However, brain autopsies showed that loneliness in life was not related to brain changes characteristic of Alzheimer's, such as plaques and tangles or tissue damaged by a lack of bloodflow.[14]

According to the researchers, the findings suggest loneliness somehow may contribute to a risk of developing an Alzheimer's-like dementia in late life unrelated to actual brain damage. All the more reason to attend (or start) a regular ladies' or guys' night out.

STAY-SHARP TIPS

If you're fortunate enough to have a rich, diverse social circle, keep those bonds tight! But if moving or retirement has loosened the ties you depended on for decades, or you simply want more social interaction in your life, these strategies from the American Psychological Association can help you build or expand your support network.[15]

Let go of the myths. You don't need a best friend or thousands of Facebook friends to have a solid social support network. Some people get all the social interaction they need from a work friend to eat lunch with, their "walking buddy" in the neighborhood, and regular attendance

Age Loud and Proud—and Reduce Your Alzheimer's Risk?

What does it mean to be "old"? Does your mind go to positive qualities, such as "wisdom" and "experience," or less-than-flattering stereotypes, such as "grouchy" and "scatter-brained"? People who view aging in a negative light are more likely to develop brain changes linked to Alzheimer's, a series of experiments led by Yale researchers found.[16]

In the first experiment, the team studied whether people who held negative stereotypes about what it means to be old would experience significant shrinkage of the hippocampus over time. To do it, they analyzed data from more than 150 cognitively healthy people enrolled in the Baltimore Longitudinal Study of Aging (BLSA). In their forties, participants took a test that assessed their attitudes toward aging in which they had to agree or disagree with statements like "older people are absent-minded." About 25 years later, the team began to track participants' hippocampus size with MRI

at their house of worship. If you interact regularly and don't feel lonely or isolated, your social network is doing its job.

Connect around your passions. Do you like to bird-watch, scrapbook, sing, make jewelry? Join a local club, sign up for a class, or take on a volunteer position in an organization that shares your interests. As you immerse yourself in an activity you love, you'll begin to interact naturally with those who love it, too.

Make the first move. Don't wait for others to reach out to you. If you'd like to see a certain person more than you do, issue a standing invitation to get together once a week or once a month for lunch or cof-

brain scans every year for 10 years.

Compared to participants who'd viewed aging more positively, those with negative views had more hippocampus shrinkage. In fact, the "negatives" experienced the same amount of shrinkage in 3 years as the "positives" did in 9.

The second experiment was to find out whether the brains of people who'd held negative views of aging would accumulate greater amounts of plaques and tangles. Brain autopsies revealed this to be the case. The brains of the "negatives" contained more of these toxic proteins compared to those of the "positives." In both studies, the team adjusted for health, age, and other risk factors for Alzheimer's. It may be that the stress generated by holding negative attitudes about aging results in damaging brain changes, according to the study's lead author.[17]

The take-home message: If you believe aging is a bummer, go out of your way to blast through those negative attitudes. You really are only as old as you feel, if you choose to believe it.

fee. Don't wait for phone calls—make them. Ask about people's health, their children, and their families, and let them know you care. If you show up for others, they'll be more likely to show up for you.

Seek targeted support. If you care for an elderly parent or a family member with a chronic illness or struggle with illness yourself, consider joining a support group. Local hospitals often host cancer, stroke, or caregiver support groups where you'll meet others dealing with the same challenges you face. They'll be there when you need someone to lean on. You'll be there for them, too, which is just as beneficial.

Attitude Adjustment #2: Seek Treatment for Depression

Everyone gets the blues now and then, but major depression is different. This serious mood disorder can fester for months, or even years, and color not just how you feel but how you think.

There's no hard proof that depressed people have a higher risk of dementia, but there's no shortage of research that link the two conditions. Studies of both animals and people have associated psychological distress—a key component of depression—with impairments in memory, learning, and executive function. Other research has found that, compared to older people with low levels of distress, those with high levels are more likely to develop mild cognitive impairment and Alzheimer's, even if they're in good mental health.[18] In fact, a scientific review of 23 studies of nearly 50,000 adults over age 50 concluded that people who suffered from depression were 65 percent more likely to develop Alzheimer's as those who didn't, and more than twice as likely to develop vascular dementia.[19]

One issue of the journal *Neurology* included three separate studies on the link between depression later in life and the risk of dementia. In one of those studies, researchers followed almost 1,000 people enrolled in the landmark Framingham Heart Study for up to 17 years. When the study began, everyone was cognitively healthy. By the end, 136 participants had developed Alzheimer's and 28 other types of dementia.

Of those who were depressed when the study began, 21.6 percent went on to develop dementia, compared to 16.6 percent of those who were not depressed. When the researchers factored in age and gender, they discovered that depression raised the risk of later dementia by a whopping

50 percent.[20] A separate study of more than 1,200 older people, published in the same issue of the journal, found that experiencing two or more episodes of late-life depression doubled the risk of dementia.[21]

What's the connection between late-life depression and dementia risk? There are several theories, but one possible explanation is that the chronic stress of depression might change the structure of the brain. In studies, the brains of mice and rats kept in stressful conditions show changes to their hippocampus, and researchers believe that chronic distress may change the human hippocampus in a similar way.[22]

STAY-SHARP TIPS

Major depression shouldn't be ignored. If you've experienced some of the signs and symptoms below most of the day, almost every day, for at least 2 weeks or if you've considered hurting yourself, take immediate action—tell your doctor or someone you trust.[23]

- You often feel sad, anxious, or "empty."
- It's harder to concentrate, remember things, or make decisions.
- You're often irritable.
- You feel guilty, worthless, or helpless.
- You've lost interest in hobbies or activities you used to take pleasure in.
- You have less energy or more fatigue.
- You move or talk more slowly or feel so restless you can't sit still.
- You can't sleep, sleep too much, or wake up early.
- You're experiencing changes in your appetite and/or weight.
- You have aches or pains, headaches, or digestive problems with no clear physical cause.

If you suspect depression, it's vital to seek treatment, both for your current quality of life and your future brain health. If your doctor does diagnose it, there's every reason to have hope—even severe depression can respond to counseling, antidepressant medications, or a combination of the two.

Researchers also are exploring whether a class of antidepressants called selective serotonin reuptake inhibitors (SSRIs) might lower Alzheimer's risk. In a small preliminary study, a team of researchers led

Nonstop Negativity and Alzheimer's Risk

We all get mired in negativity now and then. But if you feel wound-up most of the time, here's a good reason to change: Chronic anxiety and distress may raise the risk of Alzheimer's later in life.[24]

Researchers in Sweden followed 800 middle-aged women for nearly 40 years, starting when they were between 38 and 54 years old. In that time, 104 developed Alzheimer's. Women who scored the highest on a test for neuroticism at the start of the study were twice as likely to be diagnosed with Alzheimer's, compared to those who scored lowest.

Researchers noted that other studies have linked both neuroticism and stress with less-than-healthy changes in the structure and function of the hippocampus.

A proven neuroticism neutralizer: cognitive behavioral therapy (CBT). This solution-oriented form of therapy focuses less on your past than on how to get past painful feelings and unhealthy thoughts and behaviors that keep you stuck in the present. To learn more about CBT, log on to the website of the Association for Behavioral and Cognitive Therapies (abct.org).

by the University of Pennsylvania had healthy people without Alzheimer's take either 60 milligrams of the SSRI citalopram (Celexa) or a placebo pill. Then, for the next day and a half, the researchers kept track of the levels of beta-amyloid in their participants' spinal fluid.[25] Compared to those who swallowed the placebo, those who took citalopram reduced the production of beta-amyloid in their brains by 37 percent.[26] While more research is needed, the finding may pave the way for a preventive treatment for Alzheimer's.

Attitude Adjustment #3: Cultivate Conscientiousness

Remember Goofus and Gallant from the magazine *Highlights for Children*? If you leafed through it as a kid, you likely recall Goofus as the less-than-responsible boy all moms frowned upon, and Gallant as the reliable boy who worked hard, played by the rules, and kept his word.

Gallant is the perfect example of *conscientiousness,* the personality trait associated with being organized, self-disciplined, and goal-oriented. This "if it's worth doing, it's worth doing well" trait predicts more than just worldly success. Research links it with good health, a long life, and even a sharp mind and memory: in one study, conscientious people were less likely to develop Alzheimer's as they aged.[27]

Researchers analyzed the medical data of nearly 1,000 older people enrolled in the Religious Orders Study, who were dementia-free when they enrolled. As part of a scientific personality test, they read 12 statements designed to identify conscientiousness—such as, "I am a productive person who always gets the job done"—and then rated themselves on a scale from 0 to 4. Higher scores suggested higher conscientiousness. They took this test each year.

Twelve years later, 176 participants had developed Alzheimer's, and the team compared everyone's conscientiousness scores with his or her susceptibility to Alzheimer's during the study period. They found that for each point on the conscientiousness scale scored, Alzheimer's risk fell by more than 5 percent. High scorers (40 points or more) had an 89 percent lower risk of developing Alzheimer's than low scorers (28 points or lower). That association held even when the researchers factored in such considerations as participants' level of physical activity, the number of brain-stimulating activities they enjoyed, the size of their social network, and even whether they had the Alzheimer's gene APOE-e4. High scorers were also less likely to develop mild cognitive impairment, compared to low scorers.

So why might diligent, self-disciplined people have sharper brains in older age? According to the researchers, it may be because they're more likely to experience success in school and at work, both associated with a reduced risk of Alzheimer's. The researchers also noted that conscientiousness has been linked to higher levels of emotional resilience and a greater tendency to manage stress in positive ways (with exercise or social support, for example). "These factors might lessen the adverse consequences of negative life events and chronic psychological distress, which have been associated with risk of dementia in old age," the study said.

STAY-SHARP TIPS

If you're naturally conscientious, thank your lucky stars. If you're not, it's not the end of the world. With patience and persistence, it's possible to develop this trait, one step at a time.[28]

Take it slow. Rome wasn't built in a day, and no one turns from Goofus to Gallant overnight, either. Give yourself permission to work toward positive change slowly, and to experience a setback or two.

Make your bed each morning. You've got to start somewhere, and this simple, 3-minute task is a good way to do it. Once you're smoothing the covers and fluffing the pillows daily, try another task like returning your shopping cart to the corral instead of ditching it in the parking lot, picking up trash when you see it on the street, getting to work on time, or washing the dishes each night before bed. Focus on one task at a time, no matter how long it takes. You'll get there!

Learn to say no. When conscientious people say they'll do something, they do it. If you tend to make promises you can't keep, turn down requests to take on obligations you know you can't or won't honor, whether that's serving on a committee or selling candy for your nephew's football team. Ironically, saying no makes you more conscientious automatically. When you're honest with yourself and others about your schedule and limitations, you come through for others, because they're free to find a helper who can get the job done.

Attitude Adjustment #4: Build Up Your Emotional Resilience

At some point, everyone faces life's deep waters—the death of a loved one, job loss, serious illness, violent crime, or natural disaster. The question is, in a crisis, how well are you able to keep your head above water?

That's where *resilience* comes in. Resilience is a person's ability to manage adversity in positive ways and come out the other side. It's the ability to marshal your inner strength, cope with stress, and find peace even as the storm rages around you.[29]

Resilience is not a personality trait. Rather, it involves behaviors, thoughts, and actions you can develop, which is well worth doing. As resilience helps you cope with hard times in healthy ways, it also may help stave off cognitive decline.[30]

Autopsies of the brains of cognitively healthy older people show that about 30 percent contain enough plaques and tangles to meet the criteria for Alzheimer's. Yet amazingly, these folks show no symptoms of the disease.[31] This is called asymptomatic Alzheimer's disease, or ASYMAD. As you may recall, it's possible to have a brain full of plaques and tangles with no cognitive symptoms. And personality traits associated with resilience may come into play.

Researchers at the National Institute on Aging analyzed data obtained from over 100 older people who completed personality tests that assessed the Big Five. After their deaths, the team examined their brains for the physical changes associated with Alzheimer's.

When the team compared the autopsy results with the personality tests, they found that those with greater emotional resilience and conscientiousness had a lower risk of dementia, even if their brains showed signs of Alzheimer's. More specifically, they scored lower on neuroticism—which encompasses vulnerability to stress, anxiety, and depression—compared to those who had developed dementia.

Emotionally stable, conscientious people may have greater "resistance" to Alzheimer's cognitive symptoms for several reasons. For example, they are generally in better physical health, less likely to suffer from depression, and more likely to engage in lifestyle habits shown to reduce the risk of dementia, like exercise.

STAY-SHARP TIPS

According to the American Psychological Association, the following strategies can help build emotional resilience.[32] (You'll find more resilience-builders at *apa.org*.) Bear in mind that resilient people do experience emotional pain and distress. However, they manage these intense feelings in positive ways and give themselves the same TLC they'd lavish on a loved one.

Ask for help—and take it. A key way to build resilience is to seek out support. Your family and friends, work colleagues, and church are likely to know what you're going through. When they ask if they can watch your grandkids, run to the store, or make dinner, take them up on it. And allow them to sit with you as you freak out.

Alternatively, reach out to others in their time of need. Volunteer at a local animal shelter, senior citizens' community center, or hospital. You'll get back as much as you give, and the knowledge that you're of use can see you through the darkness.

Nurture yourself, body and soul. In a crisis, your physical and emotional needs don't typically come first on your to-do list. Even so, take time to tend to your own health or seek out simple pleasures. Continue your walks or workouts, and ask a friend to join you if necessary. Get regular cuddle time with your pet. Meditate to clear your mind and blow off stress. Show up for your mammogram or dental appointment (clean teeth feel good!). When you practice self-care, you're better able to push through difficult times without feeling like you might fall apart.

Take action. Focus on possible solutions to a challenge rather than the fear and worry it may cause. Is there anything you can do to improve the situation, even the smallest thing? If so, take a deep breath and take that step. You'll instantly feel more in control.

Fan the flame of hope. Remind yourself that this, too, shall pass and that the future can be better. Try to visualize that future. Who are

What You Can Learn from the Super-Resilient

If you wanted to conduct research on emotional resilience, who better to study than a group of former prisoners of war who'd faced unspeakable horror—and emerged mentally and emotionally intact?

That's just what Dennis S. Charney, MD, an expert in the subject of human resilience, did. In collaboration with colleague Steven M. Southwick, MD, Dr. Charney studied 750 men—mostly pilots in the Vietnam War—who'd been POWs for 6 to 8 years. Although these men had been tortured, held in solitary confinement, or both, they'd emerged from their captivity without clinical depression or posttraumatic stress syndrome (PTSD).

The research, drawn from interviews, psychological tests, brain scans, and DNA studies, revealed critical components of resilience that include:[33]

1. Optimism
2. Altruism
3. A moral compass or beliefs that can't be shattered
4. Faith or spirituality
5. Humor

you with? What are you doing that brings you happiness? When you're paralyzed by worry or fear, "visit" that future in your mind's eye.

Keep a "resilience journal." You may have heard "with challenge comes opportunity." You might keep a journal and write about the uncomfortable and unpredictable journey you're on. What might your hardship teach you, either about life or yourself? How can you use adversity, or even tragedy, as an opportunity for growth? Have you discovered a sense of strength or resourcefulness you didn't know you possessed, grown closer to your partner or a friend, increased your faith?

6. A role model

7. Social support

8. A sense of purpose in life

It's possible to develop such traits in yourself. These ideas can get you started.

Jot down one or two things you're grateful for at the start or end of every day and drop them in a jar. When you feel sad or anxious, sift through the jar. In one study, researchers asked a group of adults to spend a few minutes writing down three things that had gone well that day and why they happened. The experiment lasted just 1 week, but participants reported that they felt happier for 6 months afterward.[34]

Commit to serving someone every day. You might drop in on an elderly neighbor each week or lend a hand at the local food pantry.

Write out a long-overdue "thank you." In another experiment, people got a week to write and deliver a letter of gratitude to someone who'd shown them kindness but whom they'd never thanked properly. The happiness boost lasted about a month, and those who delivered and read the letter to its recipient in person, rather than mailing it, reaped the greatest benefits.[35]

Attitude Adjustment #5: Pursue (or Seek) Your Life's Purpose

What floats your boat? Kindles your passion? Gives your life direction, meaning, *purpose*? It's a serious question with serious implications for your health. Many studies have associated having a strong sense of purpose with health perks, such as more happiness and a longer, healthier life.

A strong sense of purpose may also blunt the harmful effects of the brain plaques and tangles linked to Alzheimer's, according to researchers at Rush University Medical Center in Chicago.[36] The team studied almost 250 older people enrolled in the Rush Memory and Aging Project. These folks received health evaluations, including cognitive tests and neurological exams, every year for up to 10 years.

To assess their participants' sense of purpose, the researchers had them rate their level of agreement or disagreement with 10 statements. The statements included, "I feel good when I think of what I've done in the past and what I hope to do in the future" and "I have a sense of direction and purpose in life." Higher scores suggested a higher sense of purpose.

When participants died, their brains were studied. The team found that in those whose brains had accumulated significant plaques and tangles, the rate of cognitive decline was about 30 percent slower in those who'd reported a strong purpose in life compared to those who'd had less purpose. "These findings suggest that purpose in life protects against the harmful effects of plaques and tangles on memory and other thinking abilities," stated the study's lead author, Patricia A. Boyle, PhD.[37] That's even after the team factored in physical health, the size of the participants' social network, symptoms of depression, and other factors that could have made a difference.

A strong sense of purpose may benefit cognitive reserve, the study said, noting that almost all our brains develop some plaque and tangles as we age, whether or not we develop Alzheimer's. What the findings suggest is that a strong sense of purpose may allow the brain to "rise above" such age-related damage and continue to function at a higher level.

In another study of more than 450 people in their eighties, those who said they had a strong sense of purpose were less likely to develop areas of brain damage caused by blockages in bloodflow.[38] These areas of damage, called infarcts, may spur the development of dementia. So both findings are solid reasons to live with purpose as you grow older—or, if you haven't found it yet, to start your search.

STAY-SHARP TIPS

"The meaning of life is to find your gift. The purpose of life is to give it away." This beautiful quote often has been attributed to the great painter Pablo Picasso. Although few of us are great artists, all of us have talents that, properly utilized, can add purpose to our lives. If you don't know what yours are yet, now's your chance to embark on the ultimate adventure: self-discovery.

Your purpose in life doesn't have to be lofty or complicated. It just has to kindle the light in your heart, whether it's spending time with family, perfecting a craft, or teaching others a valuable skill. The questions below can help you begin to identify your true purpose in life, says Susan Biali, MD, author of *Live a Life You Love: 7 Steps to a Healthier, Happier, More Passionate You.*

Find a quiet, comfortable spot during your downtime—perhaps after dinner, when you'd normally watch TV—and ponder Dr. Biali's questions. It's okay if you don't come up with answers right away. "Connecting with and living your purpose is a journey that typically unfolds in mysterious and surprising ways," she says. "It's not something to be forced or something to actively worry about 'having to' find. I like to think of it as a treasure hunt, a perfectly paced adventure with your eyes and heart wide open."

1. **What do you love to do, that you would do even if you don't get paid for it?** The job that pays your mortgage doesn't

necessarily match your purpose in life, says Dr. Biali. "What is so 'you' that you just have to do it, no matter what?"

2. **What do others say you excel at?** Maybe they rave about your homemade breads and pastries, the way you transform beat-up furniture into showpieces, your way with frightened animals or troubled teenagers, or the unique creations you whip up on your sewing machine. If you continually hear, "You should do this for a living," or "You have a gift," pay attention, says Dr. Biali.

3. **What is your "last day on earth" goal?** What is the one thing you want to accomplish before it arrives? Finish your degree? Hike all 2,190 miles of the Appalachian Trail? Help make the world a kinder, gentler place in your own unique way? No one can answer this question but you—and the answer is there if you seek it. You'll know when you hit upon your goal, says Dr. Biali. It's likely to strike a chord in you that gives you a feeling of deep satisfaction.

Reduce Brain-Shrinking Stress

YOU COULD CHUCK YOUR day job, relocate to a mountain-top, and become a hermit, but you still wouldn't escape stress. You're hardwired to experience it. Your body's response to it—a primal, automatic reaction to danger—is a feature of your amazing physiology, not a bug. In short bursts, stress is good. It can boost your memory (really!) and even save your life.

But your body is designed for temporary bouts of *acute* stress. Researchers have long known that *chronic* stress, the type that drags on without end, can lead to heart disease, high blood pressure, diabetes, and obesity.[1] Now, there's evidence that prolonged stress harms the brain and may even increase the risk of Alzheimer's.[2]

A recent scientific review considered the question of whether stress and anxiety can damage the brain. It looked at research that included brain-imaging studies of stress in both healthy people and those under treatment for depression, anxiety, and posttraumatic stress disorder (PTSD). The review focused on three brain regions involved in stress, fear, and anxiety: the hippocampus, amygdala, and medial prefrontal cortex. (As you may recall, the amygdala is part of your "lizard brain" that processes primal emotions like aggression and fear. The medial prefrontal cortex is involved in both memory and decision-making.[3])

Stress, fear, and anxiety are distinct conditions but cause similar patterns of abnormal brain activity, the review found. All put the amygdala into overdrive and slow the hippocampus and prefrontal cortex. This overlap of brain circuitry could explain the link between chronic stress and the development of brain-centric disorders like major depression and Alzheimer's.

But there's more: Sleep deprivation counts as chronic stress. That's right—night after night of insufficient shut-eye may speed the development of Alzheimer's.

Now for the good news. Even if chronic stress (including sleep problems) is a risk factor for Alzheimer's,[4] it's a risk factor you can change. Experts agree that stress is caused less by the adverse circumstances in your life than by how you perceive and cope with them. Learn to change the way you view and react to the stress in your life, and you can break its potentially destructive effects on your brain and body.

Once you find out how chronic stress affects the brain, chill out with the science-backed stress-busters that follow, including techniques based on the renowned mind/body stress management program called Mindfulness-Based Stress Reduction (MBSR). All have been found to tame tension and, in some cases, literally change the brain. If stress keeps you up at night, the sleep-better tips can help soothe you into the restorative shut-eye your brain needs to stay sharp.

And see page 193 to find out which sleep position may reduce Alzheimer's risk.

THIS IS YOUR BRAIN ON STRESS

Over millions of years, our brains evolved to respond to stress in a way that ensures our survival: with the *stress response,* also called the fight, flight, or freeze response.

The instant your brain perceives danger, your amygdala sends a "red alert" that activates the hypothalamic-pituitary-adrenal (HPA) axis, which helps trip the body's stress response. The resulting cascade of cortisol and other stress hormones prepares your body to fight the threat, run from it, or to stay stock-still, to keep a predator from noticing you. Your heart pounds and your breath comes faster. Your muscles tense. Your stomach knots up, and you may get queasy.[5]

If those symptoms sound familiar, they should—the stress response hasn't changed from our caveman days. But the "dangers" that set it off certainly have. Although our daily lives are packed with stress, it's typically not the life-or-death type our primitive ancestors faced. Unfortunately, your amygdala doesn't know that. It can't distinguish between real danger (a jungle cat running you down) and a perceived threat (a job you can't quit, bills you can't pay, a relationship on the rocks).

Normally, once a threat has passed, your body automatically puts the brakes on the stress response. But with chronic stress, the "all clear" signal never comes. Imagine your foot on your car's gas pedal, revving the motor for weeks, months, or years. That's your body on chronic stress—flooded with stress hormones, particularly cortisol.

Elevated cortisol is toxic to the hippocampus. Researchers at

Stress 101

We often use the word *stress* as shorthand to describe the wide variety of pressures that batter us every day, from long lines at the supermarket to the death of a loved one. But to researchers who study it, stress is the mind and body's response to a demand, and stressors are the things that trigger this response.

Stressors can be external—"out there" in the world—or internal, in your body or thoughts. They range from pain, noise, and infection and illness to a job that saps your soul, an unhappy relationship, or chronic anxiety about an event that may or may not happen.[6]

Although such stressors aren't fun, stress itself serves a purpose. When a car on the highway cuts you off, you want your stress response to kick in so you swerve and slam on the brakes. Amazingly, there's even "good stress," called *eustress*, which helps you ace a job interview or make a deadline. You might also feel eustress when you experience a positive yet trying life change like becoming a grandparent or being promoted at work.

It's negative stress, or *distress*,

McGill University in Montreal tracked people 60 years old and over for more than a dozen years, comparing their cortisol levels with their memory performance.[9] In participants whose cortisol rose to high levels during the study period, the hippocampus was 14 percent smaller compared to those whose cortisol levels stayed moderate, and they developed more memory impairment. One participant with high cortisol levels—a woman who developed both depression and Alzheimer's during the study—lost 60 percent of her total brain volume over a 5-year span. Yikes!

In a more recent study, Yale University researchers interviewed more

that grinds you down. We're all too familiar with routine stress, which stems from the daily demands of work, family, and, well, life. There's stress triggered by a sudden negative change, such as job loss, major illness (yours or a family member's), or the breakup of a marriage. Traumatic stress results from surviving a life-threatening situation, such as a major accident, a natural disaster, life in a war zone, or assault or abuse.[7]

In general, the more stressors in your life, the more stress you'll feel. However, the things that stress you out may be no big deal to someone else, and vice versa. That's because your experience of a stressor is influenced by how well you believe you can cope with it. Perceived stress is your estimation of how stressful your life is, as well as how confident you are in your ability to handle its stressors.[8] Fortunately, the techniques in this chapter can help you reduce your level of perceived stress.

than 100 healthy people on stressful events such as divorce, the loss of a job, or the death of a loved one, then gave them MRI brain scans. Comparing the interviews with the scans, the team found that those who reported higher levels of frequent, ongoing stress showed reduced gray matter in parts of the medial prefrontal cortex.[10]

THE DISTRESS/DEMENTIA LINK

One of the first studies to associate distress with heightened dementia risk was conducted on the monks, priests, and nuns enrolled in the

Religious Orders Study.[11] To measure their vulnerability to stress, they were asked to rate their level of agreement or disagreement with such statements as "I am not a worrier" and "I often feel tense and jittery." Within 5 years of taking the test, people in the top 10 percent of vulnerability to stress were twice as likely to develop Alzheimer's-related memory loss compared to those in the bottom 10 percent.

How Stress Attacks Your Body

Chronic stress doesn't just mess with your sleep, mood, and memory. It causes major wear and tear on your body, too. Here's how prolonged stress can impact three of its most important systems.

It weakens your immune system. Chronic stress can suppress your body's ability to repair and defend itself, leading to delayed wound healing and increased susceptibility to colds. It can also cause chronic inflammation and worsen the symptoms of autoimmune diseases, such as psoriasis, lupus, and rheumatoid arthritis.[12]

It harms your heart and blood vessels. Prolonged stress can cause chest pain and increase heart rate and blood pressure, which forces the heart to work harder. Long-term elevations in blood pressure can lead to heart attack, stroke, and heart failure.[13]

It wreaks havoc on your digestive system. Often called "the second brain," the enteric nervous system is made up of more than 100 million nerve cells that line your digestive tract from top (your esophagus) to bottom (your rectum). Because of this gut/brain pathway, chronic stress can play a role in the development of painful conditions of the colon and stomach, such as inflammatory bowel disease (IBD),[14] irritable bowel syndrome (IBS),[15] and peptic ulcer.[16]

Scarier still, prolonged stress in middle age may "prime" the brain for Alzheimer's and other dementias decades down the road. Swedish researchers conducted two studies on women, following them more than 30 years to trace the effect of stress on their minds and memories. Both studies were based on data from a large study of women from the Swedish city of Gothenburg that began in the 1960s.

The first study followed the women for 35 years. Three times during that period, the women were surveyed about their stress, which the researchers defined as tension, nervousness, anxiety, fear, or sleep problems that lingered a month or more due to work, health, or family issues.

By the end of the study, 161 of the women had developed dementia, mainly Alzheimer's. The risk of dementia was about 65 percent higher in women who reported that they'd experienced repeated bouts of stress in midlife compared to those who reported no stress. Among women who completed all three surveys and reported stress each time, the risk more than doubled.[17]

The second study followed 800 women for 38 years. By the end of the study, around one in five developed dementia, most often Alzheimer's. Those who reported experiencing extreme stress in middle age—events like divorce, the death of a spouse or child, or serious illness in a family member—were at 21 percent increased risk of developing Alzheimer's and at 15 percent higher risk of developing other types of dementia.

According to the study authors, stress may cause a variety of physiological reactions in the body known to harm thinking and memory. These include damage to the hippocampus, increased levels of inflammation-causing cytokines in the brain, and boosted deposits of beta-amyloid and tau proteins, the raw material of plaques and tangles.[18]

However, bear in mind that not every stressed-out woman in these studies developed Alzheimer's. And while you can't control what life dishes out, you *can* use the techniques in this chapter to handle stress in healthy ways.

PUTTING THE RESEARCH TO WORK

Bar none, physical activity is the best stress-buster there is. Rodents allowed to run are more likely to create new brain cells in response to stress compared to sedentary animals, and researchers believe the same thing may occur in us.[19] Studies of people show that regular exercise lowers stress, reduces the risk of major depression, and promotes sleep. So team your daily walk or workout with one or more of the science-backed stress-busters below.

Stress Management Technique #1: Don't Lose Your Mind–Center It

As you've read, when you're caught in a stress storm, your prefrontal cortex slows down, while your amygdala, along with other brain regions that activate the stress response, revs up. Happily, it's possible to short-circuit this brain pattern with a technique called *mindfulness*.

When you practice mindfulness, you tune in to your thoughts, feelings, or body sensations in the moment, without judging them as either good or bad. Research suggests that mindfulness increases activity in the prefrontal cortex, which helps turn down the stress response.[20]

The Mindfulness-Based Stress Reduction (MBSR) program, introduced in 1979 by Dr. Jon Kabat-Zinn at the University of Massachusetts Medical Center, combines elements of meditation and yoga techniques.

Over 100 studies have shown this 8-week program to reduce a wide variety of ailments, from anxiety and major depression to sleep problems and chronic pain.[21]

MBSR also changes brain structure in ways that may benefit thinking and memory. In one study, Harvard researchers trained healthy people in several MBSR techniques—body scan, yoga, and sitting

Manage Stress Now, Head Off Memory Loss Later

If you think you're too busy (or tense) to try the stress-busters in this chapter, here's a good reason to make time. Older people with the highest levels of perceived stress more than double their risk for developing amnestic mild cognitive impairment, or amnestic MCI. This is the most common type of MCI, and its hallmark is memory loss.[22]

Researchers at Albert Einstein College of Medicine in New York studied data collected from more than 500 people 70 years old or older, all cognitively healthy when the study began. The team followed these folks for more than 3 years, and each year evaluated their health, memory, thinking abilities, and ability to perform daily tasks. The study participants also completed a "perceived stress scale," a psychological test designed to pick up on chronic stress. The higher the score, the greater a person perceives his or her stress to be.

Participants in the highest-stress group were more than twice as likely to develop MCI as those in four other groups that reported lower levels of stress. Furthermore, that risk stayed the same even when researchers factored in participants' depression and genetic risk of Alzheimer's. That's a good reason to add one or more tension-tamers to your ageless brain lifestyle.

meditation—and told them to practice a half hour a day. They also gave their subjects an MRI brain scan 2 weeks before the study began and another scan after 8 weeks of meditation.

Compared to a control group, the group of meditators showed more gray matter in the hippocampus and *less* gray matter in the amygdala.[23] Interestingly, an earlier study of 26 people conducted by the same team found a relationship between changes in perceived stress and structural changes in a portion of the amygdala. In other words, the more par-

STAY-SHARP STRATEGY

DE-STRESS IN 20 BREATHS

If you learn only one stress-buster, make it deep breathing. Not only is this technique at the core of other stress management practices like mindfulness meditation, it'll take you from tense to calm in just minutes on its own.

Deep breathing sends your brain a message—"relax"—which it then relays to your body. As you continue to breathe deeply, your heart rate and breathing slow, your muscles relaxed, and the opposite of the stress response—called the relaxation response—kicks in.

Here's how to breathe deeply, step by step.[25] Do this exercise twice a day, or whenever you feel your stress spill over. Before long, you'll do it automatically whenever stress strikes.

1. Sit comfortably. Place one hand on your chest and the other on your belly.

2. Inhale deeply through your nose. The hand on your belly should

ticipants' stress levels decreased, the more the gray matter density in this "stress region" shrank.[24]

In another study published in the journal *Neuroscience Letters*, adults with mild cognitive impairment between 55 and 90 years old practiced MBSR at home for a half hour a day. Eight weeks later, MRI brain scans showed that shrinkage of the hippocampus had slowed. Moreover, the participants showed improved functional connectivity in the part of the brain that's always active—called the default mode

rise higher than the one on your chest. This means your diaphragm is pulling air into your lungs.

3. Exhale through your mouth, then inhale deeply through your nose, for a count of 4.

4. Slowly exhale through your mouth, for a count of 6 to 8. As you release your breath, contract your abdominal muscles to completely evacuate the rest of the air in your lungs. (You deepen your breathing when you fully exhale air, rather than when you inhale it.)

5. Repeat 19 more times, for a total of 20 breaths.

If you like, say the word *stress* silently as you exhale, and *peace* or *calm* as you inhale. The idea is to "breathe in" peace as you blow out stress and tension.

network—as well as improvements in thinking and well-being. According to the study authors, these findings suggest that MBSR may benefit brain regions most involved in mild cognitive impairment and Alzheimer's.[26]

STAY-SHARP TIPS

As you'll see from the technique on page 188, mindfulness meditation isn't weird—you don't have to burn incense or bang gongs. Nor are the techniques hard to learn. When you practice mindfulness, there is no past to regret and no future to fret about; there is simply *now*. And when you stay in the moment, stress tends to vaporize.

The landmark book on mindfulness, *Full Catastrophe Living: Using the Wisdom of Your Body and Mind to Face Stress, Pain, and Illness* is a good way to explore MBSR on your own. Written by Dr. Kabat-Zinn, the book offers instruction on MBSR techniques, such as breathing, sitting meditation, and the body-scan meditation. (If you've tried meditation before and find it hard to sit still, skip to the walking meditation.)

If you have access to the Internet, the Mindful Awareness Research Center at the University of California at Los Angeles (*marc.ucla.edu*) offers a variety of guided meditations as short as 5 minutes. Just click on the "Free Guided Meditations" link, press "play," and let the experts guide you.

You can also choose to enroll in a formal 8-week MBSR program, either online or in your area. Many local hospitals offer instruction as part of their community health and wellness programs. Online courses cost approximately $200. An 8-week class with a certified MBSR trainer in your community, which includes printed materials and CDs for guided meditation, costs about $400.

Stress Management Technique #2: Peace Out with Yoga

Less stress, more serenity—that's what you might expect to gain from a regular rendezvous with a yoga mat. But pairing yoga practice with a simple form of meditation appears to not only boost memory but brighten mood and reduce anxiety, according to a study published in the *Journal of Alzheimer's Disease (JAD)*.[27]

Led by researchers at the University of California at Los Angeles, the study looked at the effects of yoga and meditation on behavior and brain activity in people over 55. All the participants had mild cognitive impairment and reported memory issues—things like forgetting names, faces, and appointments and misplacing things. At the start and end of the study, they took memory tests and underwent a "next generation" type of brain scan—functional magnetic resonance imaging, or fMRI.

The team randomly assigned participants to one of two groups. One group was trained in memory enhancement techniques for an hour a week and spent 20 minutes a day on memory-improvement exercises (crossword puzzles, brain games). The other group took a 1-hour, once-a-week class in Kundalini yoga, which combines meditation, breathing, and poses. They also did a type of meditation called Kirtan Kriya at home for 20 minutes a day. Practiced for centuries by older people in India to keep their minds sharp, Kirtan Kriya involves chanting, finger movements, and visualization. (Note: It's easier than it sounds. See page 190.)

By the end of the 12-week study, both groups had improved their verbal memory, which helps you remember names and lists of words, the researchers found. But the yoga/meditation group showed more improvement in visual-spatial memory, used to recall locations and navigate your surroundings. This group also reported less anxiety and depression and a better ability to cope with stress.

The participants' memory gains coincided with observable changes in their brain activity, the fMRI scans showed. Although both groups had changes in brain connectivity, only the changes in the yoga and meditation group were significant.

Yoga and meditation may benefit the brain in different ways, the

STAY-SHARP STRATEGY

SCAN AWAY STRESS-BASED PAIN

Short-term stress can make your palms sweat and your stomach clench. But when stress settles into your body for the long haul, your muscles can get tight and achy, or pain may intensify in a part that already hurts, such as your lower back.

A key practice in Mindfulness-Based Stress Reduction (MBSR), the body scan brings mindful attention to each area of the body in a systematic way—not to change or judge stress or pain but just to experience and accept it. This meditation can help you zero in on which part or parts of your body "express" stress, so you can release that muscular tension. It also can play a role in pain management. In one study of people with chronic pain, the participants reported a reduction in pain-related distress after one 10-minute body scan.[28]

This exercise takes 10 minutes but can be expanded to 20. You can do it on a carpeted floor, your bed, or a yoga mat. If your mind wanders, gently direct your attention back to your body. Lie on your back, arms by your side, palms up. If you have back problems, it's okay to bend your knees. Close your eyes (open them if you start to feel drowsy). Breathe deeply, and focus on the rise and fall of your breath.

study said. Yoga may enhance the brain's production of brain-derived neurotrophic factor (BDNF) and reduce inflammation, while Kirtan Kriya may engage certain brain networks in ways that boost verbal and visual memory.

STAY-SHARP TIPS

If you're willing to try something new (which itself increases plasticity), the yoga and meditation techniques used in the study are a low-key way

1. To begin, bring your attention to the toes of your left foot. "Scan" your toes for any sensations—warmth, tingling, heaviness/lightness, aches, pain, or nothing at all. When you're finished, visualize your breath moving down to your toes, and then traveling back up and out through your nose.

2. Bring your attention from your toes to your left leg. As before, "scan" your left ankle, shin, knee, and thigh. As you scan each part, focus on any sensations you experience, and direct your breath from that part and up and out again through your nose.

3. Repeat with your right leg. Then slowly and methodically scan your lower back, belly, upper back, chest, shoulders, and both of your arms.

4. Scan your neck, throat, face, the back of your head, and the top of your head.

5. To end the scan, slowly start to return your awareness to the room, perhaps by wiggling your fingers or toes or rolling to one side. Sit up when you feel ready.

to sharpen your brain. To find a Kundalini class, call your local YMCA or yoga studio. Or log on to *spafinder.com*, which has a search function that can connect you to an instructor in your area.

The study had participants do both Kundalini yoga and Kirtan Kriya meditation. However, one study found that doing just the meditation 12 minutes a day for 2 months improved cognitive function.[29]

Kirtan Kriya involves chanting certain sounds—*sa ta na ma*—and performing finger movements called *mudras*. To see the practice in action, go to YouTube and type in "Kirtan Kriya." According to *Yoga Journal*, this is how it's done.[30] The directions seem long, but they're simple. (Don't get hung up on the "2 minutes" part. It's okay to guesstimate.)

1. Sit comfortably, with your spine straight, on the floor or in a chair. Place your hands, palms up, on your knees.

2. Inhale deeply through your nose and begin to chant: *sa ta na ma*. Chant for 2 minutes, and repeat these finger movements as you do so.

    On *sa*: Touch the index finger of each hand to your thumb.

    On *ta*: Touch your middle finger to your thumb.

    On *na*: Touch your ring finger to your thumb.

    On *ma*: Touch your pinkie to your thumb.

3. Repeat these finger movements as you continue to chant, either aloud or silently, for 10 minutes more. Here's how to do it.

    2 minutes: Chant the mantra aloud.

    2 minutes: Drop your voice to a whisper and continue to chant.

    2 minutes: Chant the mantra silently.

    2 minutes: Raise your voice to a whisper again and chant.

    2 minutes: Chant aloud again.

4. Inhale deeply as you reach your arms above your head. Exhale and press both hands together in front of your chest as if you're praying. End by saying: *sat nam*, which means "Truth is my identity."

Stress Management Technique #3: Tackle Tension with "Moving Meditation"

What brisk walking is to us, tai chi is to older people in China. The purpose of this gentle, low-impact form of exercise, often called "moving meditation," is to balance mind and body. But if all you know about tai chi comes from Mr. Miyagi and *The Karate Kid*, it's time to take its tension-taming, brain-boosting powers seriously.

In a Tufts University review of 40 studies, this ancient Chinese practice of movement, meditation, and deep breathing was found to improve psychological well-being and reduce stress, anxiety, and depression.[31] That's good news for your future brain health. According to a study published in *JAD*, the practice also might lower your risk for dementia or Alzheimer's.[32]

Researchers from the University of South Florida teamed up with researchers from China to study the effects of tai chi on the brain. They divided 120 older Shanghai residents into four groups. One group did tai chi in a local park three times a week for 50 minutes (20 minutes of warmup, 20 minutes of tai chi, and a 10-minute cooldown). One group walked for 30 minutes three times a week around a circular track, with another 20 minutes of warmup and cooldown moves. A third "social interaction" group met for lively discussions for an hour, three times a week. The last group simply carried on with their normal routines. All participants underwent two MRI brain scans—one before the study began, and one after it was completed.

After 40 weeks, the tai chi group showed the biggest improvements in brain volume, followed by the social interaction group. In a finding that surprised the researchers, the walkers did *not* show an improvement in brain volume. "The lack of an effect in the Walking group was unexpected," the study said. "However, evaluation of the number of steps taken per minute in this group suggested that the pace adopted by the participants . . . was relatively slow. Those who walked faster experienced greater gains on cognitive tests, suggesting that more vigorous aerobic exercise may be necessary to have a beneficial effect." This underscores the findings about the benefits of brisk walking, using proper technique, which we explored in Chapter 6. Also, the team suggested that the high level of sustained attention needed to perform the intricate movements of tai chi—as opposed to simply circling a track—might be why tai chi outperformed walking in this case.

STAY-SHARP TIPS

No special clothes or equipment are required for tai chi, and you can practice indoors or outdoors, alone or in a group. As a bonus, tai chi does double duty: As it reduces stress, it improves balance. In fact, tai chi is one of the exercises recommended by the American Geriatrics Society to prevent falls.[33]

Tai chi is so popular that the local YMCA/YWCA, or the community wellness program at your local hospital, is bound to offer a class. You can go to *americantaichi.net* to find one near you. You'll likely be encouraged to practice at home once or twice a day, too, for 15 or 20 minutes at a time.[34]

The great thing about tai chi is that you can modify it based on your

STAY-SHARP STRATEGY

SLEEP LIKE THIS TO PROTECT YOUR BRAIN

Compared to snoozing on your belly or back, side sleeping (called the lateral sleep position) may better help the brain's cleansing system remove waste—and help reduce the risk of Alzheimer's, suggests a study published in the *Journal of Neuroscience*.[35]

The glymphatic system removes harmful wastes and chemicals in the brain. It's so named because it acts much like the lymphatic system, which drains wastes from the body, but is managed by the brain's glial cells.[36]

In this study, researchers had rats and mice sleep on their backs, stomachs, and sides and gave the critters brain scans in each position. Side sleeping best removed brain waste like beta-amyloid and tau proteins, associated with the plaques and tangles of Alzheimer's.

Because this study was conducted on rodents, here's the obvious question: Does side sleeping also clear our brain waste more efficiently? Although more research (on people) is needed, that's likely the case, the researchers said.

---

unique health needs, including your level of mobility. Before you start a class, get the green light from your doctor, and tell the instructor about any special needs you may have.

If you'd prefer to learn and practice tai chi at home, you'll find plenty of instructional DVDs online or in the fitness sections of big-box stores. One to consider is *Tai Chi for Beginners: 8 Lessons with Dr. Paul Lam*. A retired family doctor, Dr. Lam is the founder of the nonprofit Tai Chi for Health Institute in Australia and has practiced tai chi for 40 years.

Stress Management Technique #4: Give Yourself Some TLC

When stress strikes, do you keep a stiff upper lip, or give yourself the same TLC you'd extend to a friend? Treating yourself with kind, non-judgmental understanding, or *self-compassion*, has been shown to reduce anxiety and depression and help build emotional resilience.[37]

When stress has you in its crosshairs, beating yourself up triggers more stress, because the amygdala sends signals that raise blood pressure and increase adrenaline and cortisol levels. By contrast, self-compassion may produce changes in the body that also occur when you get social support, including the release of the hormone oxytocin, studies suggest. Nicknamed the "tend and befriend" hormone, oxytocin has been shown to dampen the stress response.[38]

Kristin Neff, PhD, professor of educational psychology at the University of Texas at Austin and the author of *Self-Compassion: The Proven Power of Being Kind to Yourself,* studies the psychological benefits of being kind to yourself. "My research shows that people who show themselves compassion are much less likely to be depressed, anxious, and stressed, and are much more likely to be happy, resilient, and optimistic about their future," she says.

Lavishing kindness and understanding on yourself may protect against stress-induced inflammation, according to a study of healthy adults published in *Brain, Behavior, and Immunity.* Those with higher levels of self-compassion (as measured by a scale developed by Dr. Neff) showed lower blood levels of interleukin-6, a marker of inflammation.[39]

Self-compassion techniques also have been shown to reduce cortisol levels. In a study published in *Clinical Neuropsychiatry,*[40] researchers used "compassion-focused imagery," or CFI, to help participants cope with stress. They were asked to imagine receiving compassion from a source outside themselves, and were verbally guided during the exercise with statements such as, "Allow yourself to feel that you are the recipient of great compassion." The CFI group had lower levels of cortisol compared to a control group.

Don't mistake self-compassion with self-pity, says Dr. Neff. This attitude is about accepting that you're human—neither better nor worse than anyone else—and extending to yourself the same kindness you'd offer a friend or loved one.

STAY-SHARP TIPS

If you're online, Dr. Neff's website, *self-compassion.org*, features a 26-question assessment of how much TLC you typically give yourself, along with a variety of guided meditations and exercises to develop self-compassion skills.

For example, for an instant shot of self-compassion, give yourself a hug. As New Age-y as that sounds, it works: "Physical touch releases oxytocin, reduces cortisol, and calms cardiovascular stress," says Dr. Neff. If you're with others when stress strikes, there's a sneaky way to hug it out—casually fold your arms (pretend you're chilly) and give yourself a gentle, reassuring squeeze.

The three hallmarks of self-compassion are staying in the moment, perceiving stress as a part of being human, and being kind to yourself, says Dr. Neff. The simple exercise below, called the "Self-Compassion Break," puts you in touch with them. You can do it silently if you're around others or out loud if you're alone.

1. When your tension rises, say, "This is stress," or "This hurts."
2. Next, say, "I'm not alone," or "We all struggle in our lives."

3. Put your hands over your heart. As you tune in to the gentle touch of your hands on your chest, say, "May I be kind to myself," or "May I learn to accept myself as I am."

Stress Management Technique #5: Spend More Time in Bed–and "Sleep Clean"

"Eating clean" means filling your plate with whole, natural foods shown to help build an ageless brain. "Sleeping clean" is when you adopt practices that promote the sound sleep your noodle needs. Easy to say, not always easy to do.

When you're constantly stressed out, your ability to get enough deep, restful sleep takes a hit—and your brain health may pay the price. Studies confirm the link between poor sleep and lower cognitive performance.[41] And recall the research from Part 2 that ties sleep apnea, which deprives the brain of deep, restorative slumber, to a higher risk of memory problems and Alzheimer's. What's the connection between crummy sleep and cognitive decline?

It may come down to brain gunk. Studies on mice suggest that, by day, waste products like beta-amyloid build up in the brain. During non-rapid eye movement (non-REM) sleep, the critters' brain cells literally shrank to make room for fluids to wash away these potentially brain-harming wastes.[42]

In people, poor sleep quality is associated with a greater buildup of beta-amyloid in the brain. In a study of people between the ages of 53 and 91, those who reported sleeping less than 5 hours a night had higher levels of this toxic protein in their noodles than those who slept over 7 hours a night, brain scans showed.[43]

In another study, researchers at the University of California at

OUTSMART THE SIX DEADLY SLEEP-STEALERS

1. **Technology in bed.** If you surf the net, watch TV, or read in bed, your body learns to associate your bed with being awake. Nor should you settle into bed with your laptop, e-reader, or tablet. Such gadgets have a high concentration of blue light, which suppresses levels of the sleep-promoting hormone melatonin.[44]

2. **Large, late-night noshes.** Keep bedtime snacks light and under 200 calories—a serving of yogurt and berries, or piece of whole grain toast with a tablespoon of natural peanut butter. Skip the cold pizza or a fast-food meal within 3 hours of bedtime. Rich, heavy food taxes the digestive system.

3. **Late-afternoon naps.** A 10-minute catnap can boost your brainpower and help compensate for lost sleep. But don't nap longer than 20 minutes, and get up before 3 p.m. If you snooze any later, you may find it hard to fall asleep that night.

4. **Staring at the ceiling.** Your body and brain should associate your bed with sleep and sleep alone. Tossing and turning night after night weakens that link. So if you're wide awake 20 minutes after you go to bed and start to fret that sleep won't come, get up. But don't clean or channel surf—these activities are too stimulating. Instead, leaf through a magazine or sip a cup of noncaffeinated herbal tea until you feel sleepy.

5. **Caffeine.** The Colombian Supreme that perks you up at 3 p.m. can keep you buzzing long into the night. Sip your last cola, cup of coffee, or caffeinated tea 4 to 6 hours before bedtime. A brisk walk can push you past a midafternoon slump just as well as caffeine, minus the sleep disruption.

6. **Nightcaps.** One cocktail or a single glass of wine with dinner? Sure. Just enjoy it 2 to 3 hours before bedtime. A drink right before bed may make you sleepy, but it also can wake you up in the middle of the night, as your body metabolizes the alcohol.

Berkeley recruited cognitively healthy people between the ages of 65 and 81. First, they received PET scans to measure the levels of beta-amyloid in their brains. Then they were given over 100 word pairs to memorize, and tested on how well they remembered a portion of them.

The participants then slept 8 hours, as the researchers monitored their brain waves to assess the quality of their sleep. The next morning, they were asked to remember the rest of the word pairs as researchers scanned their brains. Participants with the highest levels of beta-amyloid in their medial frontal cortex had the poorest quality of sleep and performed the worst on the memory test.[45]

"The more beta-amyloid you have in certain parts of your brain, the less deep sleep you get and, consequently, the worse your memory," the study's senior author, Matthew Walker, stated. "Additionally, the less deep sleep you have, the less effective you are at clearing out this bad protein. It's a vicious cycle. But we don't yet know which of these two factors—the bad sleep or the bad protein—initially begins this cycle."[46] More reason to clean up your sleep habits and take control of stressors that rob your brain of the rejuvenating sleep it needs.

STAY-SHARP TIPS

Want to sleep better tonight? You can, with these strategies from the American Association of Sleep Technologists. Sure, you may have heard of them. But if you've never followed them, they can significantly improve the quality of your shut-eye.

Get on a schedule. Pick a time to go to bed and a time to wake up each day. Then, stick to those times. On weekends, go to bed and get up within 20 minutes of your scheduled times.[47] When you're on a schedule, your internal "body clock" gets used to your new bedtime, which can help you fall asleep better at night and wake up more easily each morning.

If you're a night owl, don't try to change your sleep schedule in one night. Rather, push back your bedtime in 15-minute increments. For example, if you typically go to sleep at midnight and decide on a 10 p.m. bedtime, go to bed at 11:45 p.m. for three nights. Then, for the next few nights, go to bed at 11:30 p.m. Keep going until you hit your new, healthier bedtime.[48]

Wind down before you turn in. If you typically arrive home late after a stress-packed day, you may find it hard to relax enough to sleep. The solution: create a relaxing ritual that you perform every night. Your body will learn to associate it with sleep. For example, you might dim the lights when you get home, soak in a warm tub by candlelight, slip into your PJs, and practice the deep-breathing technique on page 184.

Let the sun shine in. Your body clock is sensitive to light and darkness, so start each morning with a dose of sun. If possible, soak in the sun for a half hour before work or take a stroll at lunch. If you struggle with insomnia, aim for an hour of exposure to morning sunlight—if possible, walk before work rather than after. Also, dim the lights an hour or two before bed, so your brain is primed for sleep.

Get regular exercise. Not only is it good for your brain, it promotes continuous sleep. If you can, work out 4 to 6 hours before bed—it's best for sleep, studies show. If you must work out at night, hit the showers at least 2 hours before your bedtime.

Give your bedroom a "sleepover." That's a makeover for your bedroom. These tips can help you create an environment that promotes quality sleep.

- Keep your bedroom on the cool side. It's been shown that most people sleep better in cool temperatures.

- If your pets sleep in your bedroom and keep you awake, find them a cozy new space to spend the night. (It's not mean. When you get the sleep you need, you'll be a better "fur parent.")

- Turn your alarm clock away from you so you won't stare at the time as you try to fall asleep.

Check your medications. Some meds prescribed for heart disease or breathing disorders such as asthma or chronic bronchitis can cause insomnia or wake you up at night. So can over-the-counter medications such as nasal decongestants, pain relievers that contain caffeine, or cold and allergy medications that contain an antihistamine.

If you suspect that a medication you've been prescribed is messing with your sleep, continue to take it until you talk to your doctor. He or she may be able to change the time you take it, or prescribe a different medication.

If you still can't sleep, or get to bed at a decent hour each night but wake up exhausted, see your doctor. If stress isn't the issue, a sleep disorder such as sleep apnea might be. You may be referred to a sleep specialist, who can identify and treat the problem.

9

Preserve Your Wits with Play

JUST AS THE MUSCLES in your arms and legs grow stronger when you use them, so does your brain. And just as the muscles in your body become smaller and weaker when you neglect them, so, too, does your brain.

Do you:

- Drive your car mindlessly, as your GPS tells you where to go? Or do you map out your route ahead of time and carefully pay attention as you drive, always looking for your next turn?

- Do math throughout the day, such as calculating a tip at a restaurant, converting Celsius to Fahrenheit, figuring out how much you'll save with your "25 percent off" coupon? Or do you use apps and calculators instead?

- Use new recipes regularly? Or do you mostly eat out, order in, and subscribe to mail order meal kits that are delivered to your door and allow you to assemble dinner without thinking?

- Know any of your friends' birthdays or phone numbers? Or do you rely on social media and your phone to remember these details for you?

- Work? And if so, how challenged do you feel on the job? Do you solve problems and stretch and learn daily? Or have you been in the same position for so long that you do your job on autopilot?

- Embrace novel experiences in your leisure time? Or does every day unfold in the same predictable manner?

STAY-SHARP STRATEGY

GET OUT OF YOUR COMFORT ZONE

The comfort zone is where the brain turns to mush. It's scary to do the unfamiliar, but research tells us that our brains grow outside of the comfort zone and not within it.[1]

We feel uncomfortable whenever we tackle something new. We like to be the person who has mastered everything, and never the person who seems befuddled. But that sense of befuddlement is what challenges the brain to stretch. A little bit of anxiety is good. It wakes you up and keeps you focused. Yet, too much anxiety overwhelms the brain. Trust us: None of the world's greatest discoveries took place when someone was having a full-blown anxiety attack.

The sweet spot is not that sick feeling in the pit of your stomach when you feel so far in over your head that you worry you might drown in your own cortisol. It's also not the sense of smugness you feel when you've mastered something and can do it on autopilot. Rather, you've found your sweet spot when you feel confident in your ability to learn something new eventually, even though it feels quite difficult to you now.

Like the muscles in your body, your brain *needs* stimulation. You stimulate a muscle by moving. You stimulate your brain when you think, experience, remember, and learn. Education forces you to use your brain. So does a challenging, high-paced career that constantly has you on your toes, as do stimulating hobbies and leisure activities that make you feel fantastically alive.

And, here's the kicker: None of this must feel like a chore. Don't think: "I must *exercise* my brain to keep it sharp." Instead think: "My brain loves to *play*." *Fun* and *delight* are essential ingredients of the ageless brain recipe. Look for new experiences and pursuits that you truly enjoy and find invigorating. Your brain grows stronger during those moments of surprise and wonder, when you find yourself inhaling deeply, savoring strongly, and living greatly. Enjoy being silly. Delight in hobbies and activities for their own sake, and not because you are crossing them off a to-do list.

THIS IS YOUR BRAIN ON PLAY

As you've learned, cognitive reserve is your brain's version of a 401(k), and the more knowledge and experiences you "bank" over the years, the better. There's no better way to build cognitive reserve than to take your brain out to play—every day. Delight it by pushing it ever further by embracing new ideas, learning new skills, and meeting new people.

In addition to building a rich cognitive reserve, playful experiences may also improve the wiring in your brain. The spiderlike dendrites—the highways that connect our brain cells and allow them to communicate with each other—increase and decrease over time, depending on whether or not they're stimulated. In this way, dendrites are a lot like a path through a forest. If the path is walked often, it becomes bigger and more worn and easier to find without getting lost. Walk it rarely and the path becomes overgrown and may disappear altogether.

Taking the forest analogy a step further, consider how lost you would become if only a few, narrow paths were available between points A and B. If you accidentally meandered off a given path, you'd find yourself in a dense thicket of brush and become hopelessly lost.

This is what happens in your brain when messages have only a few, narrow paths to take, and especially when some of those paths have become damaged due to a ministroke or other problem. When messages get lost, you find yourself at a loss for words. Words and ideas remain on the tip of your tongue, but you can't quite access them. You see someone standing in front of you. You have a vague sense of knowing them but can't quite remember where you met or what the person's name is. You find yourself wandering through a parking garage, knowing your car is in there somewhere, but unable to remember its precise location. The more dendrites you have, the more paths messages can take to get from one part of the brain to another, and the easier and faster it is for messages to speed through your brain and arrive at their destinations. Having more dendrites makes the difference between staring at someone blankly versus saying, "Oh, Jack, wow, it's been years. What are you up to?"

KEEP YOUR BRAIN BUBBLING WITH LEARNING AND WORK

Now let's get to the important stuff. How do you build a rich cognitive reserve that will last into your seventies, eighties, nineties, and beyond?

A solid education helps. In one study published in *JAMA Neurology,* people with 16 years of education (high school plus a bachelor's degree) had less evidence of brain degeneration than people with less education.[2] For a different study, researchers at Johns Hopkins Tulane and Imperial College London followed 769 patients for a year after they suffered a head injury. They kept track of which patients continued to suffer from mental impairment versus which ones were free from disability, and they factored in whether educational attainment seemed to play a role. High school graduates were more likely to fully recover than nongraduates, and people with a bachelor's degree more likely than people with only a high school diploma.[3]

And it's never too late. Formal education in any stage of life will help reduce your risk of cognitive decline and dementia, according to a study published in *Alzheimer's & Dementia*.[4] Whether you study as a teenager, at midlife, or as a retiree, education still helps to build your cognitive reserve.

In addition to education, a challenging career also helps. Work is so protective, in fact, that you may wish to reconsider any wishes to retire early. Oregon State University researchers found that delaying retirement by 1 year reduced risk of death by 11 percent.[5] Another study found that people who lived in industrialized nations with earlier retirement ages tended to score more poorly on memory tests than did people who lived in countries where people worked until a later age.[6]

So, what do you do if you are already retired and have absolutely no inclination to go back to school to get another degree? Many older adults torment themselves with a daily ritual of formal brain training—often using expensive subscription-based services—that they don't particularly enjoy. Don't get us wrong; brainteasers may be *great* if you love them, but they are not the *only* way to build an ageless brain and, despite claims made by the brain-training industry, these brainteasers may not be all that effective, either. A 2014 review of 52 different studies that involved a total of 4,885 participants found that the computerized brain-training tools were only moderately effective at bolstering cognitive performance.[7] And a consensus statement signed by neuroscientists from around the world cautioned brain-game marketers to ditch their wildly exaggerated claims. "We object to the claim that brain games offer consumers a scientifically grounded avenue to reduce or reverse cognitive decline when there is no compelling scientific evidence to date that they do," the consensus statement read, in part. "The promise of a magic bullet detracts from the best evidence to date, which is that cognitive health in old age reflects the long-term effects of healthy, engaged lifestyles."[8]

As it turns out, real life is what the brain most craves and needs. In one study done by researchers at Rush Alzheimer's Disease Center in Chicago, researchers asked 700 nuns, priests, and religious brothers to describe how much time they spent doing various activities such as going to museums, playing games, and reading the newspaper. The researchers kept tabs on the study participants for 17 years, periodically asking them to take memory tests. When the study participants died, the researchers autopsied and examined their brains. They found that the study participants who participated in more activities more often had a 47 percent reduced risk of developing Alzheimer's disease compared to those who participated in the fewest activities least often.[9]

Another study found that the more often study participants read, played cards, did puzzles, went to museums, and watched TV or listened to the radio, the less likely they were to develop dementia over a 4-year period. The activities *most* likely to reduce risk included reading, board games, and playing musical instruments, and *not* brainteasers.[10]

On the next few pages, you'll find nine suggestions for bolstering your cognitive reserve with playful experiences, but you don't have to limit yourself to just these. For best results, make sure your brain play is:

Novel. Adopt an attitude of curiosity. Try to do something new every day.

Varied. Think of how you train your body in the gym. You don't do only one exercise that targets only one muscle in your body. Rather, you do several exercises to get your entire body fit. Just as your body has many different muscles, your brain has many different structures and functions, and these all need stimulation to stay firm.

Challenging. Once a task has become easy or routine, your brain is no longer challenged. Once you've mastered an activity, look for ways to make it harder or consider adding a new activity to your brain-play repertoire.

Consistent. The more often and more consistently you challenge your brain, the more ageless it will become.[11]

Fun! If a task is meaningful to you, it's more likely to hold your attention. Pick activities that you look forward to and that you find fulfilling.

Play Technique #1: Retire to Something, Not from Something

If we're being honest, most of us will admit that we dream of the ability not only to retire early, but also to spend the rest of our days lounging on a chair while we do nothing more taxing than listen to the sound of the waves crashing on the beach.

Sadly, though early retirement may seem like paradise, it's hell on the brain. That's because our work is often one of the most consistently stimulating things we do. As we mentioned earlier, Oregon State University research found that delaying retirement by even a year reduced risk of death by 11 percent.[12]

Researchers aren't completely sure why our brains go mushy once we stop working, but they have some educated hunches. It could be that, when we leave our jobs, we lose most of our social connections (see Chapter 2 for why social connections are so important). Or it's possible that, when we don't go into the office, we spend our time not as we had once envisioned (walking on the beach, reading book after book, socializing and catching up with friends), but sacked out in front of the TV, a bag of chips at the ready.

No matter the reason, when we stop engaging in daily complex mental activities, our brains get flabby.

STAY-SHARP TIPS

You don't have to work full time until the day you die—especially if you hate your job. Instead, try to find something meaningful to *retire to*.

Work for a cause. Women who volunteered 15 hours a week for Experience Corps, a program that pairs older volunteers with elementary schools, experienced an improvement in their ability to plan, reason, and solve problems over 6 months, found a study from Johns Hopkins Bloomberg School of Public Health.[13]

Make it social. As you learned in Chapter 2, a rich social life is part of the recipe for building an ageless brain. Consider fun, group activities that get you around people at least once a day.

Keep your body in shape. Physical exercise can help to offset the brain drain of early retirement. Walking 200 minutes a week, for example, has been shown to help people ages 70 and older to maintain their brain functioning.[14]

Play Technique #2:
Do the Same Things, Differently

Do you remember making and eating your breakfast or the specific route you took to get to work or another destination? Chances are, if you're like most people, you may have a vague memory of what you ate, but you can't recall much of the *how*. And perhaps you remember one or two things about your commute—such as the truck that backed up traffic—but not much else. It's almost as if the car drove itself.

That's because when we do an activity repeatedly, we don't have to consciously think about how to complete such tasks, so we do them automatically and mindlessly.

Just by making a few small tweaks, however, you can turn mindless tasks into mindful ones, which forces your brain to pay attention and grow stronger and sharper. And these tweaks can also make everyday activities more fun, too. Find ways to change things up, even just a tad, to keep your brain engaged.

STAY-SHARP TIPS

Small changes can make a big difference. If you love to eat out, try a new restaurant. Find a new way to drive to the store, and push yourself to take your favorite hobby to the next level. More specifically, you might:

Take notes longhand instead of using your tablet or laptop. Taking handwritten notes may be better than typing them, in terms of how well you remember everything. We process information more shallowly when we type than when we write, with research finding the students who take notes on laptops performing worse on conceptual questions than students who take notes by hand.[15] You might take this tactic a step further and start writing letters and sending cards again rather than sending emails and texts.

Use chopsticks. Or eat with your nondominant hand. Both tactics will slow you down and provide a touch of the unfamiliar, as well as engage more of your brain. You might even find that you savor your meal a lot more, too.

Make a new recipe every week. While it's certainly easier to make the same foods repeatedly, new recipes require you to break out of the familiar. Not only will your brain stretch and grow during the physical act of cooking, but you'll also be more alert at the grocery store as you shop for ingredients you don't usually purchase. Consider inviting one or more friends over to sample your new dish. That way, you'll also benefit from being social as well as having the added brain-boosting challenge of getting everything cooked at the same time.

Read on paper, not on a screen. A Norwegian study found that people who read a short story on an e-reader remembered less of the plot than people who read the same story in a paperback book.[16] Reading while holding a book or magazine in your hands may boost retention because you are forced to use more of your senses. It's not just a visual experience, it's also a tactile one.

Chew gum while you read, study, or concentrate. A study out of Newcastle, England, found that people who chewed gum performed better during a 20-minute memory test than people who weren't chewing gum during the test, improving their ability to recall the words they'd memorized by 35 percent.[17]

Stop automatically reaching for that app. We've come to rely on computers as a second brain. This is great, but we can challenge our brains more by trying to do at least some of this work in our heads. Rather than always reaching for the calculator, try to calculate a tip on your own. Or use your GPS, but keep it on silent, and see if you can find your way without the help, only leaning on the guidance system when needed. Or try to memorize a few phone numbers a week rather than always allowing your smartphone to cough them up for you.

Do it backward. Switch up your walking or running route, doing the whole thing backward. Or, if you usually do a circuit at the gym, swap the order of the exercises or do the same exercises differently.

Play Technique #3: Embrace Additional Hobbies

Each new hobby encourages you to acquire new knowledge, which bolsters your cognitive research. Bird-watching, for example, teaches you the names and calls of various birds, along with the types of foods they eat and their migratory patterns. Hobbies often introduce us to a new community of friends, too, which helps to bolster our social connections, which are also essential for building an ageless brain. And they tend to relax us, reducing the stress that can accelerate brain aging.

STAY-SHARP TIPS

Though any new hobby will help to age-proof your brain, hobbies that require you to make quick decisions and pay careful attention to details are particularly potent. Consider embracing any or all of the following hobbies.

Try community theatre. Not only does acting get you out of your comfort zone, it also involves memorizing lots of lines. Maybe that's why a study of 122 adults who took acting classes twice a week for 4 weeks found that they performed better on tests of memory, comprehension, creativity, and problem solving compared to other study participants who didn't take acting lessons.[18]

Take up knitting, sewing, or quilting. You'll not only boost brainpower as you learn how to quilt, knit, or sew, but you'll also improve fine motor skills as you use your fingers and hands in new ways. In one study of 259 people, participants who spent 16 hours a week learning to quilt improved their memory over people who didn't try a new hobby.[19]

Consider photography. The same study that revealed the brain-sharpening effects of quilting also found that people who spent 16 hours a week learning photography skills boosted their memories.[20]

Learn to juggle. In one study, participants used juggling packs to teach themselves how to juggle, practicing for a half hour a day. After 6 weeks, the study participants grew the size of the white matter in their parietal lobes, which connects what we see with how we move.[21] Other research shows that juggling may be able to help us with spatial problems, such as how much stuff you can fit in the trunk of your car.[22]

Take up dancing. Not only does dancing count as a form of exercise, but it can also boost mood, lower stress, and help you to expand your circle of friends. Dance is fun, and it works your brain in new ways, according to a study of people ages 75 and older out of Albert Einstein College of Medicine in New York City. Of all the physical activities examined in the study, frequent dancing seemed to offer the most benefit, reducing risk for dementia by 76 percent.[23]

Play Technique #4: Immerse Yourself in Art

It's no wonder research shows that people who dabble in the arts are less likely to develop memory problems. Learning to draw, sculpt, and paint encourages you to see the world differently. You'll start to notice the unique shape of a specific flower petal or the way a beam of sunlight changes the color of a field from green to gold. Artistic pursuits, including woodworking, also tend to be hands on, which may strengthen fine motor skills, and they involve making a series of decisions: Is this the right color? Is that the shape of the model's eye? Should I draw the apple or leave it out of the picture entirely? Finally, art also requires you to exercise your memory as you see something and transfer what you remember onto the canvas, piece of clay, or whatever medium you happen to be using.

One study asked people ages 85 and older about activities they'd participated in during their fifties. The researchers tested the participants every 15 months for 4 years for their mental status, memory, language, spatial skills, and ability to reason, plan, and solve problems. Over several years, 121 participants out of the 256 developed memory problems, but the study participants who'd engaged in arts and crafts were half as likely to have developed mild cognitive impairment.[24]

STAY-SHARP TIPS

Whether you decide to take an art class or an art appreciation class, the following advice will guide you in your quest to create an ageless brain.

Hit your local museum. Just looking at works of art can give your brain a boost, according to a study done in Germany.[25]

Explore different methods and media. You might start off with drawing, but then advance to watercolors, pastels, or oils. Or, once you become proficient at capturing a still life, consider trying a landscape or a portrait.

Don't forget crafts. If you worry that you are not "artistic," crafts might be the way to go. Everything from scrapbooking to ornament making to basket weaving can help to strength your brain as well as your creativity.

Play Technique #5:
Turn Off the TV and Turn On Your Computer

Parents have often told their children that too much television would rot their brains, and research is now revealing that parents may have been onto something.

Researchers from the Northern California Institute for Research and Education, in San Francisco, and several other institutions, followed the health outcomes of more than 3,200 people for 25 years. People who were sedentary and who watched 3 or more hours of TV a day were twice as likely to develop cognitive problems as they got older, performing poorly on cognitive tests of verbal memory, information processing, and other mental skills, compared to people who watched less television.[26]

Researchers aren't completely sure why television has such a profoundly negative effect on the brain, but it may have something to do with the association between television viewing and a sedentary lifestyle. Remember, as you learned in Chapter 6, physical fitness is an important piece of the ageless brain puzzle. From your brain's point of view, watching television is also an incredibly passive activity. Compared to the brainpower involved in completing a puzzle or even in just reading a book, the brain hardly has to do anything when you watch television.

But not all screens are bad for your brain. Take your computer or tablet. An 8-year study of nearly 6,442 people found that the brains of people who regularly went online declined more slowly than the brains of people who did not. During the study, the participants were regularly tested for their ability to recall a series of words in a given amount of time. Participants who used email performed 3 percent better at recalling the words than participants who didn't use the Internet or email.[27]

Be judicious and smart about your screen time. Prioritize other brain-healthy habits—such as exercise and socializing with friends—and look for ways to make screen time more brain healthy. Here are some ideas to get you started.

Never take a television show sitting down. Rather than vegetating on the couch, turn TV time into active time. Stretch, do yoga, or walk on a treadmill while you watch TV or movies.

Use television to learn. Rather than always watching the same old mindless shows, consider literally changing the channel and taking in a show that expands your mind. How about a travel show, to gather ideas of new places to visit? Or how about a cooking show that you plan to use for research on new recipes to try? Or maybe a documentary or a science show is what you really need.

Watch shows with subtitles. Reading the subtitles will engage your brain more than just sitting and passively listening to the show as it unfolds. Foreign language shows can also help you to learn or brush up on a new language, which is also good for the brain. (See technique #6.)

Take a computer class. A class can introduce you to new ways to use your computer and also help you to fix problems that crop up.

Play Technique #6:
Learn a New Language

Becoming fluent in another language may provide a workout for the brain, challenging gray-matter cells and keeping them from degenerating.[28]

In one study, out of the University of Ghent in Belgium, researchers tracked the health outcomes of 134 people who were all being treated for mild cognitive problems and suspected to have Alzheimer's disease. At the beginning of the study, 65 of the study participants were bilingual or multilingual, whereas the rest spoke only one language. People who only spoke one language were diagnosed with full-blown Alzheimer's disease at least 4 years earlier, on average, than people who were bilingual or multilingual. The average age of an Alzheimer's diagnosis was 73 for people who spoke only one language and 77 for people who spoke more than one.[29]

Learning a second language may help you recover from a stroke, too. A study of 608 stroke patients from India found that people who spoke more than one language were twice as likely to regain their normal cognitive functioning as people who only spoke one.[30]

STAY-SHARP TIPS

Try to make learning your second (or third or fourth) language a fun, playful process. See it as a way to experience more in life, using these suggestions.

Use your new language as an excuse to travel. For example, if you're learning Spanish, you might travel to Mexico or Spain.

Watch television shows in the language you are learning. Here's one way your television may benefit your brain rather than harm it. By watching shows in another language and reading the subtitles, you'll more easily pick up the new language and discover the right way to pronounce certain words.

Explore the cuisines from countries where your new language is spoken. For example, you might teach yourself French cooking if you're learning French or Chinese cooking if you're learning Chinese. In this way, you don't only learn a new language, but you also start to embrace an entire culture.

Play Technique #7:
Learn a Musical Instrument

Whether you simply enjoy listening to music or take the extra step and discover how to play it, music offers many benefits for your brain. The process of listening to classical, jazz, and other types of music can activate multiple areas of the brain at once, including those involved in memory and attention.[31] Certain types of music—especially the music of your youth—may also help you access certain memories. A song might take you back to your first kiss or another important event in your life, for example.

Learning to play an instrument offers even more ageless benefits. In one study of 70 people between the ages of 60 and 83, musicians who'd been studying an instrument for 10 or more years scored the highest on tests of nonverbal and visual-spatial memory, the ability to name objects, and the ability to remember and use new information. People with less musical training performed less well, and people with no training performed the worst.[32] In another study, adults who took piano lessons improved their attention, concentration, and planning abilities over 6 months compared to adults who didn't take lessons.[33]

STAY-SHARP TIPS

There's no one right or wrong type of music or instrument. Go with what you find most intriguing and fun, because that's what you will be most likely to practice and master over time.

Join a singing group. You came into this world with your voice box, so there's no need to rent or buy one for hundreds or thousands of dollars. And research shows that singing may be just as powerful as playing an instrument, as adults who joined a singing group improved their memory and attention compared to study participants who didn't join a singing group.[34]

Join a local band or orchestra. Look for music groups that cater to older adults with or without prior musical training. For example, New Horizons International Music Association offers adults the ability to learn how to play an instrument.

Try a drumming circle. No prior experience is required at these events that focus on the spontaneous creation of unscripted music.

Play Technique #8: Play Games

Board games aren't just for kids. In addition to challenging your ability to plan, strategize, make decisions, and remember previous moves, board games and cards are inherently social.

One study that tracked the health outcomes of 3,777 people for 2 decades found that board-game players had a 15 percent lower risk of developing dementia than did nonplayers. The games studied included card games, chess, parlor games, bingo, and checkers.[35] An earlier study of 469 people published in the *New England Journal of Medicine* also found an association between board games and reduced risk of dementia.[36]

STAY-SHARP TIPS

When looking to board games to bolster brain health, the key strategy is regularity. In studies, people played board games at least every other day. Consider playing a board game or cards at night rather than watching television.

Have a regular game night. Invite friends over for cards, bingo, or a dance-off on the Wii.

STAY-SHARP STRATEGY

PUZZLE YOUR MIND ONCE A DAY

Crossword puzzles, word jumbles, Sudoku, and other brain teasers are good for the brain, especially if you enjoy them. One study of 488 people found that people who had done crossword puzzles throughout life delayed the onset of memory problems by an average 2.5 years.[37] Another study found that people who began solving Sudoku, the Japanese game that has you place nine digits in a specific order, improved on tests of working memory.[38] Finally, another study found that people who enjoyed playing games every day—including crosswords and puzzles—performed better on tests of memory and other mental functions than those who didn't do puzzles.[39]

Learn a new game. For example, if you usually play poker, try bridge.

Join a club. Clubs like the American Contract Bridge League or the Internet Chess Club can help keep you motivated.

Play Technique #9: Play Video Games

Unlike watching television, playing a video game is an active experience that involves making a series of quick decisions. These games can also be fun, and they often naturally increase in difficulty, which allows your brain to continually benefit from them over time.

For all those reasons and more, researchers have busily been trying to design video games specifically for older adults. For example, Adam

Gazzaley of the University of California San Francisco created a game called *NeuroRacer* specifically for older adults who wish to boost their brainpower. It involves driving a virtual car, pressing a series of buttons to navigate and respond to signage. Study participants who played it 3 hours a week for 4 weeks improved on tests of multitasking and attention, putting them on par with the skills of 20-year-olds.[40] The improvements lasted for months after the seniors stopped playing the game.

In addition to helping you keep your mind sharp, video games may also offer emotional benefits. A study from *Computers in Human Behavior* found that older adults who gamed regularly—by playing solitaire, *Words with Friends*, puzzle games like Sudoku, and things like Wii tennis and bowling—had lower scores on tests of "negative affect," and reported better everyday functioning than older adults who didn't game.[41]

STAY-SHARP TIPS

NeuroRacer is still under study and isn't available for purchase, but *Brain Age*, marketed by Nintendo, is available. It includes a host of puzzles, brain teasers, and math. Older adults who played *Brain Age* for 15 minutes a day, 5 days a week, for 4 weeks improved their ability to plan, reason, and solve problems.[42]

But you don't necessarily need to seek video games designed for older adults, though. For one thing, we just don't have enough research at the moment to know whether video games specifically designed for older adults offer any real benefit over any other video games—and particularly over other pursuits such as learning an instrument or embracing stimulating hobbies.

If you love playing video games, however, research does offer a couple of hints as to which ones may be more likely to help you in your quest to build an ageless brain.

Play like a kid—but go 3-D. Researchers from the Max Planck Institute for Human Development have found that 3-D games like *Super Mario* can help to hone your planning and memory skills.[43] In another study, *Super Mario* outperformed *Angry Birds* in its ability to help study participants improve their memories. The difference, say researchers, is that *Super Mario* offers players a fast-paced, three-dimensional, action-packed game, whereas *Angry Birds* is more passive and two dimensional.[44] The best video games for your brain tend to be complex and get continually more difficult. Think *Medal of Honor*, but not *Pac-Man*, and *Space Fortress*, but not *Tetris*.[45]

Play against other people. Older adults who started playing a multiplayer video game called Rise of Nations improved their memories, compared to other study participants who didn't play the game.[46] The role-playing *World of Warcraft*[47] game as well as *Call of Duty* have also been shown to help boost memory.[48] In addition to helping to sharpen your memory, these games can also expand your social circle. The games offered older adults a place to socialize, helping them to build those social connections we told you about in Chapter 2.[49]

10

Brain-Healthy Meals

YOUR BELLY PLAYS A vital part in building an ageless brain. Here are more than 45 tasty meals that will nourish your noodle, dazzle your taste buds, and leave you feeling full and satisfied. And these eats are fast as well as flavorful—many require just 15 minutes of prep time, and others even less. And whether you're cooking for one, two, or more, it's simple to shrink or expand the serving sizes.

Each breakfast, lunch, or dinner selection includes foods on the research-backed MIND diet we discussed back in Chapter 5. That means you'll tap into lots of brain-boosting leafy greens and other veggies, whole grains, nuts, and berries, as well as fish and poultry. And here's some sweet news: Dessert is on the menu! You're about to discover just how delicious "brain food" can be.

Persian Herb Omelet

PREP TIME: 20 MINUTES   TOTAL TIME: 2 HOURS 45 MINUTES   *SERVES: 4*

- 1   cup halved cherry tomatoes
- 1   tablespoon olive oil
- ¾   teaspoon salt, divided
- 1   teaspoon balsamic vinegar
- 6   large eggs
- 1   tablespoon all-purpose flour
- ½   teaspoon aluminum-free baking powder
- ¾   cup chopped fresh parsley
- ¾   cup chopped chives or scallion greens
- ¾   cup chopped fresh cilantro
- ¾   cup chopped fresh dill
- ¼   cup finely chopped red onion
- ¼   cup chopped walnuts
- 2   teaspoons finely grated lemon peel
- ¼   teaspoon ground turmeric
- ¼   teaspoon ground black pepper
- ½   lemon

1. Preheat the oven to 250°F. In a small bowl, toss the tomatoes with the oil and ½ teaspoon of the salt. Place in a small baking pan and bake for 2 hours, or until browned and caramelized. Remove from the oven and drizzle with the vinegar. Increase the oven temperature to 350°F.

2. Coat a 9" pie plate with nonaerosol cooking spray. Beat the eggs, flour, and baking powder in a large bowl for 2 minutes. Add the parsley, chives or scallions, cilantro, dill, onion, walnuts, lemon peel, the remaining ¼ teaspoon salt, turmeric, and pepper. Scrape the mixture into the pie plate and bake for 20 minutes, or until lightly browned and firm to the touch. Remove from the oven. Squeeze the lemon juice over the omelet. Cut into 8 wedges and top with the roasted tomatoes.

Nutrition (per serving): 217 calories, 12 g protein, 8 g total carbohydrates, 2 g fiber, 3 g sugars, 16 g total fat, 3 g saturated fat, 543 mg sodium

Flax-Almond Pancakes

PREP TIME: 10 MINUTES   *TOTAL TIME: 20 MINUTES*   *SERVES: 2*

½ cup almond meal
¼ cup ground flaxseeds
¼ cup unsweetened shredded coconut
¼ teaspoon salt
4 egg whites
1 cup 1% milk
¼ teaspoon almond extract
1 tablespoon canola oil
½ cup fresh blueberries

1. In a large bowl, combine the almond meal, flaxseeds, shredded coconut, and salt.

2. In a small, clean glass bowl, beat the egg whites with a hand mixer until stiff peaks form.

3. Stir the milk, almond extract, and beaten egg whites gently into the flour mixture.

4. Heat the oil in a griddle or skillet over medium heat. Pour the batter onto the cooking surface, using ½ cup per pancake. Cook 3 to 4 minutes, carefully turning once, or until lightly browned on both sides. Serve 2 pancakes per serving with ¼ cup blueberries.

Nutrition (per serving): 470 calories, 21 g protein, 25 g total carbohydrates, 9 g fiber, 12 g sugars, 34 g total fat, 9 g saturated fat, 468 mg sodium

Overtime Oats

PREP TIME: 5 MINUTES   TOTAL TIME: 40 MINUTES   SERVES: 3

- 4½ cups water
- 1 cup steel-cut oats
- ½ cup oat bran
- ½ teaspoon salt
- ½ cup walnuts, coarsely chopped
- 4 large strawberries, sliced

Mix the water, oats, oat bran, and salt in a medium saucepan. Bring to a boil over medium-high heat. Reduce the heat and cover the pan. Simmer, stirring frequently, for 30 minutes or until thickened. Serve topped with the walnuts and strawberries.

Nutrition (per serving): 266 calories, 9 g protein, 38 g total carbohydrates, 7 g fiber, 2 g sugars, 12 g total fat, 1.5 g saturated fat, 300 mg sodium

Love-Your-Brain Smoothie

- 1 cup blueberries
- ¾ cup water
- ½ cup spinach
- ½ cup plain yogurt
- ¼ cup coconut milk
- 1 teaspoon matcha powder
- ½ teaspoon ground turmeric
- Ice, as needed

In a blender, combine the blueberries, water, spinach, yogurt, coconut milk, matcha powder, and turmeric. Blend, adding ice as needed, until smooth.

Nutrition (per serving): 290 calories, 8 g protein, 33 g total carbohydrates, 5 g fiber, 23 g sugars, 17 g total fat, 13 g saturated fat, 91 mg sodium

Strawberry Pancakes

PREP TIME: 10 MINUTES   TOTAL TIME: 20 MINUTES   SERVES: 4

1 cup white whole wheat flour
2 tablespoons ground flaxseeds
1 teaspoon grated orange peel
½ teaspoon aluminum-free baking powder
¼ teaspoon baking soda
⅛ teaspoon salt
1 cup plain soy milk
1 egg white
8 strawberries, sliced

1. Preheat a griddle over high heat. Combine the flour, flaxseeds, orange peel, baking powder, baking soda, and salt in a large bowl. Make a well in the center, and add the soy milk and egg white. Whisk until combined.

2. Coat the griddle with nonaerosol cooking spray. Pour ¼ cup batter per pancake onto the griddle, and top each one with the slices from 1 strawberry. Cook for 3 to 4 minutes, until small bubbles appear on the top. Flip, and cook for an additional 3 to 4 minutes, until the pancakes are cooked through. Serve immediately.

Nutrition (per serving): 189 calories, 8 g protein, 31 g total carbohydrates, 6 g fiber, 4 g sugars, 4 g total fat, 0.5 g saturated fat, 259 mg sodium

Hearty Oatmeal and Greek Yogurt

PREP TIME: 1 MINUTE   *TOTAL TIME: 5 MINUTES*   *SERVES: 1*

- ¾ cup cooked oatmeal
- ¾ cup plain 0% Greek yogurt
- 2 tablespoons ground flaxseeds
- ¼ teaspoon ground cinnamon
- ¼ cup unsweetened frozen blueberries, thawed
- 2 tablespoons almonds

In a bowl, loosely combine the oatmeal, yogurt, flaxseeds, and cinnamon. Top with the blueberries and almonds.

Nutrition (per serving): 413 calories, 26 g protein, 41 g total carbohydrates, 11 g fiber, 11 g sugars, 18 g total fat, 2 g saturated fat, 75 mg sodium

Mediterranean Scramble

PREP TIME: 5 MINUTES   TOTAL TIME: 10 MINUTES   SERVES: 1

- 1 egg
- 1 egg white
- 1 tablespoon water
- 1 teaspoon olive oil
- ½ cup coarsely chopped baby spinach
- ⅓ cup chopped tomato
- ⅓ cup rinsed and drained canned white beans
- 2 tablespoons feta cheese

In a small bowl, whisk the egg and the egg white together with the water. Heat the oil in a nonstick skillet over medium-high heat and scramble the eggs together with the baby spinach, tomato, beans, and feta.

Nutrition (per serving): 293 calories, 20 g protein, 24 g total carbohydrates, 6 g fiber, 3 g sugars, 14 g total fat, 5 g saturated fat, 362 mg sodium

Fruit 'n' Nut Muffins

PREP TIME: 15 MINUTES   TOTAL TIME: 40 MINUTES   SERVES: 12

1⅓ cups all-purpose flour

¾ cup quick cooking oats

½ cup packed brown sugar

⅓ cup wheat bran

1 tablespoon aluminum-free baking powder

½ teaspoon ground cinnamon

½ teaspoon ground allspice

¼ teaspoon salt

1 cup halved seedless grapes

½ cup grated carrots

½ cup fat-free milk

½ cup applesauce

3 tablespoons canola oil

1 egg, beaten

½ cup chopped walnuts, divided

1. Preheat the oven to 350°F.

2. Line 12 muffin cups with paper liners, and set aside.

3. Combine the flour, oats, sugar, bran, baking powder, cinnamon, allspice, and salt in a medium bowl, and mix well. Add the grapes, carrots, milk, applesauce, oil, egg, and ¼ cup of the walnuts. Stir just until combined. Spoon the batter into the prepared muffin cups (they will be very full), and sprinkle with the remaining ¼ cup walnuts.

4. Bake for 20 to 25 minutes, or until a toothpick inserted in the center comes out clean. Cool in the pan 10 minutes before transferring muffins to a cooling rack to cool completely.

Nutrition (per serving): 207 calories, 5 g protein, 31 g total carbohydrates, 2 g fiber, 12 g sugars, 8 g total fat, 1 g saturated fat, 84 mg sodium

Peanut Butter and Yogurt Smoothie

PREP TIME: 5 MINUTES   TOTAL TIME: 5 MINUTES   SERVES: 1

- ½ cup fat-free milk
- ½ cup fat-free plain yogurt
- 2 tablespoons creamy natural unsalted peanut butter
- ⅓ very ripe banana
- 1 tablespoon honey
- 4 ice cubes

Combine the milk, yogurt, peanut butter, banana, honey, and ice cubes in a blender. Process until smooth.

Nutrition (per serving): 385 calories, 17 g protein, 47 g total carbohydrates, 3 g fiber, 35 g sugars, 16 g total fat, 2 g saturated fat, 256 mg sodium

Almond, Blueberry, and Banana Smoothie

PREP TIME: 5 MINUTES   *TOTAL TIME: 5 MINUTES*   *SERVES: 1*

- 1½ cups plain unsweetened almond milk
- 1 small frozen banana
- 1 cup frozen or fresh blueberries
- 1 cup chopped kale (washed, coarsely chopped, and larger sections of stems removed)
- 5 unsalted whole almonds
- 2 teaspoons honey

Combine the almond milk, banana, blueberries, kale, almonds, and honey in a blender. Puree until smooth, 1 to 2 minutes.

Nutrition (per serving): 323 calories, 7 g protein, 60 g total carbohydrates, 10 g fiber, 35 g sugars, 10 g total fat, 0.5 g saturated fat, 300 mg sodium

Green Machine Smoothie

- 1 cup fat-free plain yogurt
- ½ cup kale (washed, coarsely chopped, and larger sections of stems removed)
- ½ peeled banana
- 1 kiwifruit
- 1 avocado
  Ice, as needed

In a blender, combine the yogurt, kale, banana, kiwi, and avocado. Blend until smooth. Add ice as needed for a frothier smoothie.

Nutrition (per serving): 288 calories, 17 g protein, 47 g total carbohydrates, 6 g fiber, 32 g sugars, 5 g total fat, 1 g saturated fat, 206 mg sodium

Spinach Salad with Almond-Encrusted Chicken Breast

PREP TIME: 10 MINUTES　　　*TOTAL TIME: 20 MINUTES*　　　*SERVES: 1*

- 5 ounces boneless, skinless chicken breast
- 1 tablespoon cornstarch
- 1 egg beaten with 1 tablespoon water
- 2 tablespoons finely chopped almonds
- 2 tablespoons balsamic vinegar
- 1 tablespoon olive oil
- ⅛ teaspoon ground black pepper
- 3 cups baby spinach leaves
- ¼ cup sliced mushrooms
- ¼ cup yellow or red grape tomatoes, halved
- 1 small red bell pepper, sliced into strips

1. To prepare the chicken: Sprinkle each side of the chicken with the cornstarch. Dip the chicken into the egg mixture to coat, allowing the excess to drip off. Sprinkle both sides with the almonds.

2. Coat a small skillet with nonaerosol spray and heat over medium heat. Cook the chicken for 5 minutes on each side, or until a thermometer inserted in the thickest portion registers 165°F and the juices run clear. Remove from the pan and set aside.

3. To prepare the salad: In a medium bowl, whisk the vinegar, oil, and black pepper. Add the spinach, mushrooms, tomatoes, and bell pepper. Toss to coat. Transfer to a serving plate. Slice the reserved chicken diagonally and place on top.

Nutrition (per serving): 577 calories, 43 g protein, 29 g total carbohydrates, 7 g fiber, 9 g sugars, 31 g total fat, 5 g saturated fat, 370 mg sodium

Tomatoes Stuffed with White Bean Salad

PREP TIME: 15 MINUTES   *TOTAL TIME: 20 MINUTES*   *SERVES: 4*

- 2 tablespoons Italian parsley, chopped, and several sprigs for garnish
- 1 tablespoon lemon juice
- 1 tablespoon extra-virgin olive oil
- 2 teaspoons capers, drained and rinsed
- 2 cloves garlic, minced
- ¼ teaspoon salt
- ¼ teaspoon ground black pepper
- 1 can (15.5 ounces) navy beans, drained and rinsed
- 4 medium tomatoes

1. In a medium bowl, combine the chopped parsley, lemon juice, oil, capers, garlic, salt, and pepper. Whisk to mix. Add the beans. Toss thoroughly to mix. For a slightly creamier texture, mash one-quarter of the beans roughly with the back of a fork.

2. Slice ¼ inch from the tops of the tomatoes. Scoop out the seeds and discard. Spoon the bean salad into the tomatoes. Garnish with the parsley sprigs.

Nutrition (per serving): 155 calories, 8 g protein, 24 g total carbohydrates, 6 g fiber, 4 g sugars, 4 g total fat, 1 g saturated fat, 572 mg sodium

Savory Sautéed Pepper and Chicken Sandwich

PREP TIME: 10 MINUTES　　　*TOTAL TIME: 15 MINUTES*　　　*SERVES: 1*

- ¼ green bell pepper, sliced
- ¼ yellow bell pepper, sliced
- 3 thick slices red onion
- 3 black olives, sliced
- ¼ teaspoon dried oregano
- 1 teaspoon olive oil
- 2 teaspoons red wine vinegar
- ¼ teaspoon ground black pepper
- 1 (2-ounce) whole wheat roll
- 4 ounces roasted chicken breast

1. In a bowl, combine the bell peppers, onion, olives, oregano, oil, vinegar, and black pepper.

2. Coat a skillet with nonaerosol cooking spray and heat over medium heat. Add the pepper mixture and cook, stirring frequently, for 6 to 7 minutes, until the peppers and onion are soft. Slice the roll and fill it with the chicken and peppers.

Nutrition (per serving): 423 calories, 41 g protein, 37 g total carbohydrates, 6 g fiber, 8 g sugars, 12 g total fat, 2 g saturated fat, 443 mg sodium

Long-Grain Rice and Lentil Soup

PREP TIME: 15 MINUTES   TOTAL TIME: 1 HOUR   SERVES: 16

  2 quarts reduced-sodium chicken broth
  1 cup water
1½ cups lentils, rinsed and drained
  1 cup long-grain brown rice
  1 can (28 ounces) diced tomatoes
  3 carrots, chopped
  1 small onion, chopped
  1 rib celery, chopped
  3 cloves garlic, minced
  1 teaspoon dried basil
  1 teaspoon dried oregano
  1 teaspoon dried thyme
  1 bay leaf
  2 tablespoons cider vinegar
  ½ cup finely chopped fresh parsley
     Ground black pepper

1. In a large pot over medium-high heat, combine the broth, water, lentils, rice, tomatoes (with juice), carrots, onion, celery, garlic, basil, oregano, thyme, and bay leaf. Bring to a boil, then reduce the heat to low. Simmer, covered, for 45 minutes, stirring occasionally.

2. Remove from the heat and add the vinegar, parsley, and pepper to taste. Remove and discard the bay leaf, adjust the seasonings, and serve.

Nutrition (per serving): 147 calories, 9 g protein, 25 g total carbohydrates, 7 g fiber, 3 g sugars, 1 g total fat, 0.5 g saturated fat, 160 mg sodium

Curried Barley Salad with Shrimp and Baby Greens

PREP TIME: 20 MINUTES   TOTAL TIME: 1 HOUR 5 MINUTES   SERVES: 6

3 cups water

1 teaspoon curry powder

½ teaspoon ground turmeric

1 cup barley

¼ cup freshly squeezed lime juice (about 4 limes)

1 tablespoon vegetable oil

2 teaspoons finely chopped seeded jalapeño chile pepper (wear plastic gloves when handling)

1 clove garlic, minced

¼ teaspoon salt

1 pound small cooked shrimp

1½ cups seeded and diced tomatoes

½ cup chopped green bell pepper

½ cup chopped peeled cucumber

12 cups baby greens

¼ cup chopped fresh basil

½ cup toasted shelled pumpkin seeds (pepitas)

1. In a large saucepan over high heat, bring the water, curry powder, and turmeric to a boil. Stir in the barley. Cover and reduce the heat to low. Cook for 45 minutes, or until the water is absorbed and the barley is tender. Remove from the heat.

2. Meanwhile, in a large bowl, whisk together the lime juice, oil, chile pepper, garlic, and salt. Add the shrimp, tomatoes, bell pepper, cucumber, and barley. Toss to coat.

3. Divide the barley salad evenly and spoon on top of 2 cups of baby greens per plate. Sprinkle on the basil and pumpkin seeds.

Nutrition (per serving): 305 calories, 27 g protein, 35 g total carbohydrates, 9 g fiber, 3 g sugars, 8 g total fat, 1 g saturated fat, 244 mg sodium

Vegetable Stew with Quinoa

PREP TIME: 15 MINUTES   *TOTAL TIME: 40 MINUTES*   *SERVES: 4*

- 1 teaspoon olive oil
- 1 small onion, finely chopped
- 2 cloves garlic, minced
- 16 ounces mushrooms, quartered
- 1 large (about 14 ounces) sweet potato, peeled and cut into ½" chunks
- 2½ cups low-sodium vegetable broth
- 1 tablespoon fresh lemon juice
- 1 teaspoon Dijon mustard
- ¼ teaspoon dried thyme
- ¼ teaspoon kosher salt
- Pinch of freshly ground black pepper
- ¾ cup quinoa, rinsed
- 8 tablespoons crumbled reduced-fat feta cheese

1. Heat the oil in a large saucepan over medium heat.

2. Add the onion, garlic, mushrooms, and sweet potato, and stir well. Add the broth, lemon juice, mustard, thyme, salt, and pepper.

3. Increase the heat to medium-high. Boil for 8 to 10 minutes, or until the sweet potato is nearly cooked through.

4. Stir in the quinoa. Cover the pan, reduce the heat to a simmer, and cook for 10 to 12 minutes, until the quinoa is tender but still a bit chewy.

5. Divide the stew among 4 bowls and garnish each portion with 2 tablespoons of the cheese.

Nutrition (per serving): 293 calories, 13 g protein, 49 g total carbohydrates, 8 g fiber, 8 g sugars, 6 g total fat, 2 g saturated fat, 522 mg sodium

Quinoa with Raisins, Apricots, and Pecans

PREP TIME: 10 MINUTES   *TOTAL TIME: 30 MINUTES*   *SERVES: 4*

- 3 tablespoons chopped pecans
- ¾ cup quinoa
- ¾ cup orange juice
- ¾ cup water
- ⅓ cup chopped dried apricots
- ⅓ cup golden raisins
- 2 scallions, finely chopped
- 1 tablespoon chopped fresh cilantro
- 1 tablespoon lemon juice
- 1 tablespoon olive oil
- ½ teaspoon salt

1. Cook the pecans in a small skillet over medium heat, stirring often, for 3 to 4 minutes, or until lightly toasted. Tip onto a plate and let cool.

2. Place the quinoa in a fine-mesh strainer and rinse under cold running water for 2 minutes.

3. In a medium saucepan, combine the quinoa, orange juice, and water.

4. Bring to a boil over high heat, reduce the heat to medium-low, cover, and simmer for 12 to 15 minutes, or until the liquid is absorbed. Transfer the quinoa to a large bowl.

5. Add the apricots, raisins, scallions, cilantro, and toasted pecans. Add the lemon juice, oil, and salt, tossing well to distribute.

Nutrition (per serving): 274 calories, 6 g protein, 45 g total carbohydrates, 4 g fiber, 20 g sugars, 9 g total fat, 1 g saturated fat, 298 mg sodium

Tabbouleh with Fruit

PREP TIME: 15 MINUTES   TOTAL TIME: 1 HOUR   SERVES: 4

- 1 cup orange juice
- ½ cup medium-grain bulgur
- 1 large tomato, seeded and finely chopped
- ½ small cantaloupe, seeded, finely chopped
- 1 cup finely chopped hulled fresh strawberries
- 1 cup fresh blueberries
- 1 cup fresh raspberries
- ⅓ cup chopped flat-leaf parsley
- ½ small red onion, finely chopped
- 1 tablespoon chopped fresh mint
- 2 tablespoons lemon juice
- 1 tablespoon extra-virgin olive oil
- ¾ teaspoon ground cumin
- ½ teaspoon ground cinnamon
- ¼ teaspoon salt
- ¼ teaspoon freshly ground black pepper

1. In a medium bowl, combine the orange juice and bulgur. Let stand for 30 minutes, or until tender and softened.

2. Drain the bulgur and place in a large bowl. Add the tomato, cantaloupe, strawberries, blueberries, raspberries, parsley, onion, mint, lemon juice, oil, cumin, cinnamon, salt, and pepper. Toss to coat well. Let stand for at least 15 minutes to allow the flavors to blend.

Nutrition (per serving): 203 calories, 5 g protein, 40 g total carbohydrates, 9 g fiber, 18 g sugars, 5 g total fat, 0.5 g saturated fat, 165 mg sodium

Mediterranean Salad Wraps

PREP TIME: 10 MINUTES   TOTAL TIME: 20 MINUTES   SERVES: 4

- ½ cup green olive tapenade
- 2 tablespoons freshly squeezed lemon juice (about 1 lemon)
- 4 cups (one 4-ounce bag) salad greens
- ½ cup canned no-salt-added chickpeas, rinsed and drained
- ½ cup drained and sliced jarred roasted red peppers (blotted dry)
- ½ cup halved and thinly sliced seedless cucumber
- ¼ cup thinly sliced red or sweet onion
- 2 ounces crumbled goat cheese
- 4 whole wheat wraps or tortillas (8" diameter)

1. Mix the tapenade and lemon juice in a large bowl with a fork. Add the greens, chickpeas, peppers, cucumber, and onion, and toss to mix well. Add the cheese and toss gently.

2. Warm the wraps or tortillas per package directions. Put one-quarter of the salad mixture on the bottom of a wrap and roll it up. Cut it in half on an angle, placing a wooden pick in each half. Repeat with the remaining wraps.

Nutrition (per serving): 297 calories, 11 g protein, 37 g total carbohydrates, 6 g fiber, 5 g sugars, 12 g total fat, 4 g saturated fat, 684 mg sodium

Quinoa Salad with Carrot Fries

PREP TIME: 10 MINUTES   TOTAL TIME: 30 MINUTES   SERVES: 2

- 3 medium to large carrots, quartered lengthwise, then cut crosswise into 2½"–3" sticks
- ¼ cup olive oil, divided
- ¼ teaspoon sea salt, divided (or more, to taste)
- 1 cup water
- ½ cup quinoa, rinsed well and drained
- 1 can (15 ounces) chickpeas, rinsed and drained
- 3 scallions, thinly sliced
- 1 cup finely chopped Italian parsley
- ¼ cup finely chopped fresh mint
- 1 cucumber, seeded and finely chopped
- 1 cup baby spinach
- ¼ cup lemon juice

1. Preheat the oven to 425°F. Coat a baking sheet with nonaerosol cooking spray.

2. In a saucepan, bring the water and quinoa to a boil, uncovered. Reduce the heat, cover, and simmer for 15 minutes. Turn off the heat and steam the quinoa for 5 minutes. Remove the lid and fluff with a fork.

3. In a medium bowl, toss the carrots, 1 tablespoon of the oil, and half the salt together. Spread on the baking sheet. Bake for 12 to 15 minutes, until golden brown, turning once. Remove from the oven and set aside.

4. In a large bowl, combine the cooked quinoa, chickpeas, scallions, parsley, mint, cucumber, spinach, the remaining oil, lemon juice, and the remaining salt. Enjoy immediately or keep in the fridge—this is great chilled for an easy salad. Serve with the carrot fries.

Nutrition (per serving): 607 calories, 17 g protein, 66 g total carbohydrates, 16 g fiber, 10 g sugars, 34 g total fat, 5 g saturated fat, 899 mg sodium

Mediterranean Bulgur Salad

PREP TIME: 10 MINUTES   TOTAL TIME: 1 HOUR 45 MINUTES   SERVES: 6

- 1½ cups boiling water
- 1 cup bulgur
- ½ yellow onion, chopped
- ⅓ green bell pepper, chopped
- 1 tablespoon extra-virgin olive oil
- ½ teaspoon salt
- ¼ teaspoon ground black pepper
- 2 bunches fresh parsley, finely chopped
- 2 tomatoes, seeded and chopped
- 1 cucumber, peeled and chopped
- 2 tablespoons lemon juice
- ½ can (2.25 ounces) sliced black olives, drained

1. In a large bowl, combine the water and bulgur. Stir. Cover and let sit for 30 minutes, or until the bulgur has soaked up the water.

2. Fluff the bulgur with a fork. Add the onion, bell pepper, oil, salt, and black pepper. Toss. Refrigerate for 1 hour.

3. Add the parsley, tomatoes, cucumber, lemon juice, and olives. Toss.

Nutrition (per serving): 128 calories, 4 g protein, 24 g total carbohydrates, 6 g fiber, 3 g sugars, 4 g total fat, 0.5 g saturated fat, 243 mg sodium

Mediterranean Turkey Burgers

PREP TIME: 15 MINUTES   *TOTAL TIME: 30 MINUTES*   *SERVES: 4*

- 1 pound lean ground turkey
- ½ cup crumbled feta cheese
- ½ cup chopped roasted red peppers
- ⅓ cup chopped fresh basil
- ⅓ cup chopped kalamata olives
- ½ teaspoon ground black pepper, divided
- ½ cup oil-packed sun-dried tomatoes, drained
- ⅓ cup olive oil
- 2 tablespoons red wine vinegar
- 2 teaspoons fresh thyme
- 1 clove garlic
- ½ teaspoon smoked paprika
- ¼ teaspoon salt

1. Coat a grill rack or grill pan with nonaerosol cooking spray. Preheat the grill or grill pan over medium-high heat.

2. In a large bowl, mix the turkey, feta, red peppers, basil, olives, and ¼ teaspoon of the black pepper. Form into 4 patties. Grill for 6 minutes per side, or until a thermometer inserted in the thickest portion registers 165°F and the meat is no longer pink.

3. In a blender or food processor, combine the sun-dried tomatoes, olive oil, vinegar, thyme, garlic, paprika, salt, and remaining ¼ teaspoon black pepper. Blend until the spread is smooth.

4. Serve each burger open faced, topped with 1 tablespoon of the spread. Store the remaining spread in a sealed container in the refrigerator for up to 2 weeks.

Nutrition (per serving): 348 calories, 26 g protein, 9 g total carbohydrates, 1 g fiber, 1 g sugars, 22 g total fat, 6 g saturated fat, 827 mg sodium

Simmered Chickpeas in Tomato Sauce

PREP TIME: 10 MINUTES   *TOTAL TIME: 30 MINUTES*   *SERVES: 4*

- 1 tablespoon olive oil
- 1 medium onion, sliced
- 2 large cloves garlic, thinly sliced
- 1 small zucchini (6 ounces), cut into rough ¼" chunks
- ¼ teaspoon salt
- ¼ teaspoon ground black pepper
- 1 can (14.5 ounces) diced no-salt-added tomatoes in juice
- 1 can (15 ounces) chickpeas, rinsed and drained
- 2 tablespoons chopped fresh basil or parsley

1. Warm the oil in a large skillet over medium heat. Add the onion and garlic and cook, stirring often, until tender, about 5 minutes. Add the zucchini and sprinkle with the salt and pepper. Stir to blend well with the onion.

2. Add the tomatoes and juice and bring to a simmer. Cook, uncovered, stirring occasionally, until the zucchini is crisp-tender, 6 to 8 minutes. Add the chickpeas. Cover and cook just until heated through. Sprinkle with the basil or parsley and serve.

Nutrition (per serving): 162 calories, 6 g protein, 25 g total carbohydrates, 5 g fiber, 4 g sugars, 4 g total fat, 1 g saturated fat, 420 mg sodium

Baked Turkey Cutlets with Savory Mushrooms and Peppers

PREP TIME: 10 MINUTES   *TOTAL TIME: 40 MINUTES*   *SERVES: 6*

- 1¼ pounds turkey breast cutlets
- 1 onion, thinly sliced
- 1 red bell pepper, thinly sliced
- 1 green bell pepper, thinly sliced
- 8 ounces mushrooms, thinly sliced
- ½ teaspoon dried thyme
- ½ teaspoon dried sage
- ⅛ teaspoon salt (optional)
- ⅛ teaspoon ground black pepper

1. Preheat the oven to 350°F.

2. Cut the turkey cutlets into 6 equal-size pieces and place them in a 2- or 3-quart casserole dish. Top with the onion, bell peppers, and mushrooms. Sprinkle with the thyme, sage, salt (if using), and black pepper.

3. Cover with foil and bake for 30 minutes, until either the vegetables are tender and the turkey is cooked through or a thermometer inserted in the thickest portion registers 165°F and the juices run clear.

Nutrition (per serving): 125 calories, 25 g protein, 5 g total carbohydrates, 2 g fiber, 3 g sugars, 1 g total fat, 0.5 g saturated fat, 136 mg sodium

Baked Eggplant with Nutty Tomato Chutney

PREP TIME: 10 MINUTES   *TOTAL TIME: 1 HOUR*   *SERVES: 4*

1 medium eggplant
2 tablespoons olive oil, divided
¼ teaspoon salt
¼ teaspoon ground black pepper
1 onion, chopped
1 clove garlic, chopped
¼ cup balsamic vinegar
1 tablespoon chopped fresh basil or 1 teaspoon dried
1 can (14.5 ounces) diced tomatoes, drained
¼ cup shelled pistachios, coarsely chopped

1. Heat the oven to 425°F. Coat a 13" x 9" baking dish with nonaerosol cooking spray. Cut the eggplant into ½" slices and brush with 1 tablespoon of the oil. Sprinkle each side with salt and pepper and lay the slices in the baking dish. Bake for 30 minutes or until the eggplant is tender.

2. Heat the remaining 1 tablespoon oil in a saucepan over medium-high heat. Cook the onion and garlic, stirring, until softened, 3 minutes. Add the vinegar and basil and cook, stirring, for 1 minute. Add the tomatoes and simmer for 5 minutes. Remove from the heat and stir in the pistachios. Spoon over the eggplant and bake for 10 minutes more.

Nutrition (per serving): 92 calories, 2 g protein, 10 g total carbohydrates, 3 g fiber, 6 g sugars, 5 g total fat, 1 g saturated fat, 159 mg sodium

Roasted Catfish with Zesty Sweet Potatoes

PREP TIME: 10 MINUTES   TOTAL TIME: 1 HOUR 10 MINUTES   SERVES: 4

- 1 pound sweet potatoes, peeled and sliced ¼" thick
- ½ teaspoon ground cumin
- 1 tablespoon canola oil
- 4 catfish fillets (5 ounces each)
- 1 teaspoon chili powder
- ½ cup diagonally sliced scallions
- 1 bag (10 ounces) frozen corn kernels, thawed
- 1 medium green bell pepper, chopped
- 2 tablespoons fresh lime juice
- 1 tablespoon chopped cilantro
- 1 teaspoon finely chopped jalapeño chile pepper, or more to taste (wear plastic gloves when handling)

1. Preheat the oven to 400°F. In a 13" x 9" baking dish, combine the potatoes, cumin, and oil. Toss to coat. Spread in an even layer and roast for about 45 minutes, or until the potatoes are browned.

2. Remove the potatoes from the oven. Increase the temperature to 450°F. Use a wide spatula to gently turn the potato slices. Arrange the fish on top of the potatoes. Sprinkle with the chili powder. Scatter the scallions over top. Return the fish and potatoes to the oven. Roast for 8 to 10 minutes per inch of thickness, or until the fish flakes easily.

3. Meanwhile, in a bowl, combine the corn, bell pepper, lime juice, cilantro, and jalapeño pepper. With a wide spatula, lift portions of potatoes and fish onto serving plates. Spoon the corn salad on top.

Nutrition (per serving): 360 calories, 26 g protein, 32g total carbohydrates, 5 g fiber, 8 g sugars, 15 g total fat, 3 g saturated fat, 106 mg sodium

Chicken with Seven-Vegetable Couscous

PREP TIME: 20 MINUTES   TOTAL TIME: 55 MINUTES   SERVES: 4

- 1 teaspoon olive oil
- 1 medium onion, finely chopped
- 1 pound boneless, skinless chicken thighs, cut into bite-size pieces
- 1 pound winter squash or pumpkin, cut into 1" cubes
- 3 medium carrots, cut into 1" pieces
- 2 small zucchini, sliced into rounds (about 2 cups)
- 1 medium turnip, cut into 1" cubes
- 1 green bell pepper, cut into 1" pieces
- 2 cups reduced-sodium chicken broth
- 2 teaspoons ground cinnamon
- 1 teaspoon ground ginger
- ½ teaspoon ground allspice
- ¼ teaspoon salt
- 2 cups baby spinach
- ½ cup chopped fresh cilantro
- ½ cup chopped fresh parsley
- 2 cups cooked whole wheat couscous
- Hot sauce (optional)

1. Heat the oil in a large pot or Dutch oven over medium heat. Add the onion and cook until soft, about 1 minute. Add the chicken, squash or pumpkin, carrots, zucchini, turnip, bell pepper, broth, cinnamon, ginger, allspice, and salt. Bring to a boil. Reduce to a simmer, cover, and cook until the vegetables reach the desired doneness, about 30 minutes.

2. Stir in the spinach, cilantro, and parsley. Spoon the chicken and vegetables over ½-cup servings of couscous. Serve with hot sauce, if desired.

Nutrition (per serving): 434 calories, 35 g protein, 63 g total carbohydrates, 13 g fiber, 11 g sugars, 7 g total fat, 2 g saturated fat, 404 mg sodium

Pasta Primavera with Pine Nuts

PREP TIME: 10 MINUTES   *TOTAL TIME: 40 MINUTES*   *SERVES: 4*

2 cups broccoli florets

3 cups whole wheat pasta (a small style, such as rotini)

2 tablespoons olive oil, divided

1 large yellow bell pepper, sliced

4 tablespoons pine nuts

½ cup chopped oil-packed sun-dried tomatoes

1. Fill a large pot with water and bring to a rolling boil. Add the broccoli and cook just until tender and bright green (2 to 3 minutes). With a slotted spoon, remove from the pot and place in a colander. Save the broccoli water. Run cold water over the broccoli for 1 minute then place in a large bowl.

2. In the same pot, return the water to a boil and cook the pasta according to package directions. Drain the pasta and add it to the broccoli. Toss with 1 tablespoon of the oil.

3. Add the remaining 1 tablespoon oil to the pot over medium heat and cook the pepper, stirring frequently, until soft (about 4 minutes). Remove from the pot and place in the pasta bowl.

4. In the same pot, toast the pine nuts until slightly browned, about 2 minutes, shaking the pan frequently to prevent burning. Add the nuts to the bowl and toss with the other ingredients. Toss in the tomatoes and serve.

Nutrition (per serving): 325 calories, 9 g protein, 40 g total carbohydrates, 6 g fiber, 3 g sugars, 16 g total fat, 2 g saturated fat, 54 mg sodium

Spicy Vegetarian Stir-Fry with Toasted Almonds

PREP TIME: 10 MINUTES   TOTAL TIME: 1 HOUR 50 MINUTES   SERVES: 4

- 1 package (16 ounces) firm tofu
- 4 cups broccoli florets
- 3 teaspoons toasted sesame oil, divided
- 1 bunch scallions, thinly sliced
- 1 tablespoon minced garlic
- 1 small jalapeño chile pepper, halved, seeded, and finely chopped (wear plastic gloves when handling)
- 3½ teaspoons soy sauce
- 2 tablespoons sliced almonds, lightly toasted
- 2 cups hot cooked brown rice

1. Line a plate with a few sheets of paper towel. Place the tofu on a plate and top with a cutting board. Place several cans of food on the board to weigh it down. Let the tofu rest for 30 minutes while the water is squeezed out. Cut the tofu into small cubes.

2. While the tofu drains, lightly steam the broccoli for about 5 minutes, or until crisp-tender. Set aside.

3. Coat a wok or large skillet with nonaerosol cooking spray. Set over medium-high heat for 1 minute. Add 2 teaspoons of the oil. When hot, add the tofu and cook for about 5 minutes, stirring constantly, until browned. Transfer to a shallow bowl.

4. Add the remaining 1 teaspoon oil to the wok, followed by the scallions, garlic, pepper, and broccoli. Stir-fry over medium-high heat for 2 minutes. Stir in the soy sauce, almonds, and tofu. Gently toss to combine. Serve each portion with ½ cup of brown rice.

Nutrition (per serving): 257 calories, 14 g protein, 32 g total carbohydrates, 5 g fiber, 2 g sugars, 9 g total fat, 1 g saturated fat, 249 mg sodium

Chicken and Potato Salad Over Greens

PREP TIME: 15 MINUTES   TOTAL TIME: 1 HOUR   SERVES: 4

- ½ cup olive or vegetable oil
- ⅓ cup white wine vinegar
- 1 shallot, minced
- 2 cloves garlic, minced
- 2 tablespoons Dijon mustard
- 2 tablespoons chopped fresh sage
- ½ teaspoon salt
- ¼ teaspoon ground black pepper
- 2 pounds small red-skinned potatoes, quartered
- 1 pound boneless, skinless chicken thighs
- 6 cups salad greens

1. Preheat the oven to 425°F.

2. In a medium bowl, whisk together the oil, vinegar, shallot, garlic, mustard, sage, salt, and pepper. Reserve 4 tablespoons of this marinade for the salad greens.

3. In a casserole dish, combine the potatoes and half of the remaining marinade and toss until evenly coated. Add the chicken to a medium bowl with the rest of the remaining marinade, turning the chicken until evenly coated. Set aside the potatoes and refrigerate the chicken for 30 minutes.

4. Preheat the grill or grill pan over medium-high heat. Remove the chicken from the marinade and grill, turning occasionally, for 15 minutes, or until a thermometer inserted in the thickest portion registers 165°F and the juices run clear. Transfer to a cutting board and rest 5 minutes before cutting.

5. Place the greens in a serving bowl and toss with the reserved marinade. Top with the potatoes and chicken.

Nutrition (per serving): 369 calories, 28 g protein, 39 g total carbohydrates, 6 g fiber, 4 g sugars, 12 g total fat, 2 g saturated fat, 260 mg sodium

Seared Salmon Over Curried Lentils

PREP TIME: 15 MINUTES   *TOTAL TIME: 1 HOUR*   *SERVES: 4*

- 1 cup water
- ½ cup brown lentils, picked over and rinsed
- 4 whole cloves garlic, peeled
- 1 bay leaf
- ½ teaspoon salt, divided
- 1 teaspoon olive oil
- 1 cup chopped onion
- ½ cup chopped carrot
- 2 cloves garlic, minced
- ¾ teaspoon curry powder
- 1 tablespoon chopped fresh mint
- 4 salmon fillets (4 ounces each)
- ¼ teaspoon ground black pepper
- 4 lemon wedges (optional)

1. Combine the water, lentils, whole garlic cloves, bay leaf, and ¼ teaspoon of the salt in a medium saucepan over medium-high heat. Bring to a boil and reduce the heat to medium-low. Cover and simmer for 20 to 22 minutes, or until tender. Remove from the heat and discard the bay leaf and garlic cloves.

2. Heat the oil in a large skillet over medium-high heat. Add the onion and carrot and cook, stirring occasionally, for 2 to 3 minutes, or until starting to soften. Add the minced garlic and curry powder and cook, stirring, for 1 minute. Add the lentils and cook for 1 minute. Remove from the heat and stir in the mint. Divide among 4 plates.

3. Using a paper towel, wipe the skillet clean. Coat with nonaerosol cooking spray and heat over medium-high heat. Sprinkle the salmon with the pepper and the remaining ¼ teaspoon salt. Add to the skillet, skin side up, and cook for 4 minutes per side, or until the fish is opaque. Serve the salmon over the lentils with the lemon wedges, if desired.

Nutrition (per serving): 333 calories, 28 g protein, 17 g total carbohydrates, 6 g fiber, 3 g sugars, 17 g total fat, 3.5 g saturated fat, 376 mg sodium

Greek Lemon Chicken

PREP TIME: 15 MINUTES　　　*TOTAL TIME: 1 HOUR*　　　*SERVES: 4*

2 tablespoons olive oil, preferably extra-virgin
2 teaspoons grated lemon peel
4 tablespoons lemon juice
1 tablespoon minced garlic
1 teaspoon dried oregano
¾ teaspoon salt
¾ teaspoon ground black pepper
¾ teaspoon paprika
8 boneless, skinless chicken thighs, trimmed (about 1½ pounds total)
1 medium orange bell pepper, cut into 8 wedges
1 medium red bell pepper, cut into 8 wedges
2 medium Yukon gold potatoes, each cut into 8 wedges
1 medium red onion, cut in 8 wedges
8 pitted kalamata olives, each quartered lengthwise
Fresh mint or parsley leaves, for garnish
Lemon wedges, for garnish

1. Preheat the oven to 400°F. Coat a large rimmed baking sheet with nonaerosol cooking spray. Stir together the oil, lemon peel and lemon juice, garlic, oregano, salt, black pepper, and paprika.

2. Place the chicken on one side of the pan and the bell peppers, potatoes, and onion on the other. Pour lemon-garlic mixture over top and toss to coat.

3. Roast for 20 minutes. Turn the chicken and stir the vegetables. Roast for another 20 to 25 minutes, or until the juices run clear, and the vegetables are lightly browned and tender. Sprinkle with the olives. Garnish with the mint or parsley and lemon wedges, if using.

Nutrition (per serving): 373 calories, 30 g protein, 28 g total carbohydrates, 5 g fiber, 6 g sugars, 15 g total fat, 3 g saturated fat, 703 mg sodium

Grilled Fish and White Bean Salad

PREP TIME: 15 MINUTES   TOTAL TIME: 15 MINUTES   SERVES: 4

- 2 tablespoons extra-virgin olive oil
- 2 tablespoons lemon juice
- 1 teaspoon grated lemon peel
- Pinch of salt and ground black pepper
- 1½ cups precooked skinless grilled salmon or tuna pieces, broken into large chunks
- 2 cups cooked white beans
- 1 cup cooked green beans
- 1 cup grape tomatoes, halved
- ⅓ cup thinly sliced red onion
- 1½ teaspoons thinly shredded fresh sage or minced rosemary leaves

1. In a large bowl, whisk together the oil, lemon juice, lemon peel, and salt and pepper.

2. Measure out 1 tablespoon of the dressing and toss with the salmon or tuna in a medium bowl.

3. To the remaining dressing in the large bowl, add the white beans, green beans, tomatoes, onion, and sage or rosemary. Toss well.

4. Divide the vegetable mixture among 4 plates and top with the salmon or tuna. Serve at room temperature or chilled.

Nutrition (per serving): 374 calories, 32 g protein, 31 g total carbohydrates, 9 g fiber, 3 g sugars, 14 g total fat, 2 g saturated fat, 116 mg sodium

Tilapia and Spinach in Spicy Tomato Sauce

PREP TIME: 5 MINUTES   *TOTAL TIME: 25 MINUTES*   *SERVES: 6*

- ⅓ cup extra-virgin olive oil
- 1 tablespoon finely chopped garlic
- 1 can (14 ounces) diced Italian-seasoned tomatoes
- 1 cup chicken broth
- ½ teaspoon red-pepper flakes
- ½ teaspoon salt
- 2½ pounds tilapia fillets
- 1 bag (10 ounces) baby spinach leaves (10 cups)

1. In a large skillet, heat the oil and garlic over medium heat for 2 minutes, or until fragrant. Add the tomatoes (with juice), broth, red-pepper flakes, and salt. Bring to a boil. Reduce the heat to a brisk simmer. Cook for 8 minutes, or until the mixture thickens.

2. Place the fish in the pan. Press lightly to submerge it in the sauce. Cover and cook for 8 minutes, or until the fish flakes easily. Remove the fish to pasta bowls. Add the spinach to the skillet. Increase the heat to high. Cook, stirring occasionally, for 2 minutes, or until the spinach is wilted. Spoon over the reserved fish.

Nutrition (per serving): 333 calories, 9 g protein, 9 g total carbohydrates, 3 g fiber, 2 g sugars, 16 g total fat, 3 g saturated fat, 638 mg sodium

Mediterranean Cod

PREP TIME: 20 MINUTES   *TOTAL TIME: 30 MINUTES*   *SERVES: 4*

- ⅓ cup sun-dried tomato pesto
- 1 pound cod fillets, cut into 4 portions
- 2 bunches fennel (¾ pound), trimmed, halved, and sliced very thin crosswise
- 2 tablespoons chopped fennel fronds
- ⅓ cup halved pitted kalamata olives
- 1 cup whole fresh parsley leaves
- 1½ teaspoons lemon juice
- 1½ teaspoons olive oil
- Pinch of salt

1. Preheat the oven to 400°F. Coat an ovenproof pan with nonaerosol cooking spray.

2. Spoon 1 tablespoon of the pesto on each fillet. Arrange in the prepared pan with space in between. Roast for 9 minutes, or until the fish flakes easily. Remove from the oven.

3. Meanwhile, in a large bowl, combine the sliced fennel and fronds, olives, parsley, lemon juice, oil, and salt. Toss to mix.

4. Divide the salad among 4 plates and top each with 1 roasted cod portion.

Nutrition (per serving): 165 calories, 22 g protein, 10 g total carbohydrates, 4 g fiber, 1 g sugars, 4 g total fat, 0.5 g saturated fat, 437 mg sodium

Grilled Salmon with Brown Rice

PREP TIME: 5 MINUTES   *TOTAL TIME: 1 HOUR*   *SERVES: 2*

- ½ cup brown rice
- 2 salmon fillets (5–6 ounces each)
- 2 sprigs rosemary
- ¼ cup lemon juice
- Salt and ground black pepper

1. Cook the rice according to package directions.

2. Heat a grill or grill pan to medium-high. Place each salmon fillet on a piece of foil lined with parchment paper and place one rosemary sprig on top of each fillet. Sprinkle with lemon juice and season with salt and pepper. Fold the foil over the fish and wrap tightly, crimping the sides as you go to form a packet.

3. Place the fish on the grill and cook for 9 to 12 minutes. Turn the packets over and grill for 5 minutes longer. Remove from the grill and carefully open the packets—they will release a lot of steam. The salmon is done when it is opaque.

4. Remove and discard the rosemary sprigs. Serve the salmon over the rice.

Nutrition (per serving): 480 calories, 33 g protein, 40 g total carbohydrates, 3 g fiber, 1 g sugars, 20 g total fat, 5 g saturated fat, 163 mg sodium

Salmon in Vegetable Broth with Potato Slices

PREP TIME: 20 MINUTES   TOTAL TIME: 50 MINUTES   SERVES: 4

- 4 medium boiling potatoes, peeled and sliced ½" thick
- 1 small leek, thinly sliced
- 1 medium carrot, thinly sliced
- 1 small zucchini, finely chopped
- 4 large mushrooms, finely chopped
- 2 shallots, thinly sliced
- 1 cup dry fruity white wine or nonalcoholic white wine
- 1 teaspoon salt
- ¼ teaspoon ground black pepper
- 4 salmon steaks (1¼" thick), skin removed
- 2 tablespoons butter
- 1 tablespoon olive oil

1. Place the potatoes in a medium saucepan. Add cold water to cover. Bring to a boil over high heat. Cover, reduce the heat to low, and cook gently for 10 minutes, or until the slices are just tender when pierced with a fork. Drain, cover, and keep warm while you poach the salmon.

2. While the potatoes are cooking, prepare the poaching liquid. In a large skillet, combine the leeks, carrots, zucchini, mushrooms, shallots, wine, 1 cup water, salt, and pepper. Bring to a boil over high heat. Cover, reduce the heat to low, and cook gently for 10 minutes. Add the salmon to the skillet in a single layer, making sure that it's immersed in the liquid. Return the liquid to a boil, cover the pan, reduce the heat to low, and simmer gently for 2½ to 3 minutes, or until the salmon is cooked through and flakes easily when tested with a fork.

3. Divide the potatoes among soup plates. Using a slotted spoon, remove the salmon from the liquid and place it on top of the potatoes.

4. Add the butter and oil to the poaching liquid and vegetables in the skillet. Bring the mixture to a boil, and cook until liquid is reduced and thickened, about 10 minutes. Spoon the vegetables and sauce over and around the salmon. Serve immediately.

Nutrition (per serving): 510 calories, 28 g protein, 35 g total carbohydrates, 4 g fiber, 5 g sugars, 25 g total fat, 8 g saturated fat, 723 mg sodium

Mustard Greens with Dill and Lemon

PREP TIME: 5 MINUTES   *TOTAL TIME: 20 MINUTES*   *SERVES: 6*

- 2 tablespoons olive oil
- 1 onion, chopped
- 1 pound fresh mustard greens, chopped, or 2 packages (10 ounces each) frozen mustard greens, thawed and chopped
- ¼ cup lemon juice
- 2 tablespoons reduced-sodium soy sauce
- 1 tablespoon chopped fresh dill
- Ground black pepper

1. Heat the oil in a large skillet over medium heat. Add the onion and cook until softened.

2. Add the mustard greens and stir to mix. Cover and cook until the greens are tender, about 10 minutes.

3. Add the lemon juice, soy sauce, and dill. Stir to combine and cook for 1 minute longer. Season to taste with pepper.

Nutrition (per serving): 109 calories, 4 g protein, 10 g total carbohydrates, 4 g fiber, 3 g sugars, 7 g total fat, 1 g saturated fat, 297 mg sodium

Recipe courtesy of Sandy Gluck

Roasted Red Peppers with Anchovies

PREP TIME: 5 MINUTES   *TOTAL TIME: 5 MINUTES*   *SERVES: 8*

- 3 cups roasted red bell pepper strips
- 1 small clove garlic, finely chopped
- 6 oil-packed anchovies, thinly sliced
- 1 tablespoon oil from the tin of anchovies
   Pinch of red-pepper flakes
- 1 teaspoon white wine vinegar

In a large bowl, toss the bell pepper strips with the garlic and anchovies. Add the oil, red-pepper flakes, and vinegar. Toss gently.

Nutrition (per serving): 63 calories, 3 g protein, 9 g total carbohydrates, 1 g fiber, 4 g sugars, 3 g total fat, 0.5 g saturated fat, 574 mg sodium

Lemon-Garlic Roasted Cauliflower with Fennel and Gremolata

PREP TIME: 15 MINUTES　　　　*TOTAL TIME: 55 MINUTES*　　　　　　　*SERVES: 4*

- 1 clove garlic, finely chopped
- 1 teaspoon grated lemon peel
- 2 tablespoons chopped flat-leaf parsley
- 1 lemon, peeled and thinly sliced (about 6 slices), seeds removed
- 1 medium head cauliflower, cut into medium florets
- 1 bulb garlic, cloves separated and peeled
- 1 bulb fennel, cored and thinly sliced (about 2 cups)
- ¼ cup extra-virgin olive oil
- 1¼ teaspoons salt
- Ground black pepper

1. Preheat the oven to 400°F. For the gremolata, mix together the garlic, lemon peel, and parsley in a small bowl and set aside.

2. In a large bowl, place the lemon slices, cauliflower, garlic cloves, fennel, oil, salt, and a sprinkle of pepper, and toss together. Spread on a parchment-covered baking pan and roast for 40 minutes, stirring every 10 minutes, until the cauliflower has browned and the garlic is tender.

3. Transfer to a serving dish or to individual plates and sprinkle with the gremolata. Serve hot.

Nutrition (per serving): 199 calories, 4 g protein, 16 g total carbohydrates, 6 g fiber, 3 g sugars, 15 g total fat, 2 g saturated fat, 804 mg sodium

Bulgur with Mushrooms and Roasted Red Peppers

PREP TIME: 10 MINUTES   *TOTAL TIME: 20 MINUTES*   *SERVES: 2*

- 1 tablespoon olive oil
- ¼ cup finely chopped onion
- ½ teaspoon smoked paprika
- 2 cups mushrooms (such as shiitake, maitake, oyster, or a blend), chopped
- 2 cups baby spinach leaves
- 1 roasted red pepper, chopped (about ⅔ cup)
- 1 cup cooked bulgur*
- ¼ cup cooked lentils*
-    Salt
-    Ground black pepper
- 1 teaspoon sherry vinegar

1. Heat the oil in a large skillet over medium heat. Add the onion and cook until it softens, about 4 minutes. Add the paprika and stir to combine. Add the mushrooms and cook until they brown, 5 to 8 minutes.

2. Add the spinach, red pepper, bulgur, and lentils, and cook, stirring, until hot, about 2 minutes. The spinach should just begin to wilt from the heat of the other ingredients. Season to taste with salt and pepper. Divide the mixture between 2 bowls and drizzle with the vinegar.

Nutrition (per serving): 244 calories, 8 g protein, 37 g total carbohydrates, 12 g fiber, 5 g sugars, 8 g total fat, 1 g saturated fat, 391 mg sodium

*To prepare, follow the package instructions.

Recipe courtesy of Joy Manning

Zucchini and Carrots with Toasted Walnuts

PREP TIME: 15 MINUTES   TOTAL TIME: 25 MINUTES   SERVES: 4

- ½ cup chopped walnuts
- 2 medium zucchini
- 2 large carrots, peeled
- 1 tablespoon olive oil
- ⅛ teaspoon dried thyme
- ¼ teaspoon salt
- ⅛ teaspoon ground black pepper

1. In a large nonstick skillet over medium heat, cook the walnuts, stirring often, for 3 to 4 minutes, or until lightly browned and fragrant. Tip onto a plate. Remove the skillet from the heat and wipe it out with a paper towel.

2. Halve the zucchini lengthwise and cut the halves crosswise in two. Cut each piece into thin strips lengthwise.

3. Use a vegetable peeler to cut long strips from the carrots, reserving the core for another meal.

4. Heat the oil in the same skillet over medium heat. Add the carrots and sprinkle with the thyme, salt, and pepper. Cook, tossing often, for 3 minutes, or until nearly tender. Add the zucchini and cook, tossing, for 3 to 4 minutes, or until tender. Sprinkle with the walnuts.

Nutrition (per serving): 156 calories, 4 g protein, 9 g total carbohydrates, 3 g fiber, 4 g sugars, 13 g total fat, 1 g saturated fat, 180 mg sodium

Yogurt-Blueberry Bites

PREP TIME: 15 MINUTES   *TOTAL TIME: 1 HOUR 15 MINUTES*   *SERVES: 2*

6 ounces plain 0% Greek yogurt

1 teaspoon vanilla extract

2 cups fresh blueberries, divided

1. Cover a large baking sheet or 2 large flat plates with aluminum foil or parchment paper.

2. In a blender, combine the yogurt, vanilla, and ⅓ cup of the blueberries. Blend until smooth. Pour into a bowl.

3. Using a toothpick or your fingers, dip the remaining blueberries into the yogurt mixture, coating each one thoroughly. Place each on the baking sheet and freeze for 1 hour, or until the yogurt has hardened.

4. Transfer the blueberries to a sealed container or resealable plastic bag. Store in the freezer until ready to eat.

Nutrition (per serving): 135 calories, 9 g protein, 25 g total carbohydrates, 4 g fiber, 18 g sugars, 1 g total fat, 0 g saturated fat, 34 mg sodium

Honey-Berry Ice Pops

PREP TIME: 10 MINUTES   TOTAL TIME: 4 HOURS 15 MINUTES   SERVES: 6

⅔ cup blueberries

30 small mint leaves

1⅓ cups raspberries

1½ cups seltzer

2 tablespoons light floral honey, such as acacia

2 tablespoons lemon juice

1. Evenly layer the blueberries, mint, and raspberries in 6 ice pop molds.

2. Gently stir together the seltzer, honey, and lemon juice in a measuring cup until the honey dissolves. Pour very slowly over the berries and mint. (Note: There should be about ½" of space at the top of each mold to allow for expansion during freezing. Adjust the liquid accordingly.) Insert handles or sticks into the molds. Freeze for at least 4 hours.

Nutrition (per serving): 46 calories, 1 g protein, 12 g total carbohydrates, 2 g fiber, 9 g sugars, 0 g total fat, 0 g saturated fat, 1 mg sodium

Baked Apples with Almonds and Maple Syrup

PREP TIME: 15 MINUTES   TOTAL TIME: 30 MINUTES   SERVES: 4

- 2 tablespoons sliced almonds
- 4 organic Granny Smith apples
- 2 tablespoons lemon juice
- 1 teaspoon canola oil
- ¼ cup organic apple cider
- 1 tablespoon maple syrup
- ¼ teaspoon grated lemon peel
- ¼ teaspoon vanilla extract
- ¼ teaspoon ground cinnamon
- ¼ teaspoon ground cloves

1. In a dry skillet over medium heat, toast the almonds, shaking often, for 3 to 5 minutes or until fragrant and golden. Set aside to cool.

2. Peel, core, and slice the apples and toss them with the lemon juice in a large bowl. Heat the oil in a large skillet over medium-high heat. Add the apples and cook, stirring, for 2 minutes. Reduce the heat to low, then cover and simmer, stirring occasionally, for 5 to 8 minutes or until the apples are just tender. Using a slotted spoon, carefully divide the apples among 4 dessert dishes.

3. To the skillet, add the cider, maple syrup, lemon peel, vanilla, cinnamon, and cloves. Cook over medium-high heat, stirring constantly, until syrupy. Spoon over the apples. Sprinkle with the almonds.

Nutrition (per serving): 114 calories, 1 g protein, 24 g total carbohydrates, 2 g fiber, 17 g sugars, 3 g total fat, 0.5 g saturated fat, 1 mg sodium

Warm and Creamy Fruit Dessert

PREP TIME: 10 MINUTES   TOTAL TIME: 15 MINUTES   SERVES: 2

- 1 Granny Smith apple, cored and chopped
- 1 navel orange, peeled and chopped
- 1 teaspoon ground cinnamon
- ½ cup fat-free vanilla yogurt
- 2 tablespoons pecan or walnut pieces

Combine the apple, orange, and cinnamon in a medium microwaveable bowl. Cover with a microwaveable lid and microwave on high for 4 minutes, or until the fruit is hot and soft. Divide between 2 bowls, and spoon the yogurt evenly over each. Sprinkle with the pecans or walnuts and serve warm.

Nutrition (per serving): 175 calories, 5 g protein, 30 g total carbohydrates, 4 g fiber, 24 g sugars, 6 g total fat, 0.5 g saturated fat, 44 mg sodium

Candied Spiced Nuts

PREP TIME: 15 MINUTES   TOTAL TIME: 1 HOUR 15 MINUTES   SERVES: 18

- 1 egg white
- ½ pound shelled walnut halves
- ½ pound shelled almonds
- ½ cup sugar (preferably superfine)
- 1 tablespoon ground cinnamon
- 1 teaspoon ground ginger
- 1 teaspoon salt
- ½ teaspoon ground coriander
- ¼ teaspoon ground allspice
- ¼ teaspoon ground black pepper

1. Preheat the oven to 250°F.

2. In a medium bowl, whisk the egg white and water until frothy. Add the walnuts and almonds and stir to coat completely.

3. Add the sugar, cinnamon, ginger, salt, coriander, allspice, and pepper to the bowl and toss to coat.

4. Spread the nuts in a single layer on a baking sheet. Bake them 15 minutes and then stir, smoothing the nuts back into a single layer. Lower the oven temperature to 200°F and bake until the nuts are caramelized, about 45 minutes.

5. Allow the nuts to cool. Store in an airtight container at room temperature for up to 2 weeks.

Nutrition (per serving): 175 calories, 5 g protein, 8 g total carbohydrates, 3 g fiber, 5 g sugars, 15 g total fat, 1 g saturated fat, 133 mg sodium

Wine-Poached Ginger Pears

PREP TIME: 10 MINUTES   TOTAL TIME: 50 MINUTES + CHILLING TIME   SERVES: 4

- 4 ripe, firm medium pears
- 4 pieces (1" each) crystallized ginger
- 1 cup red wine
- 1 cup water
- 2 tablespoons honey
- 3 thin strips lemon peel
- ½ teaspoon ground cinnamon

1. Peel the pears, leaving the stems intact. Use a corer or sharp knife to remove the bottom "flower" and about 1½" of the core. Place 1 piece of the ginger into each hollow.

2. Place the pears upright in a medium pot. Add the wine, water, honey, lemon peel, and cinnamon. Cover the pot and place over medium-low heat. Simmer the pears for 20 minutes. Uncover the pot and gently lay the pears on their sides. Cover and simmer for 10 minutes. Uncover and gently turn each pear over to its other side. Simmer, uncovered, for 10 minutes.

3. Stand the pears upright in a medium glass bowl. Pour the wine syrup over the pears. Cover and refrigerate for several hours or overnight.

Nutrition (per serving): 197 calories, 1 g protein, 41 g total carbohydrates, 6 g fiber, 28 g sugars, 0 g total fat, 0 g saturated fat, 8 mg sodium

Greek Yogurt with Apricots, Honey, and Crunch

PREP TIME: 5 MINUTES   *TOTAL TIME: 5 MINUTES*   *SERVES: 1*

1 cup plain 0% Greek yogurt
5 canned apricot halves in juice, thinly sliced
4 tablespoons Grape-Nuts cereal
1 tablespoon slivered almonds
1 teaspoon honey

Spoon about half of the yogurt into a parfait glass. Top with 2 tablespoons each of the apricots and cereal. Repeat. Top with the almonds and honey.

Nutrition (per serving): *388 calories, 20 g protein, 72 g total carbohydrates, 6 g fiber, 48 g sugars, 4 g total fat, 0.5 g saturated fat, 373 mg sodium*

Grilled Peaches

PREP TIME: 5 MINUTES   TOTAL TIME: 15 MINUTES   SERVES: 4

1   tablespoon olive oil
1   tablespoon lemon juice
2   peaches, halved
¼   teaspoon ground cinnamon
    Pinch of ground black pepper

1. Preheat the grill or grill pan over medium-high heat.

2. In a small bowl, whisk together the oil and lemon juice. Brush the mixture over the cut sides of the peaches and place them on the grill grates or grill pan. Brush the mixture over the peach tops. Season with the cinnamon and pepper.

3. Grill for 3 minutes, turn, and then grill for 3 minutes more.

4. Remove from the heat and let cool. Slice thinly.

Nutrition (per serving): 50 calories, 1 g protein, 5 g total carbohydrates, 1 g fiber, 4 g sugars, 4 g total fat, 0.5 g saturated fat, 0 mg sodium

APPENDIX

THE AGELESS BRAIN STRENGTH-TRAINING WORKOUT

WHETHER YOU STRENGTH-TRAIN REGULARLY or have never even held a dumbbell, this total-body workout can help shape your muscles as it protects your brain. Our workout includes two routines—seated and standing—and each routine features 10 simple exercises. Perform the seated routine twice a week for 2 to 3 weeks. When you have it down cold, switch to the more challenging standing routine. In another 2 to 3 weeks, return to the seated routine, but increase the challenge for as many of the moves as you can (we've offered ways to do that in each exercise).

After that? Keep up the good work, and strive to improve. For example, you might move up to the next dumbbell size, or add another set of 10 repetitions. Changing up your routine every so often doesn't just challenge your muscles—it helps keep your brain nimble, too.

For each exercise, perform two sets of 10 repetitions. If any of these moves feels too easy, increase the challenge by sitting on a blowup stability ball rather than a chair.

CHEST SQUEEZE

1. Sit up straight on a chair, with your feet flat on the floor and shoulder-width apart.

2. Hold a lightweight ball (or pillow) close to your chest. Squeeze the ball with your palms to contract your chest muscles. While continuing to squeeze, slowly push the ball in front of you at chest level until your elbows are almost straight. Bend your elbows and pull back to the chest. That is 1 rep.

To challenge your brain (and body) even more: For even more of a challenge, lift one foot from the floor.

SHOULDER RETRACTION

1. Sit up straight on a chair, with your feet flat on the floor and shoulder-width apart.

2. Make a fist, with your palms facing the floor. Push your arms out in front of you at chest level. Do not completely straighten your elbows. Bend your elbows and pull them back, squeezing your shoulder blades together, slightly behind your torso. Hold for 3 seconds. That is 1 rep.

To challenge your brain (and body) even more: For even more of a challenge, lift one foot from the floor.

CURL AND PRESS

1. Sit up straight on a chair, with your feet flat on the floor and shoulder-width apart.

2. With your right elbow close to your body and your forearm extended out to the side, hold a dumbbell of 3 pounds in your right hand, palm up. Curl your arm up to a biceps curl. When you reach shoulder height, continue to push your arm up and over your head. Slowly bring the weight back down to the starting position. That is 1 rep.

3. Repeat on the other side.

TRICEPS EXTENSION

1. Sit up straight on a chair, with your feet flat on the floor and shoulder-width apart.

2. Grip a dumbbell of 5 or more pounds with both hands. Lift your arms straight up overhead. Keep your elbows slightly bent. Pause for a moment, then bend your elbows, lowering the weight behind your head so that your elbows are at 90 degrees. Straighten your arms and return to the starting position. That is 1 rep.

To challenge your brain (and body) even more: Perform the exercise using just one arm at a time.

LEG TAPS

1. Sit up straight on a chair, with your feet flat on the floor and shoulder-width apart. Place a ball or another object about 6 inches in front of you on the floor.

2. Lift your right foot and tap your toes on the top of the ball. Then take your foot back down and tap the floor. That is 1 rep. Do this as fast as you can for one set.

3. Repeat on the other side.

To challenge your brain (and body) even more: Switch feet back and forth as you tap.

LEG EXTENSIONS

1. Sit up straight on a chair, with your feet flat on the floor and your knees together.

2. Squeeze your right quadriceps as hard as you can to straighten your leg, foot flexed. Hold for 3 seconds. Bend your knee, lowering your foot until you lightly touch the floor. That is 1 rep.

3. Repeat on the other side.

THIGH SQUEEZE

1. Sit up straight on a chair with your feet flat on the floor and shoulder-width apart.

2. Place a ball or pillow between your knees. Squeeze the ball by contracting your inner thighs as much as you can. Hold for 3 seconds. That is 1 rep.

THIGH PUSH

Note: Start with the lowest-tension resistance band available. As you get stronger, you can progress to a band with more tension.

1. Sit up straight on a chair with your feet flat on the floor.

2. Place a resistance band around your mid-thighs. Lift your right foot slightly off the floor and step out to the right side. Tap your toe on the floor. Hold for 3 seconds. Then bring your foot back to the starting position. That is 1 rep.

3. Repeat on the other side.

ABS ROTATION

1. Sit up straight on a chair with your feet flat on the floor and shoulder-width apart. With both hands, hold a 3- to 5-pound dumbbell in front of your chest, arms extended and elbows slightly bent.

2. Contract your abs and rotate your torso to the right, keeping your hips facing forward. Contract your abs to bring yourself back to the center, then rotate to the left. That is 1 rep.

To challenge your brain (and body) even more: Lean back slightly to work your abs a little more.

BACKWARD LEAN

1. Sit up straight on a chair with your feet flat on the floor and shoulder-width apart. Cross your arms in front of your chest.

2. Contract your abs. Lean back as far as you can while keeping your feet on the floor. Hold for 3 seconds. Return to the starting position and repeat. That is 1 rep.

To challenge your brain (and body) even more: Lift one foot a few inches off the floor as you lean back.

Note: Some of these exercises require dumbbells. To start, use dumbbells that weigh 3 to 5 pounds (or use 12-ounce water bottles—full, of course). As you get stronger, you can increase the weight of your dumbbells. For each exercise, perform two sets of 10 repetitions.

STANDING PUSHUP

1. Stand an arm's length from the wall with your feet shoulder-width apart.

2. Lean forward, placing your palms against the wall at shoulder height.

3. Bend your elbows until your nose nearly touches the wall.

4. Push back to the starting position. That is 1 rep.

To challenge your brain (and body) even more: Use only one arm for half the reps and then switch to the other arm for the rest of the reps.

BACK PULL

1. Stand upright. Place your feet shoulder-width apart. Grip a towel with your hands shoulder-width apart.

2. Extend the towel out in front of you. Pull back and squeeze your shoulder blades together as tightly as you can. Hold for 3 seconds. That is 1 rep.

To challenge your brain (and body) even more: Try doing it while balanced on just one foot.

FRONT ARM RAISE

1. Stand upright with your feet shoulder-width apart.

2. Hold a dumbbell in each hand, palms down. Lift your arms directly in front of you to shoulder height. That is 1 rep.

To challenge your brain (and body) even more: *Try doing it while balanced on just one foot.*

BICEPS CURL TO SHOULDER PUSH

1. Stand upright with your feet shoulder-width apart.

2. Hold a dumbbell in each hand with your palms facing each other. Starting with your arms at your sides, lift the dumbbells to shoulder height, then take them directly over your head. That is 1 rep.

To challenge your brain (and body) even more: Try doing it while balanced on just one foot or while marching in place.

KNEE LIFT

1. Stand upright on your right leg while supporting yourself with the back of a chair.

2. With your right knee slightly bent, raise your left knee to hip height. Hold for 3 seconds. That is 1 rep.

3. After finishing your reps, repeat on the other side.

***To challenge your brain (and body) even more:** Work your balance as you lift your leg, only placing your hand against the chair as needed.*

LEG PUSHBACK

1. Stand upright on your right leg while supporting yourself with the back of a chair.

2. With your right knee slightly bent, push your left leg back. Squeeze the gluteal muscles as tightly as you can. Hold for 3 seconds. That is 1 rep.

3. After finishing your reps, repeat on the other side.

To challenge your brain (and body) even more: Work your balance as you lift your leg, only placing your hand against the chair as needed.

LEG SIDE PRESS

1. Stand upright on your right leg while supporting yourself with the back of a chair.

2. With your right knee slightly bent, extend your left leg to the side as far as you can. Hold for 3 seconds. That is 1 rep.

3. After finishing your reps, repeat on the other side.

To challenge your brain (and body) even more: Work your balance as you lift your leg, only placing your hand against the chair as needed.

LEG SIDE PULL

1. Stand upright on your left leg while supporting yourself with the back of a chair.

2. With your left knee slightly bent, slightly raise your right leg; pull your right knee toward your middle and hold for 3 seconds. That is 1 rep.

3. After finishing your reps, repeat on the other side.

To challenge your brain (and body) even more: Work your balance as you lift your leg, only placing your hand against the chair as needed.

SIDE BENDS

1. Stand upright with your feet shoulder-width apart. Push your shoulders back.

2. Squeeze your sides while bending to the right. Hold for 1 second. That is 1 rep.

3. Repeat on the opposite side.

To challenge your brain (and body) even more: Do the same move with one or both arms elevated overhead.

ELBOW-TO-KNEE CRUNCH

1. Stand upright on your right leg while supporting yourself with the back of a chair. Extend your left elbow to the side at shoulder level and touch your hand to the side of your head.

2. Squeeze your side while lifting your left knee to your left elbow. Hold for 3 seconds. Return to the starting position. That is 1 rep.

3. Repeat on the opposite side.

To challenge your brain (and body) even more: Work your balance as you lift your leg, only placing your hand against the chair as needed.

ENDNOTES

Chapter 1

1   "Differences between mild memory loss and more serious memory problems," Understanding Memory Loss: What To Do When You Have Trouble Remembering, National Institute on Aging, updated October 22, 2015, https://www.nia.nih.gov /alzheimers/publication/understanding-memory-loss/differences-between-mild -forgetfulness-and-more.

2   "Nearly 60 percent of people worldwide incorrectly believe that Alzheimer's disease is a typical part of aging," Alzheimer's Association, June 19, 2014, http://www.alz.org/news _and_events_60_percent_incorrectly_believe.asp.

3   "Alzheimer's Disease Facts and Figures," Alzheimer's Association, http://www.alz.org /mglc/in_my_community_60862.asp.

4   Matthew Baumgart et al., "Summary of the evidence on modifiable risk factors for cognitive decline and dementia: A population-based perspective," *Alzheimer's & Dementia* 11, no. 06(June 2015): 718–726, http://www.sciencedirect.com/science/article/pii/ S1552526015001971.

5   "Risk Factors," Alzheimer's Association, http://www.alz.org/alzheimers_disease _causes_risk_factors.asp.

6   "What Is Alzheimer's?" Alzheimer's Association, http://www.alz.org/alzheimers _disease_what_is_alzheimers.asp.

7   J. R. Richardson et al., "Elevated Serum Pesticide Levels and Risk for Alzheimer Disease," *JAMA Neurology* 71, no. 3(2014): 284–90, http://www.ncbi.nlm.nih.gov/pmc /articles/PMC4132934/.

8   W. Gomm et al., "Association of Proton Pump Inhibitors With Risk of Dementia: A Pharmacoepidemiological Claims Data Analysis," *JAMA Neurology*, published online February 15, 2016, http://archneur.jamanetwork.com/article.aspx?articleid=2487379.

9   "Serious memory problems—causes and treatments," Understanding Memory Loss: What To Do When You Have Trouble Remembering, National Institute on Aging, updated October 22, 2015, https://www.nia.nih.gov/alzheimers/publication/understanding -memory-loss/serious-memory-problems-causes-and-treatments.

10   J. S. Saczynski et al., "Depressive symptoms and risk of dementia: The Framingham Heart Study," *Neurology* 75, no. 1(2010): 35–41, podcast, http://www.ncbi.nlm.nih.gov/pmc /articles/PMC2906404/.

11   "Younger/Early Onset Alzheimer's & Dementia," Alzheimer's Association, http://www .alz.org/alzheimers_disease_early_onset.asp.

12   Tiia Ngandu et al., "A 2 year multidomain intervention of diet, exercise, cognitive training, and vascular risk monitoring versus control to prevent cognitive decline in at-risk elderly people (FINGER): a randomised controlled trial," *The Lancet* 385, no. 9984:2255–63, http://www.thelancet.com/journals/lancet/article/PIIS0140-6736(15)60461-5/fulltext.

13   "Cognitive Aging: An Action Guide for Individuals and Families," National Academy of Sciences, 2015, http://www.nationalacademies.org/hmd/~/media/Files/Report%20 Files/2015/Cognitive_aging/Action%20Guide%20for%20Individuals%20and%20Families _V3.pdf.

14   "FAU Neuroscientist Shares Myths and Truths About Alzheimer's," Florida Atlantic University, November 12, 2015, http://www.fau.edu/newsdesk/articles/AD-MythsTruths.php.

15   "Alzheimer's Disease Fact Sheet," https://www.nia.nih.gov/alzheimers/publication/alzheimers-disease-fact-sheet.

16   "Cognitive Skills and Normal Aging," Emory University Alzheimer's Disease Research Center, http://alzheimers.emory.edu/healthy_aging/cognitive-skills-normal-aging.html.

17   "Cognitive Skills Peak at Different Ages Across Adulthood," Association for Psychological Science, March 6, 2015, http://www.psychologicalscience.org/index.php/news/releases/cognitive-skills-peak-at-different-ages-across-adulthood.html.

18   M.A. Shafto et al., "On the Tip-of-the-Tongue: Neural Correlates of Increased Word-Finding Failures in Normal Aging," *Journal of Cognitive Neuroscience* 19, no. 12(2007): 2060–70, https://www.ncbi.nlm.nih.gov/pmc/articles/PMC2373253/.

19   *Brain Facts: A Primer on the Brain and Nervous System.* Society of Neuroscience, 2012.

20   *2016 Alzheimer's Facts and Figures*, Alzheimer's Association, https://www.alz.org/documents_custom/2016-facts-and-figures.pdf.

21   A. Altmann et al., "Sex Modifies the APOE-Related Risk of Developing Alzheimer's Disease," *Annals of Neurology* 75, no. 4(2014): 563–73, https://www.ncbi.nlm.nih.gov/pmc/articles/PMC4117990/.

22   *2016 Alzheimer's Facts and Figures*, https://www.alz.org/documents_custom/2016-facts-and-figures.pdf.

23   K. A. Lin, P. M. Doraiswamy, "When Mars Versus Venus is Not a Cliché: Gender Differences in the Neurobiology of Alzheimer's Disease," *Frontiers in Neurology* 5(2014): 288, http://www.ncbi.nlm.nih.gov/pmc/articles/PMC4290582.

24   G. Chêne et al., "Gender and incidence of dementia in the Framingham Heart Study from mid-adult life," *Alzheimer's & Dementia* 11, no. 3(2015): 310–20, https://www.ncbi.nlm.nih.gov/pmc/articles/PMC4092061/.

25   Susan Jeffry, "More Evidence Brain Games Boost Cognitive Health," Medscape, July 14, 2014, http:/www.medscape.com/viewarticle/828285.

26   "A Consensus on the Brain Training Industry from the Scientific Community," Max Planck Institute for Human Development and Stanford Center on Longevity, accessed 8/30/2016, http://longevity3.stanford.edu/blog/2014/10/15/the-consensus-on-the-brain-training-industry-from-the-scientific-community/.

27   "Computerized brain training designed to improve visual attention reduces dementia risk," University of South Florida at Tampa, July 22, 2016, https://hscweb3.hsc.usf.edu/blog/2016/07/22/computerized-brain-training-designed-to-improve-visual-attention-reduces-dementia-risk/.

28   *2016 Alzheimer's Facts and Figures*, https://www.alz.org/documents_custom/2016-facts-and-figures.pdf.

29   Lisa Ronan et al., "Obesity associated with increased brain age from midlife," *Neurobiology of Aging* 47:63–70, http://www.neurobiologyofaging.org/article/S0197-4580(16)30140-3/abstract.

30   J. Z. Willey et al., "Leisure-time physical activity associates with cognitive decline: The Northern Manhattan Study," *Neurology* 86, no. 20(2016 May 17): 1897–903, http://www.neurology.org/content/early/2016/03/23/WNL.0000000000002582.abstract.

31   M. C. Morris et al., "Associations of vegetable and fruit consumption with age-related cognitive change," *Neurology* 67, no. 8(2006): 1370–76, https://www.ncbi.nlm.nih.gov/pmc/articles/PMC3393520/.

32   E. E. Devore et al., "Dietary intakes of berries and flavonoids in relation to cognitive decline," *Annals of Neurology* 72, no. 1(July 2012): 135–43, http://onlinelibrary.wiley.com/doi/10.1002/ana.23594/abstract.

33 ———. "Sleep duration in midlife and later life in relation to cognition," *Journal of the American Geriatrics Society* 62, no. 6(2014): 1073–81, http://www.ncbi.nlm.nih.gov/pmc/articles/PMC4188530/.

Chapter 2

1 "Explorers of the Brain: Research from the Frontiers of Neuroscience," National Science Foundation, transcript, http://www.nsf.gov/news/newsmedia/transcript_brainexplorers.jsp.

2 Vyara Valkanova et al., "Mind over matter—what do we know about neuroplasticity in adults?" *International Psychogeriatrics* 26, no. 06(June 2014): 891–909, http://journals.cambridge.org/action/

3 "Brain Basics: Know Your Brain," National Institute of Neurological Disorders and Stroke, National Institutes of Health, last modified April 17, 2015, http://www.ninds.nih.gov/disorders/brain_basics/know_your_brain.htm.

4 Ibid.

5 Ibid.

6 Steven A. Goldman, "Brain," Merck Manuals, https://www.merckmanuals.com/home/brain,-spinal-cord,-and-nerve-disorders/biology-of-the-nervous-system/brain.

7 "The Changing Brain in Healthy Aging," National Institute on Aging, updated January 22, 2015, https://www.nia.nih.gov/alzheimers/publication/part-1-basics-healthy-brain/changing-brain-healthy-aging.

8 S. A. Goldman, "Effects of Aging on the Nervous System," Merck Manual, consumer version, https://www.merckmanuals.com/home/brain,-spinal-cord,-and-nerve-disorders/biology-of-the-nervous-system/effects-of-aging-on-the-nervous-system.

9 *Brain Facts: A Primer on the Brain and Nervous System*, Society of Neuroscience (2012), 41.

10 "The Changing Brain in Healthy Aging," https://www.nia.nih.gov/alzheimers/publication/part-1-basics-healthy-brain/changing-brain-healthy-aging.

11 Ibid.

12 D. A. Bennett et al., "Overview and findings from the religious orders study," *Current Alzheimer Research* 9, no. 6(2012): 628–45, http://www.ncbi.nlm.nih.gov/pmc/articles/PMC3409291/.

13 ———. "Selected Findings from the Religious Orders Study and Rush Memory and Aging Project," *Journal of Alzheimer's Disease* 33, no. 0(2013): S397–S403, http://www.ncbi.nlm.nih.gov/pmc/articles/PMC3434299/.

14 "What Is Alzheimer's?" http://www.alz.org/alzheimers_disease_what_is_alzheimers.asp#brain.

15 Ibid.

16 R. S. Wilson et al., "Participation in Cognitively Stimulating Activities and Risk of Incident Alzheimer Disease," *Journal of the American Medical Association* 287, no. 6(2002): 742–48, http://jama.jamanetwork.com/article.aspx?articleid=194636#REF-JOC11682-9.

17 B. D. James et al., "Late-Life Social Activity and Cognitive Decline in Old Age," *Journal of the International Neuropsychological Society* 17, no. 6(2011): 998–1005, http://www.ncbi.nlm.nih.gov/pmc/articles/PMC3206295/.

18 Robert S. Wilson et al., "Clinical-pathologic study of depressive symptoms and cognitive decline in old age," *Neurology* 83, no. 8(August 19, 2014): 702–9, http://www.neurology.org/content/83/8/702.

19 ———. "Loneliness and risk of Alzheimer disease," *Archives of General Psychiatry* 64, no. 2(2007): 234–240, http://archpsyc.jamanetwork.com/article.aspx?articleid=482179.

20 "Inside the Brain: Alzheimer's Brain Tour," Alzheimer's Association, http://www.alz .org/research/science/alzheimers_brain_tour.asp.

21 "The life and death of a neuron," National Institute of Neurological Disorders and Stroke, http://www.ninds.nih.gov/education/brochures/NeuronBrocSinglePG-508.pdf.

22 "Neurons and Their Jobs," National Institute on Aging, https://www.nia.nih.gov /alzheimers/publication/part-1-basics-healthy-brain/neurons-and-their-jobs.

23 "The life and death of a neuron," http://www.ninds.nih.gov/education/brochures /NeuronBrocSinglePG-508.pdf.

24 "Neurons Firing," video, https://www.youtube.com/watch?v=yy994HpFudc.

25 Stephanie Liou, "Neuroplasticity," Stanford University, June 26, 2010, http://web .stanford.edu/group/hopes/cgi-bin/hopes_test/neuroplasticity/.

26 Valkanova et al., "Mind over matter—what do we know about neuroplasticity in adults?" http://journals.cambridge.org/action/displayAbstract?fromPage=online&aid=9246 576&fileId=S104161021300248.

27 Klaus Ebmeier, "Mind over matter," blog post, Cambridge University Press, June 27, 2014, http://blog.journals.cambridge.org/2014/06/27/mind-over-matter/.

28 Valkanova et al., "Mind over matter—what do we know about neuroplasticity in adults?" http://journals.cambridge.org/action/displayAbstract?fromPage=online&aid=9246 576&fileId=S104161021300248.

29 Ibid.

30 "Neurotransmitters, Synapses, and Impulse Transmission," *Molecular Cell Biology*, 4th Edition, http://www.ncbi.nlm.nih.gov/books/NBK21521/.

31 "Brain Basics," National Institute of Mental Health (NIMH), http://www.nimh.nih .gov/health/educational-resources/brain-basics/brain-basics.shtml.

32 "Brain Basics: Know Your Brain," http://www.ninds.nih.gov/disorders/brain_basics /know_your_brain.htm.

33 "Brain Basics," http://www.nimh.nih.gov/health/educational-resources/brain-basics /brain-basics.shtml.

34 *Brain Facts: A Primer on the Brain and Nervous System.* Society of Neuroscience, 2012.

35 "Brain makes its own version of Valium, scientists discover," Stanford Medicine News Center, May 30, 2013, http://med.stanford.edu/news/all-news/2013/05/brain-makes-its -own-version-of-valium-scientists-discover.html.

36 "Brain Basics: Know Your Brain," http://www.ninds.nih.gov/disorders/brain_basics /know_your_brain.htm.

37 "Lumosity to Pay $2 Million to Settle FTC Deceptive Advertising Charges for Its 'Brain Training' Program," Federal Trade Commission, January 5, 2016, https://www.ftc.gov /news-events/press-releases/2016/01/lumosity-pay-2-million-settle-ftc-deceptive -advertising-charges.

38 "Language experience and the brain: variability, neuroplasticity, and bilingualism," *Language, Cognition and Neuroscience* 31, no. 3(2016), http://www.tandfonline.com/doi/full /10.1080/23273798.2015.1086009.

39 R. Katzman et al., "Clinical, pathological, and neurochemical changes in dementia: a subgroup with preserved mental status and numerous neocortical plaques," *Annals of Neurology* 23, no. 2(February 1988): 138–44, https://www.ncbi.nlm.nih.gov/ pubmed/2897823.

40   "Inside the Human Brain," National Institute on Aging, last updated January 22, 2015, https://www.nia.nih.gov/alzheimers/publication/part-1-basics-healthy-brain /inside-human-brain.

41   Ibid.

42   "Brain Basics: Know Your Brain," http://www.ninds.nih.gov/disorders/brain_basics /know_your_brain.htm.

43   A. M. Tucker, Y. Stern, "Cognitive reserve in aging," *Current Alzheimer Research* 8, no. 3(2011): 1–7 https://www.ncbi.nlm.nih.gov/pubmed/21222591.

44   Y. Stern, "Cognitive Reserve," *Neuropsychologia* 47, no. 10(2009): 2015–28, http://www .ncbi.nlm.nih.gov/pmc/articles/PMC2739591/.

45   "Learning the London Knowledge," http://www.theknowledgetaxi.co.uk/.

46   Eleanor A. Maguire et al., "Navigation-related structural change in the hippocampi of taxi drivers," *Proceedings of the National Academy of Sciences of the United States of America* 97, no. 8(April 11, 2000), http://www.pnas.org/content/97/8/4398.full.

47   Ibid.

48   Megan E. Lenehan et al., "Sending your grandparents to university increases cognitive reserve: The Tasmanian Healthy Brain Project," *Neuropsychology*, published online Nov. 16, 2015, http://www.ncbi.nlm.nih.gov/pubmed/26569028.

49   David A. Bennett et al., "The effect of social networks on the relation between Alzheimer's disease pathology and level of cognitive function in old people: a longitudinal cohort study," *Lancet Neurology* 5(5): 406–412, http://www.thelancet.com/journals/laneur /article/PIIS1474-4422(06)70417-3/abstract.

50   Stern, "Cognitive Reserve," http://www.ncbi.nlm.nih.gov/pmc/articles/PMC2739591/.

51   "Normal aging vs dementia," Alzheimer Society of Canada, http://www.alzheimer.ca /en/About-dementia/What-is-dementia/Normal-aging-vs-dementia.

52   "Mild Cognitive Impairment," Alzheimer's Association, http://www.alz.org/dementia /mild-cognitive-impairment-mci.asp.

53   "Mild Cognitive Impairment," UCSF Memory and Aging Center, http://memory.ucsf .edu/education/diseases/mci.

54   Ibid.

55   "Mild Cognitive Impairment," http://www.alz.org/dementia/mild-cognitive -impairment-mci.asp.

56   "Mild Cognitive Impairment," http://memory.ucsf.edu/education/diseases/mci.

57   "Mild Cognitive Impairment," http://www.alz.org/dementia/mild-cognitive -impairment-mci.asp.

58   Rebecca Erwin Wells et al., "Meditation's impact on default mode network and hippocampus in mild cognitive impairment: A pilot study," *Neuroscience Letters* 556(27 November 2013): 15–19, http://www.sciencedirect.com/science/article/pii/S0304394013009026.

59   "Dementia: Hope through research," National Institute of Neurological Disorders and Stroke, http://www.ninds.nih.gov/disorders/dementias/detail_dementia.htm#19213_2.

60   "What Is Dementia?" Alzheimer's Association, http://www.alz.org/what-is-dementia.asp.

61   "BDNF gene," Genetics Home Reference, National Institutes of Health, accessed June 8, 2016, https://ghr.nlm.nih.gov/gene/BDNF.

62   Aron S. Buchman et al., "Higher brain *BDNF* gene expression is associated with slower cognitive decline in older adults," *Neurology* (January 27, 2016), http://www.neurology.org /content/early/2016/01/27/WNL.0000000000002387.

63   Deb Song, "Protein Is Piece of Alzheimer's Puzzle," Rush University Medical Center, January 27, 2016, https://www.rush.edu/news/protein-piece-alzheimers-puzzle.

64   G. Weinstein et al., "Serum Brain-Derived Neurotrophic Factor and the Risk for Dementia: The Framingham Heart Study," *JAMA Neurology* 71, no. 1(2014): 55–61, http://archneur.jamanetwork.com/article.aspx?articleid=1779513.

65   "Dementia: Hope through research," http://www.ninds.nih.gov/disorders/dementias/detail_dementia.htm#19213_2.

66   "Dementia with Lewy bodies," Alzheimer's Association, http://www.alz.org/dementia/dementia-with-lewy-bodies-symptoms.asp#causes.

67   "Vascular Dementia," UCSF Memory and Aging Center, http://memory.ucsf.edu/education/diseases/vascular.

68   "LBDA clarifies autopsy report on comedian, Robin Williams," Lewy Body Dementia Association, http://www.lbda.org/content/lbda-clarifies-autopsy-report-comedian-robin-williams.

69   "Dementia with Lewy bodies," http://www.alz.org/dementia/dementia-with-lewy-bodies-symptoms.asp#causes.

70   "LBDA clarifies autopsy report on comedian, Robin Williams," http://www.lbda.org/content/lbda-clarifies-autopsy-report-comedian-robin-williams.

71   "Frontotemporal Dementia," UCSF Memory and Aging Center, http://memory.ucsf.edu/ftd/.

72   "Mixed dementia," Alzheimer's Association, http://www.alz.org/dementia/mixed-dementia-symptoms.asp#symptoms.

73   "Alzheimer's Disease Facts and Figures," http://www.alz.org/mglc/in_my_community_60862.asp.

74   "A Primer on Alzheimer's disease and the Brain," National Institute on Aging, https://www.nia.nih.gov/alzheimers/publication/2013-2014-alzheimers-disease-progress-report/primer-alzheimers-disease-and#characteristics.

75   "More about plaques," Alzheimer's Association, https://www.alz.org/braintour/plaques.asp.

76   "Alzheimer's Disease," University of California at San Francisco, UCSF Memory and Aging Center, http://memory.ucsf.edu/education/diseases/alzheimer.

77   "Traumatic Brain Injury," Alzheimer's Association, http://www.alz.org/dementia/traumatic-brain-injury-head-trauma-symptoms.asp#dementiaandinjury.

78   "Diagnosis of Alzheimer's Disease and Dementia," Alzheimer's Association, http://www.alz.org/alzheimers_disease_diagnosis.asp.

79   "Treatments for Alzheimer's disease," Alzheimer's Association, http://www.alz.org/alzheimers_disease_treatments.asp.

80   "Alzheimer's Disease Genetics Fact Sheet," National Institute on Aging, updated April 8, 2016, https://www.nia.nih.gov/alzheimers/publication/alzheimers-disease-genetics-fact-sheet#alzheimers.

81   Jill S. Goldman et al., "Genetic counseling and testing for Alzheimer disease: Joint practice guidelines of the American College of Medical Genetics and the National Society of Genetic Counselors," *Genetics in Medicine* 13(2011): 597–605, http://www.nature.com/gim/journal/v13/n6/full/gim9201195a.html.

82   Robert C. Green et al., "Disclosure of *APOE* Genotype for Risk of Alzheimer's Disease," *New England Journal of Medicine* 361(July 16, 2009): 245–54, http://www.nejm.org/doi/full/10.1056/NEJMoa0809578.

Chapter 3

1   V. Shane Pankratz et al., "Predicting the risk of mild cognitive impairment in the Mayo Clinic Study of Aging," *Neurology* 84, no. 14(April 7, 2015): 1433–42, http://www.neurology .org/content/84/14/1433.displayAbstract?fromPage=online&aid=9246576&fileId= S104161021300248.

Chapter 4

1   C. Ricordi et al., "Diet and inflammation: Possible effects on immunity, chronic diseases, and life span," *Journal of the American College of Nutrition* 34, suppl. no. 1(2015): 10–13, http://www.ncbi.nlm.nih.gov/pubmed/26400428.

2   "Understanding the biology of Alzheimer's disease and the aging brain," National Institute on Aging, updated January 22, 2015, https://www.nia.nih.gov/alzheimers/publication/2011 -2012-alzheimers-disease-progress-report/understanding-biology-alzheimers.

3   F. L. Heppner et al., "Immune attack: the role of inflammation in Alzheimer disease," *Nature Reviews Neuroscience* 16, no. 6(2015 Jun): 358–72, http://www.ncbi.nlm.nih.gov /pubmed/25991443.

4   G. M. Turner-McGrievy et al., "Randomization to plant-based dietary approaches leads to larger short-term improvements in Dietary Inflammatory Index scores and macronutrient intake compared to diets that contain meat," *Nutrition Research*, published online December 2, 2014, http://www.ncbi.nlm.nih.gov/pubmed/25532675.

5   "Blocking receptor in brain's immune cells counters Alzheimer's in mice, study finds," Stanford Medicine News Center, December 8, 2014, http://med.stanford.edu/news /all-news/2014/12/blocking-receptor-in-brains-immune-cells-counters-alzheimers.html. "Blocking inflammation prevents cell death, improves memory in Alzheimer's disease," University of California at Irvine, February 29, 2016, https://news.uci.edu/health/blocking -inflammation-prevents-cell-death-improves-memory-in-alzheimers-disease/.

6   Ibid.

7   S. E. O'Bryant et al., "The Link between C-Reactive protein and Alzheimer's disease among Mexican Americans," *Journal of Alzheimer's Disease* 34, no. 3(2013): 701–6, http:// www.ncbi.nlm.nih.gov/pmc/articles/PMC3608400/#R3.

8   R. Schmidt et al., "Early inflammation and dementia: a 25-year follow-up of the Honolulu-Asia Aging Study," *Annals of Neurology* 52, no. 2(2002 Aug): 168–74, http://www .ncbi.nlm.nih.gov/pubmed/12210786.

9   M. T. Heneka et al., "Neuroinflammation in Alzheimer's disease," *Lancet Neurology* 14, no. 4(2015 Apr): 388–405, http://www.ncbi.nlm.nih.gov/pubmed/25792098.

10   M. R. Irwin et al., "Sleep disturbance, sleep duration, and inflammation: A Systematic Review and Meta-Analysis of Cohort Studies and Experimental Sleep Deprivation," *Biological Psychiatry* (2015 Jun 1), pii: S0006-3223(15)00437-0, http://www.ncbi.nlm.nih .gov/pubmed/26140821.

11   J. David Creswell et al., "Alterations in resting-state functional connectivity link mindfulness meditation with reduced Interleukin-6: A randomized controlled trial," *Biological Psychiatry*, published online January 29, 2016, http://www .biologicalpsychiatryjournal.com/article/S0006-3223(16)00079-2/abstract.

12   M. Hamer et al., "Physical activity and inflammatory markers over 10 years follow up in men and women from the Whitehall II cohort study," *Circulation* 126, no. 8(2012): 928–33, http://www.ncbi.nlm.nih.gov/pmc/articles/PMC3890998/.

13   Shilo Rea, "Neurobiological changes explain how mindfulness meditation improves health," Carnegie Mellon University, February 4, 2016, http://www.cmu.edu/news/stories /archives/2016/february/meditation-changes-brain.html.

14   S. Kern et al., "Does low-dose acetylsalicylic acid prevent cognitive decline in women with high cardiovascular risk? A 5-year follow-up of a non-demented population-based cohort of Swedish elderly women," *BMJ Open* 2, no. 5(2012): e001288, http://www.ncbi.nlm .nih.gov/pmc/articles/PMC3488756/.

15   V. Reichert et al., "A pilot study to examine the effects of smoking cessation on serum markers of inflammation in women at risk for cardiovascular disease," *Chest* 136, no. 1(2009): 212–19, http://www.ncbi.nlm.nih.gov/pmc/articles/PMC2707500/.

16   "Overweight and Obesity Statistics," National Institute of Diabetes and Digestive and Kidney Diseases, http://www.niddk.nih.gov/health-information/health-statistics/Pages /overweight-obesity-statistics.aspx.

17   "Assessing your weight and health risk," National Heart, Lung, and Blood Institute, https://www.nhlbi.nih.gov/health/educational/lose_wt/risk.htm.

18   "Larger belly in mid-life increases risk of dementia," American Academy of Neurology, March 26, 2008, https://www.aan.com/PressRoom/home/PressRelease/585.

19   R. A. Whitmer et al., "Central obesity and increased risk of dementia more than three decades later" *Neurology* 71, no. 14(2008 Sep 30): 1057–64, http://www.ncbi.nlm.nih.gov /pubmed/18367704.

20   B. Kaya et al., "Usefulness of the epicardial fat tissue thickness as a diagnostic criterion for geriatric patients with metabolic syndrome," *Journal of Geriatric Cardiology* 12, no. 4(2015): 373–77, http://www.ncbi.nlm.nih.gov/pmc/articles/PMC4554790/.

21   "How is metabolic syndrome diagnosed?" National Heart, Lung and Blood Institute, updated November 6, 2015, http://www.nhlbi.nih.gov/health/health-topics/topics/ms /diagnosis.

22   "Waist size matters," Harvard School of Public Health, http://www.hsph.harvard.edu /obesity-prevention-source/obesity-definition/abdominal-obesity/.

23   Y. F. Chuang et al., "Midlife adiposity predicts earlier onset of Alzheimer's dementia, neuropathology and presymptomatic cerebral amyloid accumulation," *Molecular Psychiatry* (2015 Sep 1), http://www.ncbi.nlm.nih.gov/pubmed/26324099.

24   "Adults obese or overweight at midlife may be at risk for earlier onset of Alzheimer's disease," National Institute on Aging, September 1, 2015, https://www.nia.nih.gov /alzheimers/announcements/2015/09/adults-obese-or-overweight-midlife-may-be -risk-earlier-onset.

25   Ibid.

26   Jiantao Ma et al., "Sugar-sweetened beverage consumption is associated with abdominal fat partitioning in healthy adults," *Journal of Nutrition* 144, no. 8(August 1, 2014): 1283–90, http://jn.nutrition.org/content/144/8/1283.full.html.

27   Kristen G. Hairston et al., "Lifestyle factors and 5-year abdominal fat accumulation in a minority cohort: The IRAS family study," *Obesity* 20, no. 2(February 2012): 421–427, http:// onlinelibrary.wiley.com/doi/10.1038/oby.2011.171/full.

28   "High blood pressure facts," CDC, http://www.cdc.gov/bloodpressure/facts.htm.

29   "Protect your heart, protect your brain," American Stroke Association, http://www .strokeassociation.org/STROKEORG/AboutStroke/UnderstandingRisk/Protect-Your -Heart-Protect-Your-Brain_UCM_439306_Article.jsp?appName=MobileApp.

30   "What are the signs, symptoms, and complications of blood pressure?" National Heart, Lung, and Blood Institute, updated September 10, 2015, http://www.nhlbi.nih.gov/health /health-topics/topics/hbp/signs.

31   "Vascular dementia," Alzheimer's Association, http://www.alz.org/dementia/vascular -dementia-symptoms.asp.

32 "NIH launches public health campaign on link between hypertension and brain health," National Institutes of Health, February 2, 2016, http://www.nih.gov/news-events/news-releases/nih-launches-public-health-campaign-link-between-hypertension-brain-health.

33 "Anti-hypertension drugs may benefit people with dementia," Alzheimer's Society, July 28, 2008, https://www.alzheimers.org.uk/site/scripts/press_article.php?pressReleaseID=248.

34 Constantino Iadecola, "Hypertension and dementia," *Hypertension* 64(2014): 3–5, published online before print April 28, 2014, http://hyper.ahajournals.org/content/64/1/3.full#F1.

35 "TIA (Transient Ischemic Attack)," American Stroke Association, updated March 28, 2016, http://www.strokeassociation.org/STROKEORG/AboutStroke/TypesofStroke/TIA/TIA-Transient-Ischemic-Attack_UCM_310942_Article.jsp#.VxT6lDb2aM8.

36 "Ischemic stroke," National Stroke Association, http://www.stroke.org/understand-stroke/what-stroke/ischemic-stroke.

37 "What is a stroke?" National Heart, Lung, and Blood Institute, updated October 28, 2015, http://www.nhlbi.nih.gov/health/health-topics/topics/stroke.

38 Ibid.

39 "TIA (Transient Ischemic Attack)," http://www.strokeassociation.org/STROKEORG/AboutStroke/TypesofStroke/TIA/TIA-Transient-Ischemic-Attack_UCM_310942_Article.jsp#.VxT6lDb2aM8.

40 J. R. Sattelmair et al., "Physical activity and risk of stroke in women," *Stroke* 41, no. 6(2010): 1243–50, http://www.ncbi.nlm.nih.gov/pmc/articles/PMC2876221/.

41 "Hidden brain risk: Midlife high blood pressure," Johns Hopkins Medicine, http://www.hopkinsmedicine.org/health/healthy_aging/healthy_mind/hidden-brain-risk-midlife-high-blood-pressure.

42 "Stroke treatments," American Stroke Association, http://www.strokeassociation.org/STROKEORG/AboutStroke/Treatment/Stroke-Treatments_UCM_310892_Article.jsp#.VwXLqaTD-xk.

43 Dena Ettehad et al., "Blood pressure lowering for prevention of cardiovascular disease and death: a systematic review and meta-analysis," *The Lancet* 387(10022): 957–967, http://thelancet.com/journals/lancet/article/PIIS0140-6736(15)01225-8/fulltext.

44 Ibid.

45 P. Maillard et al., "Effects of arterial stiffness on brain integrity in young adults from the Framingham Heart Study," *Stroke* 47, no. 4(2016 Apr): 1030–6, http://www.ncbi.nlm.nih.gov/pubmed/26965846.

46 Arvind Nishtala et al., "Midlife hypertension risk and cognition in the non-demented oldest old: Framingham Heart Study," *Journal of Alzheimer's Disease* 47, no. 1(2015): 197–204, http://content.iospress.com/articles/journal-of-alzheimers-disease/jad141881.

47 "Blood pressure and Alzheimer's risk: What's the connection?" Johns Hopkins Medicine, http://www.hopkinsmedicine.org/health/healthy_aging/healthy_body/blood-pressure-and-alzheimers-risk-whats-the-connection.

48 Ibid.

49 "Alcohol and heart health," American Heart Association, updated January 12, 2015, http://www.heart.org/HEARTORG/HealthyLiving/HealthyEating/Nutrition/Alcohol-and-Heart-Health_UCM_305173_Article.jsp#.Vw_GWqTcixk.

50 "New research summary: Lifestyle changes help reduce risk of cognitive decline," Alzheimer's Association, June 1, 2015, http://www.alz.org/news_and_events_lifestyle_changes_help_reduce_risk.asp.

51   "How to prevent and control coronary heart disease risk factors," National Heart, Lung, and Blood Institute, updated October 23, 2015, http://www.nhlbi.nih.gov/health /health-topics/topics/hd/prevent.

52   Ibid.

53   F. Forette et al., "The prevention of dementia with antihypertensive treatment: New evidence from the systolic hypertension in europe (Syst-Eur) study," *Archives of Internal Medicine* 162, no. 18(2002): 2046–52, http://archinte.jamanetwork.com/article .aspx?articleid=213524.

54   S. Yasar et al., "Antihypertensive drugs decrease risk of Alzheimer disease: Ginkgo evaluation of memory study," *Neurology* 81, no. 10(2013): 896–903, http://www.ncbi.nlm .nih.gov/pmc/articles/PMC3885216/.

55   "What is atherosclerosis?" National Heart, Lung, and Blood Institute, updated September 22, 2015, http://www.nhlbi.nih.gov/health/health-topics/topics/atherosclerosis/.

56   Ibid.

57   What is cardiovascular disease?" American Heart Association, updated March 23, 2016, http://www.heart.org/HEARTORG/Caregiver/Resources /WhatisCardiovascularDisease/What-is-Cardiovascular-Disease_UCM_301852_Article .jsp#.VwgCeKTD8ac.

58   "Risk factors for dementia," Alzheimer's Disease Education and Referral Center, updated January 22, 2015, https://www.nia.nih.gov/alzheimers/publication/dementias /risk-factors-dementia.

59   Wei Xu et al., "Meta-analysis of modifiable risk factors for Alzheimer's disease," *Journal of Neurology, Neurosurgery and Psychiatry* http://jnnp.bmj.com/content /early/2015/07/27/jnnp-2015-310548.

60   "What is carotid artery disease?" National Heart, Lung, and Blood Institute, updated October 29, 2015, https://www.nhlbi.nih.gov/health/health-topics/topics/catd.

61   "Living with carotid artery disease," National Heart, Lung, and Blood Institute, https:// www.nhlbi.nih.gov/health/health-topics/topics/catd/livingwith.

62   A. Solomon et al., "Midlife serum cholesterol and increased risk of alzheimer's and vascular dementia three decades later," *Dementia and Geriatric Cognitive Disorders*, 28, no. 1(2009): 75–80, doi:10.1159/000231980, http://www.ncbi.nlm.nih.gov/pmc/articles /PMC2814023/.

63   "High cholesterol in midlife raises risk of late-life dementia, Kaiser Permanente study finds," Kaiser Permanente Division of Research, August 4, 2009, https://www.dor.kaiser .org/external/news/press_releases/High_Cholesterol_in_Midlife_Raises_Risk_of_Late -life_Dementia,_Kaiser_Permanente_Study_Finds/.

64   R. F. de Bruijn, M. A. Ikram, "Cardiovascular risk factors and future risk of Alzheimer's disease," *BMC Medicine* 12(2014): 130, doi:10.1186/s12916-014-0130-5, http:// www.ncbi.nlm.nih.gov/pmc/articles/PMC4226863/.

65   M. C. Morris et al., "MIND diet associated with reduced incidence of Alzheimer's disease," *Alzheimer's & Dementia* 11, no. 9(2015 Sep): 1007–14, http://www.ncbi.nlm.nih .gov/pubmed/25681666.

66   I. Lourida et al., "Mediterranean diet, cognitive function, and dementia: a systematic review" *Epidemiology* 24, no. 4(2013 Jul): 479–89, http://www.ncbi.nlm.nih.gov /pubmed/23680940.

67   F. Panza et al., "Nutrition, frailty, and Alzheimer's disease," *Frontiers in Aging Neuroscience* 6(2014): 221, http://www.ncbi.nlm.nih.gov/pmc/articles/PMC4143595/.

68   "How to prevent and control coronary heart disease risk factors," http://www.nhlbi .nih.gov/health/health-topics/topics/hd/prevent.

69   Y. Li et al., "Saturated fats compared with unsaturated fats and sources of carbohydrates in relation to risk of coronary heart disease: A prospective cohort study," *Journal of the American College of Cardiology* 66, no. 14(2015): 1538–48, http://content .onlinejacc.org/article.aspx?articleid=2445322#tab1.

70   "Cholesterol Fact Sheet," CDC, updated April 30, 2015, http://www.cdc.gov/dhdsp /data_statistics/fact_sheets/fs_cholesterol.htm.

71   B. Reed et al., "Low HDL and high LDL serum cholesterol are associated with cerebral amyloidosis," *JAMA Neurology* 71, no. 2(2014): 195–200, doi:10.1001 /jamaneurol.2013.5390, http://www.ncbi.nlm.nih.gov/pmc/articles/PMC4083819/.

72   "High good and low bad cholesterol levels are healthy for the brain, too," UC Davis Health System, December 30, 2013, http://www.ucdmc.ucdavis.edu/publish/news /newsroom/8555.

73   Cordula Dick-Muehlke, "Stress and the influence on Alzheimer's disease," UC Irvine, Institute for Memory Impairments and Neurological Disorders, http://www.mind.uci.edu /alzheimers-disease/articles-of-interest/stress-and-the-influence-on-alzheimers-disease/.

74   "Statistics about diabetes," The American Diabetes Association, reviewed May 18, 2015, http://www.diabetes.org/diabetes-basics/statistics/.

75   G. J. Biessels et al., "Risk of dementia in type 2 diabetes mellitus: a systematic review," *Lancet Neurology* 5, no. 1(2006 Jan): 64–74, http://www.ncbi.nlm.nih.gov/pubmed /16361024.

76   A. A. Willette et al., "Association of insulin resistance with cerebral glucose uptake in late middle–aged adults at risk for Alzheimer disease," *JAMA Neurology* 72, no. 9(2015): 1013–20, http://archneur.jamanetwork.com/article.aspx?articleid=2398420.

77   S. M. de la Monte, J. R. Wands, "Alzheimer's disease is type 3 diabetes–evidence reviewed," *Journal of Diabetes Science and Technology* 2, no. 6(2008): 1101–13, http://www .ncbi.nlm.nih.gov/pmc/articles/PMC2769828/.

78   S. M. Gray et al., "Insulin regulates brain function, but how does it get there?" http:// diabetes.diabetesjournals.org/content/63/12/3992.full.

79   S. M. de la Monte, J. R. Wands, "Alzheimer's disease is type 3 diabetes–evidence reviewed," http://www.ncbi.nlm.nih.gov/pmc/articles/PMC2769828/.

80   "Brain insulin resistance contributes to cognitive decline in Alzheimer's disease," Penn Medicine, March 21, 2012, http://www.uphs.upenn.edu/news/News_Releases/2012/03/insulin/.

81   Konrad Talbot et al., "Demonstrated brain insulin resistance in Alzheimer's disease patients is associated with IGF-1 resistance, IRS-1 dysregulation, and cognitive decline," *Journal of Clinical Investigation* 122(4) (April 2012), https://www.jci.org/articles/view/59903.

82   R. O. Roberts et al., "Association of type 2 diabetes with brain atrophy and cognitive impairment," *Neurology* 82, no. 13(2014): 1132–41, http://www.ncbi.nlm.nih.gov/pmc /articles/PMC3966799/.

83   S. Chatterjee et al., "Type 2 diabetes as a risk factor for dementia in women compared with men: A pooled analysis of 2.3 million people comprising more than 100,000 cases of dementia," *Diabetes Care* 39, no. 2(February 2016): 300–307, http://care.diabetesjournals .org/content/39/2/300.long#.

84   "Complications," American Diabetes Association, http://www.diabetes.org/living-with -diabetes/complications/.

85   Erika Gebel, "Diabetes on the brain," *Diabetes Forecast Magazine* (August 2012), http:// www.diabetesforecast.org/2012/aug/diabetes-on-the-brain.html.

86   "Diabetes and dementia—Is there a connection?" Alzheimer Society Canada, updated February 10, 2016, http://www.alzheimer.ca/en/About-dementia/Alzheimer-s-disease /Risk-factors/diabetes-dementia-connection.

87   "Alzheimer's disease and type 2 diabetes: A growing connection," Alzheimer's Association, https://www.alz.org/national/documents/latino_brochure_diabetes.pdf.

88   C. C. Chung et al., "Inflammation-associated declines in cerebral vasoreactivity and cognition in type 2 diabetes," *Neurology* 85, no. 5(2015 Aug 4): 450–8, http://www.ncbi.nlm.nih.gov/pubmed/26156513.

89   "Facts and statistics," National Institute of Diabetes and Digestive and Kidney Diseases, http://www.niddk.nih.gov/health-information/health-communication-programs/ndep/health-care-professionals/game-plan/facts-statistics/Pages/index.aspx.

90   I. Ciubotaru et al., "Significant differences in fecal microbiota are associated with various stages of glucose tolerance in African American male veterans," *Translational Research* 166, no. 5(2015 Nov): 401–11, http://www.ncbi.nlm.nih.gov/pubmed/26209747.

91   "Prediabetes and insulin resistance," National Institute of Diabetes and Digestive and Kidney Diseases, http://www.niddk.nih.gov/health-information/health-topics/diabetes/insulin-resistance-prediabetes/Pages/index.aspx#steps.

92   Ibid.

93   Ricardo S. Osorio et al., "Sleep-disordered breathing advances cognitive decline in the elderly," *Neurology*, published online before print April 15, 2015, http://www.neurology.org/content/early/2015/04/15/WNL.0000000000001566.abstract.

94   "Poor dental health may lead to Alzheimer's," *Journal of Alzheimer's Disease* press release, July 30, 2013, http://www.j-alz.com/content/poor-dental-health-may-lead-alzheimer%E2%80%99s.

95   E. K. Kaye et al., "Tooth loss and periodontal disease predict poor cognitive function in older men," *Journal of the American Geriatrics Society* 58(2010): 713–18, http://www.ncbi.nlm.nih.gov/pmc/articles/PMC3649065/.

96   Ibid.

97   S. Poole et al., "Determining the presence of periodontopathic virulence factors in short-term postmortem Alzheimer's disease brain tissue," *Journal of Alzheimer's Disease* 36, no. 4(2013): 665–77, http://www.ncbi.nlm.nih.gov/pubmed/23666172.

98   A. Watts et al., "Inflammation as a potential mediator for the association between periodontal disease and Alzheimer's disease," *Neuropsychiatric Disease and Treatment* 4, no. 5(2008): 865–76, http://www.ncbi.nlm.nih.gov/pmc/articles/PMC2626915/.

99   "Poor dental health may lead to Alzheimer's," http://www.j-alz.com/content/poor-dental-health-may-lead-alzheimer%E2%80%99s.

100 Annlia Paganini-Hill et al., "Dentition, dental health habits, and dementia: The leisure world cohort study," *Journal of the American Geriatrics Society* 60, no. 8(August 2012): 1556–63, http://onlinelibrary.wiley.com/doi/10.1111/j.1532-5415.2012.04064.x/full.

101 "Periodontal disease," CDC, updated March 10, 2015, http://www.cdc.gov/OralHealth/periodontal_disease/.

102 "Periodontal (gum) disease: causes, symptoms, and treatments," http://www.nidcr.nih.gov/oralhealth/Topics/GumDiseases/PeriodontalGumDisease.htm.

103 M. A. Miller, "The role of sleep and sleep disorders in the development, diagnosis, and management of neurocognitive disorders," *Frontiers in Neurology* 6(2015): 224, http://www.ncbi.nlm.nih.gov/pmc/articles/PMC4615953/.

104 K. Yaffe et al., "Sleep-disordered breathing, hypoxia, and risk of mild cognitive impairment and dementia in older women," *Journal of the American Medical Association* 306, no. 6(2011): 613–19, http://jama.jamanetwork.com/article.aspx?articleid=1104205.

105 Osorio et al., "Sleep-disordered breathing advances cognitive decline in the elderly," http://www.neurology.org/content/early/2015/04/15/WNL.0000000000001566.abstract.

106 "Heavy snoring, sleep apnea may signal earlier memory and thinking decline," American Academy of Neurology, April 15, 2015, https://www.aan.com/PressRoom/home /PressRelease/1367.

107 Jennifer O'Brien, "Sleep apnea linked to increased risk of dementia in elderly women," University of California at San Francisco, August 9, 2011, http://www.coe.ucsf.edu/coe /research/sleep_apnea-women.html.

108 Ibid.

109 Miller, "The role of sleep and sleep disorders in the development, diagnosis, and management of neurocognitive disorders," http://www.ncbi.nlm.nih.gov/pmc/articles /PMC4615953/.

110 Osorio et al., "Sleep-disordered breathing advances cognitive decline in the elderly," http://www.neurology.org/content/early/2015/04/15/WNL.0000000000001566.abstract.

111 "Living with PAP," UCLA Sleep Disorders Center, http://sleepcenter.ucla.edu/body .cfm?id=58.

112 "Continuous positive airway pressure (CPAP)," Rush University Medical Center, https://www.rush.edu/services/test-treatment/continuous-positive-airway-pressure-cpap.

113 "How is sleep apnea treated?" National Heart, Lung and Blood Institute, https://www .nhlbi.nih.gov/health/health-topics/topics/sleepapnea/treatment.

114 "Tips for CPAP," American Academy of Sleep Medicine, http://www.sleepeducation .org/essentials-in-sleep/cpap/tips.

115 Ibid.

116 J. R. Richardson et al., "Elevated serum pesticide levels and risk for Alzheimer disease," *JAMA Neurology* 71, no. 3(2014): 284–90, http://www.ncbi.nlm.nih.gov/pmc/articles /PMC4132934/.

117 "Public health statement for DDT, DDE, and DDD," Agency for Toxic Substances and Disease Registry, September 2002, updated January 21, 2015, http://www.atsdr.cdc.gov /PHS/PHS.asp?id=79&tid=20.

118 Ibid.

119 Ibid.

120 Richardson et al., "Elevated serum pesticide levels and risk for Alzheimer disease," http://www.ncbi.nlm.nih.gov/pmc/articles/PMC4132934/.

121 Robin Lally, "Pesticide exposure linked to Alzheimer's disease," *Rutgers Today*, January 27, 2014, http://news.rutgers.edu/research-news/pesticide-exposure-linked-alzheimer %E2%80%99s-disease/20140127#.VwJvzKTD-dt.

122 "Public Health Statement for DDT, DDE, and DDD," http://www.atsdr.cdc.gov/PHS /PHS.asp?id=79&tid=20.

123 Ibid.

124 "Executive Summary: EWG's 2016 shopper's guide to pesticides in produce,"" EWG, http://www.ewg.org/foodnews/summary.php.

125 "Organic and conventionally grown food," National Pesticide Information Center, updated October 16, 2015, http://npic.orst.edu/health/ovc.html.

126 "10 things to know about local food systems," Iowa State University Extension and Outreach, https://www.extension.iastate.edu/localfoods/10-things-to-know-about-local -food-systems/.

127 Ibid.

128 "Pesticide illness & injury surveillance," CDC, updated August 14, 2015, http://www .cdc.gov/niosh/topics/pesticides/.

129 K. M. Hayden et al., "Occupational exposure to pesticides increases the risk of incident AD: The Cache County Study," *Neurology* 74, no. 19(2010): 1524–30, http://www.ncbi.nlm .nih.gov/pmc/articles/PMC2875926/.

130 F. Kamel, J. A. Hoppin, "Association of pesticide exposure with neurologic dysfunction and disease," *Environmental Health Perspectives* 112, no. 9(2004): 950–58, http://www.ncbi .nlm.nih.gov/pmc/articles/PMC1247187/.

131 "Minimizing pesticide residues in food," National Pesticide Information Center, updated November 6, 2015, http://npic.orst.edu/health/foodprac.html.

132 "Minimizing pesticide risks," National Pesticide Information Center, updated November 6, 2015, http://npic.orst.edu/health/minexp.html.

133 "Introduction to integrated pest management," Environmental Protection Agency, https://www.epa.gov/managing-pests-schools/introduction-integrated-pest-management.

134 "Minimizing exposure at work," National Pesticide Information Center, updated November 6, 2015, http://npic.orst.edu/health/minwork.html.

135 "Dirty work clothes: How should I wash out pesticides?" National Pesticide Information Center, http://npic.orst.edu/capro/dirtyclothes.html.

136 "Proton pump inhibitors (PPIs)," MedicineNet.com, reviewed June 12, 2015, http:// www.medicinenet.com/proton-pump_inhibitors/article.htm#which_proton_pump _inhibitors_ppis_are_approved_in_the_united_states.

137 W. Gomm et al., "Association of proton pump inhibitors with risk of dementia: A Pharmacoepidemiological Claims Data Analysis," *JAMA Neurology*, published online February 15, 2016, http://archneur.jamanetwork.com/article.aspx?articleid=2487379.

138 "Do proton pump inhibitors increase the risk of dementia?" editorial, *JAMA Neurology* (February 15, 2016), http://archneur.jamanetwork.com/article.aspx?articleid=2487375.

139 "Anticholinergic and antispasmodic drugs," MedicineNet.com, reviewed September 18, 2015, http://www.medicinenet.com/anticholinergics-antispasmodics-oral/article.htm#what _are_anticholinergic_drugs.

140 S. L. Gray et al., "Cumulative use of strong anticholinergics and incident dementia: A prospective cohort study," *JAMA Internal Medicine* 175, no. 3(2015): 401–7, http://archinte .jamanetwork.com/article.aspx?articleid=2091745.

141 Ibid.

142 "Benzodiazepines," MedicineNet.com, reviewed September 18, 2015, http://www .medicinenet.com/benzodiazepines_sleep-inducing-oral/article.htm#what_are_examples _of_benzodiazepines_available_in_the_us.

143 "Mental health medications," NIMH, revised January 2016, http://www.nimh.nih.gov /health/topics/mental-health-medications/index.shtml.

144 "Higher dementia risk linked to more use of common drugs," University of Washington School of Pharmacy, https://sop.washington.edu/higher-dementia-risk-linked-use-common -drugs/.

145 "How to talk to your patients about PPIs and dementia," American Gastroenterological Association, February 18, 2016, http://www.gastro.org/news_items/2016/2/18/how-to-talk -with-your-patients-about-ppis-and-dementia.

146 K. J. Anstey et al., "Smoking as a risk factor for dementia and cognitive decline: a meta-analysis of prospective studies," *American Journal of Epidemiology* 166(2007): 367–78, http://www.ncbi.nlm.nih.gov/pubmed/17573335.

147 J. K. Cataldo et al., "Cigarette smoking is a risk factor for Alzheimer's disease: An analysis controlling for tobacco industry affiliation," *Journal of Alzheimer's Disease* 19, no. 2(2010): 465–80, doi:10.3233/JAD-2010-1240, http://www.ncbi.nlm.nih.gov/pmc/articles /PMC2906761/.

148 D. E. Barnes, K. Yaffe, "The projected effect of risk factor reduction on Alzheimer's disease prevalence," *Lancet Neurology* 10(2011): 819, http://www.ncbi.nlm.nih.gov/pmc/articles/PMC3647614/.

149 T. C. Durazzo et al., "Smoking and increased Alzheimer's disease risk: A review of potential mechanisms," *Alzheimer's & Dementia* 10, no. 30(2014): S122–S145, doi:10.1016/j.jalz.2014.04.009, http://www.ncbi.nlm.nih.gov/pmc/articles/PMC4098701/.

150 A. David Smith et al., "Homocysteine-lowering by B vitamins slows the rate of accelerated brain atrophy in mild cognitive impairment: A randomized controlled trial," *PloS One* (September 8, 2010), http://journals.plos.org/plosone/article?id=10.1371/journal.pone.0012244.

151 S. Karama et al., "Cigarette smoking and thinning of the brain's cortex," *Molecular Psychiatry* 20(2015): 778–85, http://www.nature.com/mp/journal/v20/n6/full/mp2014187a.html.

152 M. Rusanen et al., "Heavy smoking in midlife and long-term risk of Alzheimer disease and vascular dementia," *Archives of Internal Medicine* 171, no. 4(2011): 333–39, http://archinte.jamanetwork.com/article.aspx?articleid=226695.

153 Ibid.

154 World Alzheimer Report 2014, "Dementia and risk reduction: An analysis of protective and modifiable factors." http://www.alz.co.uk/research/world-report-2014.

155 "Comparison of smoking cessation therapies finds similar quit rates," press release, the JAMA Network, January 26, 2016, http://media.jamanetwork.com/news-item/comparison-of-smoking-cessation-therapies-finds-similar-quit-rates/.

156 N. Lindson-Hawley et al., "Gradual versus abrupt smoking cessation: A randomized, controlled noninferiority trial," *Annals of Internal Medicine*, published online before print 15 March 2016, doi:10.7326/M14-2805, http://annals.org/article.aspx?articleid=2501853.

157 R. Whittaker et al., "Mobile phone-based interventions for smoking cessation," *Cochrane Database of Systematic Reviews* (November 14 2012), https://www.ncbi.nlm.nih.gov/pubmed/23152238.

Chapter 5

1   D. L. Katz, S. Meller, "Can we say what diet is best for health?" *Annual Review of Public Health* 35:83–103, http://www.annualreviews.org/doi/full/10.1146/annurev-publhealth-032013-182351.

2   Eurídice Martínez Steele et al., "Ultra-processed foods and added sugars in the US diet: evidence from a nationally representative cross-sectional study," *BMJ Open* 6(2016): e009892, http://bmjopen.bmj.com/content/6/3/e009892.

3   A. Safouris, "Mediterranean diet and risk of dementia," *Current Alzheimer Research* 12, no. 8(2015): 736–44, http://www.ncbi.nlm.nih.gov/pubmed/26159192.

4   C. C. Tangney et al., "Relation of DASH- and Mediterranean-like dietary patterns to cognitive decline in older persons," *Neurology* 83, no. 16(2014): 1410–16, http://www.ncbi.nlm.nih.gov/pmc/articles/PMC4206157/.

5   P. J. Tuso et al., "Nutritional update for physicians: Plant-based diets," *The Permanente Journal* 17, no. 2(2013): 61–66, http://www.ncbi.nlm.nih.gov/pmc/articles/PMC3662288/.

6   Morris et al., "MIND diet associated with reduced incidence of Alzheimer's disease," http://www.ncbi.nlm.nih.gov/pubmed/25681666.

7   C. Samieri et al., "The relation of midlife diet to healthy aging: a cohort study," *Annals of Internal Medicine* 159, no. 9(2013): 584–91, http://www.ncbi.nlm.nih.gov/pmc/articles/PMC4193807/.

8   N. Scarmeas et al., "Physical activity, diet, and risk of Alzheimer disease," *Journal of the American Medical Association* 302, no. 6(2009): 627–637, http://www.ncbi.nlm.nih.gov /pmc/articles/PMC2765045/.

9   H. Wengreen et al., "Prospective study of Dietary Approaches to Stop Hypertension– and Mediterranean-style dietary patterns and age-related cognitive change: the Cache County Study on Memory, Health and Aging," *American Journal of Clinical Nutrition* 98, no. 5(2013): 1263–71, http://ajcn.nutrition.org/content/98/5/1263.long.

10   "Nutrition and brain power," Johns Hopkins Medicine Special Report, 2010, http:// www.cognitivehealthjh.org/perch/resources/johnshopkinsnutritionandbrainpower.pdf.

11   "All about beans nutrition, health benefits, preparation and use in menus," North Dakota State University, revised November 2013, https://www.ag.ndsu.edu/publications /food-nutrition/all-about-beans-nutrition-health-benefits-preparation-and-use-in-menus.

12   "The protein myth," The Physicians' Committee for Responsible Medicine, http:// www.pcrm.org/health/diets/vegdiets/how-can-i-get-enough-protein-the-protein-myth.

13   http://www.nhlbi.nih.gov/health/health-topics/topics/dash/followdash.

14   https://health.clevelandclinic.org/2015/10/can-get-started-mediterranean-diet/.

15   http://www.nhlbi.nih.gov/health/health-topics/topics/dash/followdash.

16   https://health.clevelandclinic.org/2015/10/can-get-started-mediterranean-diet/.

17   http://www.nhlbi.nih.gov/health/health-topics/topics/dash/followdash.

18   https://health.clevelandclinic.org/2015/10/can-get-started-mediterranean-diet/.

19   http://www.nhlbi.nih.gov/health/health-topics/topics/dash/followdash.

20   https://health.clevelandclinic.org/2015/10/can-get-started-mediterranean-diet/.

21   http://www.nhlbi.nih.gov/health/health-topics/topics/dash/followdash.

22   https://health.clevelandclinic.org/2015/10/can-get-started-mediterranean-diet/.

23   http://www.nhlbi.nih.gov/health/health-topics/topics/dash/followdash.

24   https://health.clevelandclinic.org/2015/10/can-get-started-mediterranean-diet/.

25   http://www.nhlbi.nih.gov/health/health-topics/topics/dash/followdash.

26   https://health.clevelandclinic.org/2015/10/can-get-started-mediterranean-diet/.

27   http://www.nhlbi.nih.gov/health/health-topics/topics/dash/followdash.

28   file:///C:/Users/julia/AppData/Local/Microsoft/Windows/INetCache/IE/0DKJIHD3 /NewMedKit_0.pdf.

29   http://www.nhlbi.nih.gov/health/health-topics/topics/dash/followdash.

30   https://health.clevelandclinic.org/2015/10/can-get-started-mediterranean-diet/.

31   Nancy Presse et al., "Vitamin K status and cognitive function in healthy older adults," *Neurobiology of Aging* 34, no. 12:2777–83, http://www.neurobiologyofaging.org/article /S0197-4580(13)00244-3/abstract.

32   H. Wu et al., "Association between dietary whole grain intake and risk of mortality: Two large prospective studies in US men and women," http://archinte.jamanetwork.com /article.aspx?articleid=2087877.

33   Pamela J. Johnson, "Good stress," The University of Southern California, October 1, 2015, https://dornsife.usc.edu/news/stories/2155/good-stress/.

34   Ibid.

35   J. P. E. Spencer, "Flavonoids and brain health: multiple effects underpinned by common mechanisms," *Genes and Nutrition* 4, no. 4(2009): 243–50, http://www.ncbi.nlm .nih.gov/pmc/articles/PMC2775888/.

36   M. C. Morris et al., "Dietary fat intake and 6-year cognitive change in an older biracial

community population," *Neurology* 62, no. 9(2004 May 11): 1573–79, http://www.ncbi.nlm
.nih.gov/pubmed/15136684/.

37   M. C. Morris et al., "MIND diet slows cognitive decline with aging," *Alzheimer's &
Dementia* 11, no. 9(2015 Sep): 1015–22, http://www.ncbi.nlm.nih.gov/pubmed/26086182.

38   Morris et al., "MIND diet associated with reduced incidence of Alzheimer's disease,"
http://www.ncbi.nlm.nih.gov/pubmed/25681666.

39   Judith C. Thalheimer, "The MIND diet—Fighting dementia with food," *Today's
Geriatric Medicine* 8, no. 4:10, http://www.todaysgeriatricmedicine.com/archive/0715p10
.shtml.

40   "Tips to help you eat whole grains," USDA, http://www.choosemyplate.gov/grains-tips.

41   R. S. Mozaffarian et al., "Identifying whole grain foods: a comparison of different
approaches for selecting more healthful whole grain products," *Public Health Nutrition* 16,
no. 12(2013): 2255–64, http://www.ncbi.nlm.nih.gov/pmc/articles/PMC4486284/.

42   "Identifying whole grain products," Oldways Whole Grains Council, http://
wholegrainscouncil.org/whole-grains-101/identifying-whole-grain-products.

43   H. Wu et al., "Association between dietary whole grain intake and risk of mortality"
http://archinte.jamanetwork.com/article.aspx?articleid=2087877.

44   "What's a whole grain? A refined grain?" Oldways Whole Grains Council, http://
wholegrainscouncil.org/whole-grains-101/definition-of-whole-grains.

45   H. Wu et al., "Association between dietary whole grain intake and risk of mortality"
http://archinte.jamanetwork.com/article.aspx?articleid=2087877.

46   M. Ozawa et al., "Dietary pattern, inflammation and cognitive decline: The Whitehall
II prospective cohort study," *Clinical Nutrition* (2016 Jan 29), pii: S0261-5614(16)00035-2,
http://www.ncbi.nlm.nih.gov/pubmed/26874911.

47   H. Wengreen et al., "Prospective study of dietary approaches to stop hypertension–and
Mediterranean-style dietary patterns and age-related cognitive change," http://ajcn
.nutrition.org/content/98/5/1263.long.

48   "Fiber in whole grains," Oldways Whole Grains Council, http://wholegrainscouncil
.org/whole-grains-101/fiber-in-whole-grains.

49   "Popcorn: The snack with even higher antioxidants levels than fruits and vegetables,"
American Chemical Society, March 25, 2012, http://www.acs.org/content/acs/en
/pressroom/newsreleases/2012/march/popcorn-the-snack-with-even-higher-antioxidants
-levels-than-fruits-and-vegetables.html.

50   "All about the vegetable group," USDA, http://www.choosemyplate.gov/vegetables.

51   M. C. Morris et al., "Relations to cognitive change with age of micronutrients found in
green leafy vegetables," *The FASEB Journal* 29(1), suppl. 260.3(April 2015), http://www
.fasebj.org/content/29/1_Supplement/260.3.abstract.

52   Ibid.

53   "Eating green leafy vegetables keeps mental abilities sharp," Newswise, March 25, 2015,
http://www.newswise.com/articles/eating-green-leafy-vegetables-keeps-mental-abilities
-sharp.

54   Morris et al., "MIND diet associated with reduced incidence of Alzheimer's disease,"
http://www.ncbi.nlm.nih.gov/pubmed/25681666.

55   Jennifer di Noia, "Defining powerhouse fruits and vegetables: A nutrient density
approach," *Preventing Chronic Disease*, 11(2014): 130390, http://www.cdc.gov/pcd/
issues/2014/13_0390.htm#table2_down.

56   "Health benefits of coffee," Rush University Medical Center, https://www.rush.edu
/health-wellness/discover-health/health-benefits-coffee.

57   M. H. Eskelinen et al., "Midlife coffee and tea drinking and the risk of late-life dementia: a population-based CAIDE study," *Journal of Alzheimer's Disease* 16, no. 1(2009): 85–91, http://www.ncbi.nlm.nih.gov/pubmed/19158424.

58   C. Cao et al., "High blood caffeine levels in MCI linked to lack of progression to dementia," *Journal of Alzheimer's Disease* 30, no. 3(2012): 559–72, http://www.ncbi.nlm.nih.gov/pubmed/22430531.

59   B. Shukitt-Hale et al., "Coffee, but not caffeine, has positive effects on cognition and psychomotor behavior in aging," *Age* 35, no. 6(2013): 2183–92, http://www.ncbi.nlm.nih.gov/pmc/articles/PMC3824984/.

60   M. Ding et al., "Association of coffee consumption with total and cause-specific mortality in 3 large prospective cohorts," *Circulation* 132, no. 24(2015 Dec 15): 2305–15, http://www.ncbi.nlm.nih.gov/pubmed/26572796.

61   K. Ritchie et al., "The neuroprotective effects of caffeine: a prospective population study (the Three-City Study)," *Neurology* 69, no. 6(2007 Aug 7): 536–45, http://www.ncbi.nlm.nih.gov/pubmed/17679672.

62   "Does poor sleep raise risk for Alzheimer's disease?" National Institute on Aging, February 29, 2016, https://www.nia.nih.gov/alzheimers/features/does-poor-sleep-raise-risk-alzheimers-disease.

63   "Eating your greens," Leafy Greens Council, http://leafy-greens.org/eating-your-greens/.

64   "Farm to health: Maximizing nutrients and phytonutrients in Ohio produce," Ohio State University Extension, http://ohioline.osu.edu/factsheet/HYG-5581.

65   Luo Cheng et al., "Nut consumption and risk of type 2 diabetes, cardiovascular disease, and all-cause mortality: a systematic review and meta-analysis," *American Journal of Clinical Nutrition* 100(1) (July 2014): 256–69, http://ajcn.nutrition.org/content/100/1/256.long.

66   C. E. Berryman et al., "Effects of daily almond consumption on cardiometabolic risk and abdominal adiposity in healthy adults with elevated LDL-cholesterol: A randomized controlled trial," *Journal of the American Heart Association* (2015), http://jaha.ahajournals.org/content/4/1/e000993.

67   A. C. J. Nooyens et al., "Fruit and vegetable intake and cognitive decline in middle-aged men and women: the Doetinchem Cohort Study," *British Journal of Nutrition* 106(2011): 752–61, http://journals.cambridge.org/action/displayAbstract?fromPage=online&aid=8359144&fileId=S0007114511001024.

68   Shibu M. Poulouse et al., "Role of walnuts in maintaining brain health with age," *Journal of Nutrition* 144, no. 4(April 1, 2014): 561S–566S, http://jn.nutrition.org/content/144/4/561S.long#ref-56.

69   Cinta Valls-Pedret et al., "Polyphenol-rich foods in the mediterranean diet are associated with better cognitive function in elderly subjects at high cardiovascular risk," *Journal of Alzheimer's Disease* 29(2012): 773–82, http://content.iospress.com/download/journal-of-alzheimers-disease/jad111799?id=journal-of-alzheimers-disease%2Fjad111799.

70   Poulouse et al., "Role of walnuts in maintaining brain health with age," http://jn.nutrition.org/content/144/4/561S.long#ref-56.

71   Elizabeth E. Devore et al., "Dietary intakes of berries and flavonoids in relation to cognitive decline," http://onlinelibrary.wiley.com/doi/10.1002/ana.23594/abstract.

72   Marshall G. Miller and Barbara Shukitt-Hale, "Berry fruit enhances beneficial signaling in the brain," *Journal of Agricultural and Food Chemistry* 60, no. 23(2012): 5709–15, http://pubs.acs.org/doi/abs/10.1021/jf2036033.

73   Ali Bouzari et al., "Vitamin retention in eight fruits and vegetables: A comparison of

refrigerated and frozen storage," *Journal of Agricultural and Food Chemistry* 63, no. 3(2015): 957–62, http://pubs.acs.org/doi/abs/10.1021/jf5058793.

74   B. J. Venn et al., "The effect of increasing consumption of pulses and wholegrains in obese people: a randomized controlled trial," *Journal of the American College of Nutrition* 29(2010): 365–72, http://www.ncbi.nlm.nih.gov/pubmed/21041811.

75   Viranda H. Jayalath et al., "Effect of dietary pulses on blood pressure: A systematic review and meta-analysis of controlled feeding trials," *American Journal of Hypertension* 27, no. 1(2014): 56–64, http://ajh.oxfordjournals.org/content/27/1/56.abstract?ijkey =515cbc43c49a5535d412f710e8c6dca5f21293c3&keytype2=tf_ipsecsha.

76   X. Chen, "Lower intake of vegetables and legumes associated with cognitive decline among illiterate elderly Chinese: a 3-year cohort study," *Journal of Nutrition, Health & Aging* 16, no. 6(2012): 549–52, http://www.ncbi.nlm.nih.gov/pubmed/22659995.

77   "All about beans nutrition, health benefits, preparation and use in menus," https:// www.ag.ndsu.edu/publications/food-nutrition/all-about-beans-nutrition-health-benefits -preparation-and-use-in-menus.

78   Xianli Wu et al., "Lipophilic and hydrophilic antioxidant capacities of common foods in the United States," *Journal of Agricultural and Food Chemistry* 52(2004): 4026–37, http:// pubs.acs.org/doi/abs/10.1021/jf049696w.

79   Clifford W. Beninger et al., "Antioxidant activity of extracts, condensed tannin fractions, and pure flavonoids from *Phaseolus vulgaris* L. Seed Coat Color Genotypes," *Journal of Agricultural and Food Chemistry* 51, no. 27(2003): 7879–83, published online December 3, 2003, http://pubs.acs.org/doi/abs/10.1021/jf0304324.

80   Maria-Isabel Covas, "Olive oil and the cardiovascular system," *Pharmacological Research* 55(2007): 175–86, http://www.ncbi.nlm.nih.gov/pubmed/17321749.

81   Ibid.

82   V. Solfrizzi et al., "High monounsaturated fatty acids intake protects against age-related cognitive decline," *Neurology* 52, no. 8(May 12, 1999): 1563–69, http://www.ncbi .nlm.nih.gov/pubmed/10331679.

83   "Olive Oil 101," Oldways, http://oldwayspt.org/resources/good-food/olive-oil-101.

84   C. Berr et al., "Olive oil and cognition: Results from the Three-City Study," *Dementia and Geriatric Cognitive Disorders* 28, no. 4(2009): 357–64, http://www.ncbi.nlm.nih.gov /pmc/articles/PMC2796327/.

85   N. Scarmeas et al., "Mediterranean diet, Alzheimer disease, and vascular mediation," *Archives of Neurology* 63, no. 12(2006): 1709–17, http://www.ncbi.nlm.nih.gov/pmc/articles /PMC3024906/.

86   A. H. Abuznait et al., "Olive-oil-derived oleocanthal enhances β-amyloid clearance as a potential neuroprotective Mechanism against Alzheimer's disease: In vitro and in vivo studies," *ACS Chemical Neuroscience* (Feb. 15, 2013), http://pubs.acs.org/doi/abs/10.1021 /cn400024q.

87   "12 great ways to use olive oil," Oldways, http://oldwayspt.org/resources/12-ways-use -olive-oil.

88   Coreyann Poly et al., "The relation of dietary choline to cognitive performance and white-matter hyperintensity in the Framingham Offspring Cohort," *American Journal of Clinical Nutrition* 94, no. 6(December 2011): 1584–91, http://ajcn.nutrition.org/content /94/6/1584.abstract.

89   C. Castellini et al., "A multicriteria approach for measuring the sustainability of different poultry production systems," *Journal of Cleaner Production* 37(December 2012): 192–201, http://www.sinab.it/sites/default/files/115_jcleanpro1.pdf.

90   Z. S. Tan et al., "Red blood cell omega-3 fatty acid levels and markers of accelerated brain aging," *Neurology* 78, no. 9(2012): 658–64, http://www.ncbi.nlm.nih.gov/pmc/articles /PMC3286229/.

91   D. H. Kim et al., "Seafood types and age-related cognitive decline in the women's health study," *Journals of Gerontology Series A, Biological Sciences and Medical Sciences* 68, no. 10(2013): 1255–62, http://www.ncbi.nlm.nih.gov/pmc/articles/PMC3779629/.

92   E. J. Schaefer et al., "Plasma phosphatidylcholine docosahexaenoic acid content and risk of dementia and Alzheimer disease: The Framingham Heart Study," *Archives of Neurology* 63, no. 11(2006): 1545–50, http://archneur.jamanetwork.com/article .aspx?articleid=792707.

93   M. Morris et al., "Association of seafood consumption, brain mercury level, and APOE ε4 status with brain neuropathology in older adults," *Journal of the American Medical Association* 315, no. 5(2016), http://jama.jamanetwork.com/article.aspx?articleid=2484683& resultClick=3.

94   E. Kröger, R. Laforce, "Fish consumption, brain mercury, and neuropathology in patients with Alzheimer's disease and dementia," *Journal of the American Medical Association* editorial 315, no. 5(February 2, 2016), http://jama.jamanetwork.com/article .aspx?articleid=2484661&utm_campaign=articlePDF&utm_ medium=articlePDFlink&utm_source=articlePDF&utm_content=jama.2015.19451.

95   "Omega-3 content of frequently consumed seafood products," http://www .seafoodhealthfacts.org/seafood-nutrition/healthcare-professionals/omega-3-content -frequently-consumed-seafood-products.

96   "Tuna shopping guide," Greenpeace, http://www.greenpeace.org/usa/oceans/tuna -guide/.

97   "Seafood & your health," http://www.seafoodwatch.org/consumers/seafood-and-your -health.

98   M. K. Adjemian et al., "Relationships between diet, alcohol preference, and heart disease and type 2 diabetes among Americans," C. Pizzi, ed., *PLOS One* 10, no. 5(2015): e0124351, http://www.ncbi.nlm.nih.gov/pmc/articles/PMC4427330/.

99   Elizabeth R. De Oliveira e Silva et al., "Alcohol consumption raises HDL cholesterol levels by increasing the transport rate of apolipoproteins A-I and A-II," *Circulation* 102(2000): 2347–52, http://circ.ahajournals.org/content/102/19/2347.full.

100 S. Volpato et al., "Relationship of alcohol intake with inflammatory markers and plasminogen activator inhibitor-1 in well-functioning older adults: the health, aging, and body composition study," *Circulation* 109(2004): 607–12, https://www.ncbi.nlm.nih.gov /pubmed/14769682.

101 Edward Neafsey, Michael Collins, "Moderate alcohol consumption and cognitive risk," *Neuropsychiatric Disease and Treatment* 7, no. 1(2011): 465–84, http://www.ncbi.nlm.nih .gov/pmc/articles/PMC3157490/.

102 K. Mehlig et al., "Alcoholic beverages and incidence of dementia: 34-year follow-up of the prospective population study of women in Göteborg," *American Journal of Epidemiology* 167, no. 6(2008): 684–91, http://aje.oxfordjournals.org/content/167/6/684.long.

103 Philippe Marambaud et al., "Resveratrol promotes clearance of Alzheimer's disease amyloid-β peptides," *Journal of Biological Chemistry* 280:37377–82, http://www.jbc.org /content/280/45/37377.long.

104 D. G. Harwood et al., "The effect of alcohol and tobacco consumption, and apolipoprotein E genotype, on the age of onset in Alzheimer's disease," *International Journal of Geriatric Psychiatry* 25, no. 5(2010 May): 511–18, http://www.ncbi.nlm.nih.gov /pubmed/19750560.

Chapter 6

1   S. J. Blondell et al., "Does physical activity prevent cognitive decline and dementia?: A systematic review and meta-analysis of longitudinal studies," *BMC Public Health* 14(2014): 510, http://www.ncbi.nlm.nih.gov/pmc/articles/PMC4064273/.

2   K. I. Erickson et al., "Physical activity, brain plasticity, and Alzheimer's disease," *Archives of Medical Research* 43, no. 8(2012): 615–21, http://www.ncbi.nlm.nih.gov/pmc/articles/PMC3567914/.

3   R. Andel et al., "Physical exercise at midlife and risk of dementia three decades later: a population-based study of Swedish twins," *Journals of Gerontology Series A: Biological Sciences and Medical Sciences* 63, no. 1(2008 Jan): 62–66, http://www.ncbi.nlm.nih.gov/pubmed/18245762.

4   P. J. Smith et al., "Aerobic exercise and neurocognitive performance: A meta-analytic review of randomized controlled trials," *Psychosomatic Medicine* 72, no. 3(2010): 239–52, http://www.ncbi.nlm.nih.gov/pmc/articles/PMC2897704/.

5   R. L. Ownby et al., "Depression and risk for Alzheimer disease: Systematic review, meta-analysis, and metaregression analysis," *Archives of General Psychiatry* 63, no. 5(2006): 530–38, accessed June 5, 2016, http://www.ncbi.nlm.nih.gov/pmc/articles/PMC3530614/.

6   A. P. Spira et al., "Impact of sleep on the risk of cognitive decline and dementia," *Current Opinion in Psychiatry* 27, no. 6(2014): 478–83, accessed June 5, 2016, http://www.ncbi.nlm.nih.gov/pmc/articles/PMC4323377/.

7   S. Sindi et al., "Midlife work-related stress increases dementia risk in later life: The CAIDE 30-year study," *Journals of Gerontology Series B: Psychological Sciences and Social Sciences* (2016 Apr 8), accessed June 5, 2016, http://www.ncbi.nlm.nih.gov/pubmed/27059705.

8   N. F. Johnson et al., "Cardiorespiratory fitness modifies the relationship between myocardial function and cerebral blood flow in older adults," *Neuroimage* 131(2016 May 1): 126–32, http://www.ncbi.nlm.nih.gov/pubmed/26032886.

9   "Regular exercise at any age could keep the mind young," University of Kentucky College of Health Sciences, May 17, 2016, http://www.uky.edu/chs/effect-of-exercise-on-the-brain.

10   S. Colcombe, A. F. Kramer, "Fitness effects on the cognitive function of older adults: a meta-analytic study," *Psychological Science* 14, no. 2(2003 Mar): 125–30, http://www.ncbi.nlm.nih.gov/pubmed/12661673.

11   A. A. Willette et al., "Association of insulin resistance with cerebral glucose uptake in late middle–aged adults at risk for Alzheimer disease," *JAMA Neurology* 72, no. 9(2015): 1013–20, http://archneur.jamanetwork.com/article.aspx?articleid=2398420.

12   Erika Gebel, "The science of exercise," Diabetes Forecast, July 2010, http://www.diabetesforecast.org/2010/jul/the-science-of-exercise.html.

13   Carl W. Cotman, "Exercise builds brain health," Institute for Memory Impairments and Neurological Disorders, University of California at Irvine, accessed June 5, https://www.mind.uci.edu/alzheimers-disease/articles-of-interest/behaviors-mindfulness-biomarkets-stem-cells-other-dementia/exercise-builds-brain-health/.

14   "BDNF gene," https://ghr.nlm.nih.gov/gene/BDNF.

15   K. I. Erickson et al., "The aging hippocampus: interactions between exercise, depression, and BDNF," *Neuroscientist* 18, no. 1(2012): 82–97, http://www.ncbi.nlm.nih.gov/pmc/articles/PMC3575139/.

16   Bridget M. Kuehn, "The brain fights back: New approaches to mitigating cognitive decline," *Journal of the American Medical Association* 314, no. 23(December 15, 2015): 2492–94.

17   A. S. Buchman et al., "Higher brain BDNF gene expression is associated with slower cognitive decline in older adults," *Neurology* 86, no. 8(2016 Feb 23): 735–41, accessed June 8, http://www.ncbi.nlm.nih.gov/pubmed/26819457.

18   Erickson et al., "The aging hippocampus," http://www.ncbi.nlm.nih.gov/pmc/articles /PMC3575139/.

19   Carl W. Cotman, "Exercise builds brain health," Institute for Memory Impairments and Neurological Disorders, University of California at Irvine, accessed June 5, https:// www.mind.uci.edu/alzheimers-disease/articles-of-interest/behaviors-mindfulness -biomarkets-stem-cells-other-dementia/exercise-builds-brain-health/.

20   "The hallmarks of AD," National Institute on Aging, accessed June 1, 2016, https:// www.nia.nih.gov/alzheimers/publication/part-2-what-happens-brain-ad/hallmarks-ad.

21   "More brain changes," Alzheimer's Association, accessed June 1, 2016, https://www.alz .org/braintour/healthy_vs_alzheimers.asp.

22   Stanley J. Colcombe et al., "Aerobic exercise training increases brain volume in aging humans," *Journals of Gerontology Series A: Biological Sciences and Medical Sciences* 61, no. 11(2006): 1166–70, http://biomedgerontology.oxfordjournals.org/content/61/11/1166.long.

23   K. I. Erickson et al., "Physical activity and brain plasticity in late adulthood," *Dialogues in Clinical Neuroscience* 15, no. 1(2013): 99–108, http://www.ncbi.nlm.nih.gov/pmc/articles /PMC3622473/.

24   "Shall we dance? Doing the tango improves the aging brain," McGill University, November 23, 2005, https://www.mcgill.ca/newsroom/channels/news/shall-we-dance -17607.

25   *Brain Facts: A Primer on the Brain and Nervous System,* Society of Neuroscience, 2012, 68.

26   Ibid.

27   K. I. Erickson et al., "Exercise training increases size of hippocampus and improves memory," *Proceedings of the National Academy of Sciences* 108, no. 7(2011): 3017–22, http://www.pnas.org/content/108/7/3017.full.

28   "Different kinds of physical activity shown to improve brain volume and cut Alzheimer's risk in half," IOS Press, March 11, 2016, http://www.iospress.nl/ios_news/different-kinds -of-physical-activity-shown-to-improve-brain-volume-and-cut-alzheimers-risk-in-half/.

29   C. A. Raji et al., "Longitudinal relationships between caloric expenditure and gray matter in the cardiovascular health study," *Journal of Alzheimer's Disease* 52, no. 2(2016 Mar 11): 719–29, http://www.ncbi.nlm.nih.gov/pubmed/26967227.

30   Katherine Reiter et al., "Improved cardiorespiratory fitness is associated with increased cortical thickness in mild cognitive impairment," *Journal of the International Neuro-psychological Society* 21(2015): 757–67, http://journals.cambridge.org/action/displayAbstract ;jsessionid=85FB37B6CBE8AD334B6B8031116150B4.journals?fromPage=online&aid =10033579.

31   "Improving fitness may counteract brain atrophy in older adults," University of Maryland, November 20, 2015, http://www.umdrightnow.umd.edu/news/improving -fitness-may-counteract-brain-atrophy-older-adults.

32   "Recommendations for physical activity," National Heart, Lung, and Blood Institute, updated October 29, 2015, accessed June 12, 2016, https://www.nhlbi.nih.gov/health /health-topics/topics/phys/recommend.

33   A. S. Buchman et al., "Total daily physical activity and the risk of AD and cognitive decline in older adults," *Neurology* 78, no. 17(2012): 1323–29, http://www.ncbi.nlm.nih.gov /pmc/articles/PMC3335448/.

34   K. I. Erickson et al., "Physical activity predicts gray matter volume in late adulthood:

The cardiovascular health study," *Neurology* 75, no. 16(2010): 1415–22, http://www.ncbi .nlm.nih.gov/pmc/articles/PMC3039208/.

35   "Measuring physical activity intensity," Centers for Disease Control, http://www.cdc .gov/physicalactivity/basics/measuring/.

36   J. Weuve et al., "Physical activity, including walking, and cognitive function in older women," *Journal of the American Medical Association* 292, no. 12(2004): 1454–61, http:// jama.jamanetwork.com/article.aspx?articleid=199487.

37   Erickson et al., "Physical activity predicts gray matter volume in late adulthood," http://www.ncbi.nlm.nih.gov/pmc/articles/PMC3039208/.

38   Sandra B. Chapman et al., "Shorter term aerobic exercise improves brain, cognition, and cardiovascular fitness in aging," *Frontiers in Aging Neuroscience* (12 November 2013), http://journal.frontiersin.org/article/10.3389/fnagi.2013.00075/full.

39   *Walk This Way! A Guide to Developing Individual and Community Walking Programs*, American Council on Exercise, https://www.acefitness.org/advocacy/pdf/Walking _Toolkit_Community.pdf.

40   "Good form walking," New Balance, http://www.newbalance.com/good_form_ walking.html.

41   T. Liu-Ambrose et al., "Resistance training and executive functions: A 12-month randomised controlled trial," *Archives of Internal Medicine* 170, no. 2(2010): 170–78, http:// www.ncbi.nlm.nih.gov/pmc/articles/PMC3448565/.

42   R. C. Cassilhas et al., "The impact of resistance exercise on the cognitive function of the elderly," *Medicine and Science in Sports and Exercise* (39(2007): 1401–7, http://www .ncbi.nlm.nih.gov/pubmed/17762374.

43   Ziya Altug, "Resistance exercise to improve cognitive function," *Strength and Conditioning Journal* 36, no. 6(December 2014): 46–50, http://journals.lww.com/nsca-scj /Abstract/2014/12000/Resistance_Exercise_to_Improve_Cognitive_ Function.5.aspx?trendmd-shared=0.

44   "Results of three new trials reported at the Alzheimer's Association International Conference 2015 May Help People Live Better with Alzheimer's and Vascular Dementia," Alzheimer's Association International Conference, July 23, 2015, accessed June 5, 2016, https://www.alz.org/aaic/_downloads/thurs-1130am-exercise.pdf.

45   Charles L. McLafferty Jr. et al., "Resistance training is associated with improved mood in healthy older adults," *Perceptual and Motor Skills* 98, no. 3 (June 2004): 947–57, http:// pms.sagepub.com/content/98/3/947.refs.

46   *Growing Stronger: Strength Training for Older Adults*, CDC, http://www.cdc.gov /physicalactivity/downloads/growing_stronger.pdf.

47   Yasuharu Tabara et al., "Association of postural instability with asymptomatic cerebrovascular damage and cognitive decline: The Japan shimanami health promoting program study," *Stroke*, published online before print December 18, 2014, http://stroke .ahajournals.org/content/early/2014/12/18/STROKEAHA.114.006704.

48   Ewoud J. van Dijk et al., "Progression of cerebral small vessel disease in relation to risk factors and cognitive consequences: Rotterdam scan study," *Stroke* 39, no. 10(2008 Oct): 2712–19, http://stroke.ahajournals.org/content/39/10/2712.full.pdf.

49   "Sample exercises–balance," National Institute on Aging, https://www.nia.nih.gov /health/publication/exercise-physical-activity/sample-exercises-balance.

50   Ibid.

51   Y. Hong et al., "Balance control, flexibility, and cardiorespiratory fitness among older Tai Chi practitioners," *British Journal of Sports Medicine*, http://www.ncbi.nlm.nih.gov /pmc/articles/PMC1724150/.

52   M. J. Biondolillo, D. B. Pillemer, "Using memories to motivate future behaviour: an experimental exercise intervention," *Memory* 23, no. 3(2015): 390–402, http://www.ncbi.nlm.nih.gov/pubmed/24571515.

53   C. J. Stevens et al., "A pilot study of women's affective responses to common and uncommon forms of aerobic exercise," *Psychology & Health* 31, no. 2(2016): 239–57, http://www.ncbi.nlm.nih.gov/pmc/articles/PMC4684981/.

54   C. I. Karageorghis, D-L Priest, "Music in the exercise domain: a review and synthesis (Part I)," *International Review of Sport and Exercise Psychology* 5, no. 1(2012): 44–66, http://www.ncbi.nlm.nih.gov/pmc/articles/PMC3339578/.

55   Stephanie A Hooker, Kevin S Masters, "Purpose in life is associated with physical activity measured by accelerometer," *Journal of Exercise Psychology* 21, no. 6(June 2016): 962–71, http://hpq.sagepub.com/content/21/6/962.abstract.

Chapter 7

1   B. W. Roberts, D. Mroczek, "Personality trait change in adulthood," *Current Directions in Psychological Science* 17, no. 1(2008): 31–35, http://www.ncbi.nlm.nih.gov/pmc/articles/PMC2743415/,

2   Ibid.

3   Sanjay Srivastava et al., "Development of personality in early and middle adulthood: set like plaster or persistent change?" *Journal of Personality and Social Psychology* 84(5), http://psycnet.apa.org/journals/psp/84/5/1041/.

4   "Personality changes for the better with age," *American Psychological Association* 34, no. 7 (July/August 2003), http://www.apa.org/monitor/julaug03/personality.aspx.

5   Christopher J. Soto, "Is happiness good for your personality? Concurrent and prospective relations of the big five with subjective well-being," *Journal of Personality* 83, no. 1(February 2015): 45–55, http://onlinelibrary.wiley.com/doi/10.1111/jopy.12081/full.

6   "Brain structure corresponds to personality," Association for Psychological Science, June 22, 2010, http://www.psychologicalscience.org/index.php/news/releases/brain-structure-corresponds-to-personality.html.

7   P. R. Duberstein et al., "Personality and risk for Alzheimer's disease in adults 72 years of age and older: A six-year follow-up," *Psychology and Aging* 26, no. 2(2011): 351–62, http://www.ncbi.nlm.nih.gov/pmc/articles/PMC3115437/.

8   Ibid.

9   H. X. Wang et al., "Personality and lifestyle in relation to dementia incidence," *Neurology* 72, no. 3 (January 20, 2009): 253–59, http://www.neurology.org/content/72/3/253.abstract.

10   S. Cohen et al., "Social Ties and Susceptibility to the Common Cold," *Journal of the American Medical Association* 277, no. 24(1997): 1940–44, http://jama.jamanetwork.com/article.aspx?articleid=417085.

11   Teresa E. Seeman et al., "Histories of social engagement and adult cognition: Midlife in the U.S. study," *Journals of Gerontology Series B: Psychological Sciences and Social Sciences* 66B, suppl. no. 1(2011): i141-i152, http://psychsocgerontology.oxfordjournals.org/content/66B/suppl_1/i141.full.

12   Karen A. Ertel et al., "Effects of social integration on preserving memory function in a nationally representative US elderly population," *American Journal of Public Health* 98, no. 7(July 2008): 1215–20, http://ajph.aphapublications.org/doi/abs/10.2105/AJPH.2007.113654.

13   Seeman et al., "Histories of social engagement and adult cognition," http://psychsocgerontology.oxfordjournals.org/content/66B/suppl_1/i141.full.

14   R. S. Wilson et al., "Loneliness and risk of Alzheimer disease," http://archpsyc.jamanetwork.com/article.aspx?articleid=482179.

15 "Stress management: How to strengthen your social support network," American Psychological Association, http://www.apa.org/helpcenter/emotional-support.aspx.

16 Becca R. Levy et al., "A culture–brain link: Negative age stereotypes predict Alzheimer's disease biomarkers," *Psychology and Aging* 31, no. 1(Feb 2016): 82–88, https://www.researchgate.net/profile/Alan_Zonderman/publication/286219266_A_Culture-Brain_Link_Negative_Age_Stereotypes_Predict_Alzheimer's_Disease_Biomarkers/links/566ab42608ae430ab4f869c0.pdf.

17 Michael Greenwood, "Negative beliefs about aging predict Alzheimer's disease in Yale-led study," Yale News, December 7, 2015, http://news.yale.edu/2015/12/07/negative-beliefs-about-aging-predict-alzheimer-s-disease-yale-led-study.

18 A. Soetanto et al., "Association of anxiety and depression with microtubule-associated protein 2– and synaptopodin-immunolabeled dendrite and spine densities in hippocampal CA3 of older humans," *Archives of General Psychiatry* 67, no. 5(2010): 448–57, http://archpsyc.jamanetwork.com/article.aspx?articleid=210754#ref-yoa90095-6.

19 Breno S. Diniz, et al., "Late-life depression and risk of vascular dementia and Alzheimer's disease: systematic review and meta-analysis of community-based cohort studies," *British Journal of Psychiatry* 202, no. 5(May 2013): 329–35, http://bjp.rcpsych.org/content/202/5/329.

20 Saczynski et al., "Depressive symptoms and risk of dementia," http://www.ncbi.nlm.nih.gov/pmc/articles/PMC2906404/.

21 V. M. Dotson et al., "Recurrent depressive symptoms and the incidence of dementia and mild cognitive impairment," *Neurology* 75, no. 1(2010): 27–34, http://www.ncbi.nlm.nih.gov/pmc/articles/PMC2906403/.

22 Soetanto et al., "Association of anxiety and depression with microtubule-associated protein 2– and synaptopodin-immunolabeled dendrite and spine densities in hippocampal CA3 of older humans," http://archpsyc.jamanetwork.com/article.aspx?articleid=210754#.

23 "Depression," NIMH, https://www.nimh.nih.gov/health/topics/depression/index.shtml#part_145399.

24 L. Johansson et al., "Midlife personality and risk of Alzheimer disease and distress: a 38-year follow-up," *Neurology* 83, no. 17(2014 Oct 21): 1538–44, http://www.ncbi.nlm.nih.gov/pubmed/25274849.

25 Y. I. Sheline et al., "An antidepressant decreases CSF Aβ production in healthy individuals and in transgenic AD mice," *Science Translational Medicine* 6, no. 236(2014): 236re4, http://www.ncbi.nlm.nih.gov/pmc/articles/PMC4269372/.

26 Rebecca Hiscott, "When does depression signal dementia?: Research says certain features of depression may hint of later dementia," *Neurology Now* 11, no. 2(April/May 2015): 12–13, http://tools.aan.com/elibrary/neurologynow/?event=home.showArticle&id=ovid.com:/bib/ovftdb/01222928-201511020-00011.

27 R. S. Wilson et al., "Conscientiousness and the incidence of alzheimer disease and mild cognitive impairment," *Archives of General Psychiatry* 64, no. 10(2007 Oct): 1204–12, http://archpsyc.jamanetwork.com/article.aspx?articleid=210072.

28 "Raising your conscientiousness," Harvard Health Letter, http://www.health.harvard.edu/staying-healthy/raising-your-conscientiousness.

29 "The road to resilience," American Psychological Association, http://www.apa.org/helpcenter/road-resilience.aspx.

30 A. Terracciano et al., "Personality and resilience to Alzheimer's disease neuropathology: A prospective autopsy study," *Neurobiology of Aging* 34, no. 4(2013): 1045–50, http://www.ncbi.nlm.nih.gov/pmc/articles/PMC3541457/.

31 Ibid.

32 "The road to resilience," http://www.apa.org/helpcenter/road-resilience.aspx.

33   Jerrold F. Rosenbaum, Jennifer M. Covino, "Stress and resilience: implications for depression and anxiety," Medscape, December 29, 2005, http://www.medscape.com /viewarticle/518761.

34   M. E. Seligman et al., "Positive psychology progress: empirical validation of interventions," *American Psychologist* 60, no. 5(2005 Jul-Aug): 410–21, http://www.ncbi.nlm.nih.gov /pubmed/16045394.

35   Ibid.

36   P. A. Boyle et al., "Effect of purpose in life on the relation between Alzheimer disease pathologic changes on cognitive function in advanced age," *Archives of General Psychiatry* 69, no. 5(2012): 499–504, http://archpsyc.jamanetwork.com/article.aspx?articleid=1151486.

37   "Purpose in life may protect against harmful changes in the brain associated with Alzheimer's disease," Rush University Medical Center, May 7, 2012, https://www.rush.edu /news/press-releases/purpose-life-may-protect-against-harmful-changes-brain-associated -alzheimers.

38   Lei Yu et al., "Purpose in life and cerebral infarcts in community-dwelling older people," *Stroke* 46(2015): 1071–76, http://stroke.ahajournals.org/content/46/4/1071.abstract.

Chapter 8

1   "Stress and Your Health," MedlinePlus, updated November 23, 2014, https:// medlineplus.gov/ency/article/003211.htm.

2   L. Mah et al., "Can anxiety damage the brain?" *Current Opinion in Psychiatry* 29, no. 1(2016 Jan): 56–63, http://www.ncbi.nlm.nih.gov/pubmed/26651008.

3   D. R. Euston et al., "The Role of Medial Prefrontal Cortex in Memory and Decision Making," *Neuron* 76, no. 6(20 December 2012): 1057–70, http://www.sciencedirect.com /science/article/pii/S0896627312011087.

4   A. Machado et al., "Chronic stress as a risk factor for Alzheimer's disease," *Reviews in the Neurosciences* 25, no. 6(2014): 785–804, http://www.ncbi.nlm.nih.gov /pubmed/25178904.

5   "Fight or Flight," University of Texas Counseling and Mental Health Center, https:// cmhc.utexas.edu/stressrecess/Level_One/fof.html.

6   "Stress," University of Maryland Medical Center, http://umm.edu/health/medical /reports/articles/stress.

7   "Fact Sheet on Stress," NIMH, https://www.nimh.nih.gov/health/publications/stress /index.shtml.

8   Anna C. Phillips, "Perceived Stress," in *Encyclopedia of Behavioral Medicine*, Marc Gellman, J. Rick Turner, eds., 1453–54, http://link.springer.com/referenceworkentry /10.1007%2F978-1-4419-1005-9_479.

9   S. J. Lupien et al., "The Douglas Hospital Longitudinal Study of Normal and Pathological Aging: summary of findings," *Journal of Psychiatry and Neuroscience* 30, no. 5(2005): 328–34, http://www.ncbi.nlm.nih.gov/pmc/articles/PMC1197277/#r39-4.

10   E. B. Ansell et al., "Cumulative Adversity and Smaller Gray Matter Volume in Medial Prefrontal, Anterior Cingulate, and Insula Regions," *Biological Psychiatry* 72, no. 1(2012): 57–64, http://www.ncbi.nlm.nih.gov/pmc/articles/PMC3391585/.

11   R. S. Wilson et al., "Proneness to psychological distress is associated with risk of Alzheimer's disease," *Neurology* 61, no. 11(2003 Dec 9): 1479–85, http://www.ncbi.nlm.nih .gov/pubmed/14663028.

12   F. S. Dhabhar, "Effects of stress on immune function: the good, the bad, and the beautiful," *Immunologic Research* 58, no. 2-3(2014 May): 193–210, http://www.ncbi.nlm.nih .gov/pubmed/24798553.

13   J. M. Torpy et al., "Chronic Stress and the Heart," *Journal of the American Medical Association* 298, no. 14(2007): 1722, http://jama.jamanetwork.com/article.aspx?articleid =209139.

14   P. C. Konturek et al., "Stress and the gut: pathophysiology, clinical consequences, diagnostic approach and treatment options," *Journal of Physiology and Pharmacology* 62, no. 6(2011 Dec): 591–99, http://www.ncbi.nlm.nih.gov/pubmed/22314561.

15   H-Y Qin et al., "Impact of psychological stress on irritable bowel syndrome," *World Journal of Gastroenterology* 20, no. 39(2014): 14126–31, http://www.ncbi.nlm.nih.gov/pmc /articles/PMC4202343/.

16   Susan Levenstein et al., "Psychological Stress Increases Risk for Peptic Ulcer, Regardless of *Helicobacter pylori* Infection or Use of Nonsteroidal Anti-inflammatory Drugs," *Clinical Gastroenterology and Hepatology* 13, no. 3:498–506.e1, http://www .cghjournal.org/article/S1542-3565(14)01136-7/fulltext#sec3.

17   L. Johansson, et al., "Midlife psychological stress and risk of dementia: a 35-year longitudinal population study," *Brain* (2010), http://brain.oxfordjournals.org/content /brain/133/8/2217.full.pdf.

18   ———. "Common psychosocial stressors in middle-aged women related to long-standing distress and increased risk of Alzheimer's disease: a 38-year longitudinal population study," *BMJ Open* 3(2013): e003142, http://bmjopen.bmj.com/content/3/9 /e003142.full.

19   Simona Gradari et al., "Can Exercise Make You Smarter, Happier, and Have More Neurons? A Hormetic Perspective," *Frontiers in Neuroscience* (14 March 2016), http:// journal.frontiersin.org/article/10.3389/fnins.2016.00093/full.

20   R. Nauert, "Mindfulness Reduces the Way Stress Affects the Brain," Psych Central, 2015, accessed August 10, 2016, http://psychcentral.com/news/2015/02/13/mindfulness -reduces-the-way-stress-affects-the-brain/81200.html.

21   "FAQs," Center for Mindfulness in Medicine, Health Care, and Society, University of Massachusetts Medical School, http://www.umassmed.edu/cfm/stress-reduction/faqs/.

22   M. J. Katz et al., "Influence of Perceived Stress on Incident Amnestic Mild Cognitive Impairment: Results From the Einstein Aging Study," *Alzheimer Disease and Associated Disorders* 30, no. 2(2016 Apr-Jun): 93–8, http://www.ncbi.nlm.nih.gov/pubmed/26655068.

23   B. K. Hölzel et al., "Mindfulness practice leads to increases in regional brain gray matter density," *Psychiatry Research* 191, no. 1(2011): 36–43, http://www.ncbi.nlm.nih.gov /pmc/articles/PMC3004979/.

24   ———. "Stress reduction correlates with structural changes in the amygdala," *Social Cognitive and Affective Neuroscience* 5, no. 1(2010): 11–17, doi:10.1093/scan/nsp034, http://www.medscape.com/viewarticle/723847.

25   "Stress Management: Breathing Exercises for Relaxation," University of Wisconsin School of Medicine and Public Health, http://www.uwhealth.org/health/topic/actionset /stress-management-breathing-exercises-for-relaxation/uz2255.html.

26   R. E. Wells et al., "Meditation's impact on default mode network & hippocampus in mild cognitive impairment: a pilot study," *Neuroscience Letters* 556(2013): 15–19, http:// www.ncbi.nlm.nih.gov/pmc/articles/PMC4022038/.

27   H. A. Eyre et al., "Changes in Neural Connectivity and Memory Following a Yoga Intervention for Older Adults: A Pilot Study," *Journal of Alzheimer's Disease* 52, no. 2(2016 Apr 5): 673–84, http://www.ncbi.nlm.nih.gov/pubmed/27060939.

28   M. Ussher et al., "Immediate effects of a brief mindfulness-based body scan on patients with chronic pain," *Journal of Behavioral Medicine* 37, no. 1(2014 Feb): 127–34, http://www .ncbi.nlm.nih.gov/pubmed/23129105.

29 H. Lavretsky, et al., "A pilot study of yogic meditation for family dementia caregivers with depressive symptoms: Effects on mental health, cognition, and telomerase activity," *International Journal of Geriatric Psychiatry* 28(2013): 57–65, http://www.ncbi.nlm.nih.gov /pmc/articles/PMC3423469/.

30 Hillari Dowdle, "Quiet + Focus Your Mind: Kirtan Kriya," *Yoga Journal* (October 17, 2008), http://www.yogajournal.com/article/practice-section/how-to-do-kirtan-kriya/.

31 C. Wang et al., "Tai Chi on psychological well-being: systematic review and meta-analysis," *BMC Complementary and Alternative Medicine* 10(2010): 23, http://www.ncbi .nlm.nih.gov/pmc/articles/PMC2893078/.

32 James A. Mortimer et al., "Changes in Brain Volume and Cognition in a Randomized Trial of Exercise and Social Interaction in a Community-Based Sample of Non-Demented Chinese Elders," *Journal of Alzheimer's Disease* 30, no. 4(June 2012): 757–66, http://www .ncbi.nlm.nih.gov/pmc/articles/PMC3788823/.

33 "AGS/BGS Clinical Practice Guideline: Prevention of Falls in Older Persons," American Geriatrics Society, http://www.americangeriatrics.org/health_care_professionals/clinical _practice/clinical_guidelines_recommendations/prevention_of_falls_summary_of _recommendations.

34 "Tai chi," University of Maryland Medical Center, http://umm.edu/health/medical /altmed/treatment/tai-chi.

35 Hedok Lee et al., "The Effect of Body Posture on Brain Glymphatic Transport," *Journal of Neuroscience*, 35, no. 31(5 August 2015): 11034–44, http://www.jneurosci.org/content/35 /31/11034.short.

36 "Scientists Discover Previously Unknown Cleansing System in Brain," University of Rochester Medical Center, August 15, 2012, https://www.urmc.rochester.edu/news /story/3584/scientists-discover-previously-unknown-cleansing-system-in-brain.aspx.

37 Juliana G. Breines et al., "Self-compassion as a predictor of interleukin-6 response to acute psychosocial stress," *Brain, Behavior and Immunity* (2013), http://self-compassion .org/wp-content/uploads/publications/BreinesImmunity.pdf.

38 Ibid.

39 Ibid.

40 Helen Rockliff et al., "A pilot exploration of heart rate variability and salivary Cortisol responses to compassion-focused imagery," *Clinical Neuropsychiatry* 5, no. 3(Jun 2008): 132–39, https://www.researchgate.net/publication/228642817_A_pilot_exploration_of _heart_rate_variability_and_salivary_cortisol_responses_to_compassion-focsed_imagery.

41 A. P. Spira et al., "Self-Reported Sleep and β-Amyloid Deposition in Community-Dwelling Older Adults," http://www.ncbi.nlm.nih.gov/pmc/articles/PMC3918480/.

42 L. Xie et al., "Sleep Drives Metabolite Clearance from the Adult Brain," *Science* 342, no. 6156(2013): 10.1126/science.1241224, http://www.ncbi.nlm.nih.gov/pmc/articles /PMC3880190/.

43 Spira et al., "Self-Reported Sleep and β-Amyloid Deposition in Community-Dwelling Older Adults," http://www.ncbi.nlm.nih.gov/pmc/articles/PMC3918480/.

44 P. Gringras et al., "Bigger, Brighter, Bluer-Better? Current Light-Emitting Devices— Adverse Sleep Properties and Preventative Strategies," *Frontiers in Public Health* 3(2015): 233, http://www.ncbi.nlm.nih.gov/pmc/articles/PMC4602096/.

45 Bryce A. Mander et al., "β-amyloid disrupts human NREM slow waves and related hippocampus-dependent memory consolidation," *Nature Neuroscience* 18(2015): 1051–57, http://www.nature.com/neuro/journal/v18/n7/full/nn.4035.html?cookies=accepted.

46   Yasmin Anwar, "Poor sleep linked to toxic buildup of Alzheimer's protein, memory loss," UC Berkeley News, June 1, 2015, http://news.berkeley.edu/2015/06/01/alzheimers -protein-memory-loss/.

47   "Sleep Hygiene Tips to help you sleep better," American Association of Sleep Technologists, http://www.aastweb.org/blog/sleep-hygiene-tips-to-help-you-sleep-better.

48   "How to Get on a Sleep Schedule," the National Sleep Foundation, https://sleep.org /articles/get-sleep-schedule/.

Chapter 9

1   D. C. Park et al., "The Impact of Sustained Engagement on Cognitive Function in Older Adults: The Synapse Project," *Psychological Science* 25, no. 1(January 2014): 103–112.

2   C. M. Roe et al., "Alzheimer Disease and cognitive reserve: variation of education effect with carbon 11-Labeled Pittsburgh Compound B uptake," *Archives of Neurology* 65, no. 11(November 2008): 1467–71.

3   E. B. Schneider, et al., "Functional recovery after moderate/severe traumatic brain injury: a role for cognitive reserve?" *Neurology* 82, no. 18(May 2014): 1636–42.

4   E. Marques de Silva, "Formal education after 60 years improves cognitive performance," *Alzheimer's & Dementia* 7, no. 4, supplement (July 2011): S503.

5   C. Wu et al., "Association of retirement age with mortality: a population-based longitudinal study among older adults in the USA," *Journal of Epidemiology and Community Health* (March 2016): doi:10.1136/jech-2015-207097.

6   S. Rohwedder, R. J. Willis, "Mental Retirement," *Journal of Economic Perspectives* 24, no. 1(Winter 2010): 119–38.

7   A. Lampit et al., "Computerized Cognitive Training in Cognitively Healthy Older Adults: A Systematic Review and Meta-Analysis of Effect Modifiers," *PLOS Medicine* (November 2014): http://dx.doi.org/10.1371/journal.pmed.1001756.

8   "A consensus on the Brain Training industry from the scientific community," http:// longevity3.stanford.edu/blog/2014/10/15/the-consensus-on-the-brain-training-industry -from-the-scientific-community/.

9   Bennett et al., "Overview and findings from the religious orders study," http://www .ncbi.nlm.nih.gov/pmc/articles/PMC3409291/.

10   Joe Verghese et al., "Leisure Activities and the Risk of Dementia in the Elderly," *New England Journal of Medicine* 348(June 2003): 2508–16, http://www.nejm.org/doi/full /10.1056/NEJMoa022252#t=article.

11   T. Hughes et al., "Engagement in reading and hobbies and risk of incident dementia: The MoVIES Project," *American Journal of Alzheimer's Disease and Other Dementias* 25, no. 5(August 2010): 432–38.

12   H. Wu et al., "Association of retirement age with mortality: a population-based longitudinal study among older adults in the USA," *Journal of Epidemiology & Community Health* 70, no. 9(March 2016): jech-2015-207097.

13   M. C. Carlson, "Evidence for neurocognitive plasticity in at-risk older adults: the experience corps program," *Journals of Gerontology Series A, Biological Sciences and Medical Sciences* 64A, no. 12(December 2009): 1275–82.

14   Erikson, et al., "Exercise training increases size of hippocampus and improves memory," http://www.pnas.org/content/108/7/3017.full.

15   P. A. Mueller, D. M. Oppenheimer, "The Pen Is Mightier Than the Keyboard: Advantages of Longhand Over Laptop Note Taking," *Psychological Science* (April 2014): doi: 10.1177 /0956797614524581.

16   A. Mangen et al., "Reading linear texts on paper versus computer screen: Effects on reading comprehension," *International Journal of Educational Research* 58(December 31, 2013): 61–68.

17   L. Wilkinson et al., "Chewing gum selectively improves aspects of memory in healthy volunteers," *Appetite* 38(2002): 235–36.

18   H. Noice, T. Noice, "An Arts Intervention for Older Adults Living in Subsidized Retirement Homes," *Neuropsychology, Development, and Cognition Section B, Aging, Neuropsychology and Cognition* 16, no. 1(2009): 56–79.

19   D. C. Park et al., "The Impact of Sustained Engagement on Cognitive Function in Older Adults: The Synapse Project," *Psychological Science* 25, no. 1(January 2014): 103–122.

20   Ibid.

21   J. Scholz et al., "Training induces changes in white matter architecture," *Nature Neuroscience* 12(2009): 1370–71.

22   P. Jansen et al., "The influence of juggling on mental rotation performance," *International Journal of Sport Psychology* 40, no. 2(2009): 351–59.

23   Verghese et al, "Leisure activities and the risk of dementia in the elderly." http://www .nejm.org/doi/full/10.1056/NEJMoa022252#t=article.

24   R. O. Roberts et al., "Risk and protective factors for cognitive impairment in persons aged 85 years and older," *Neurology* 84, no. 18(May, 2015): 1854–61, https://www.ncbi.nlm .nih.gov/pubmed/25854867.

25   A. Bolwerk et al., "How Art Changes Your Brain: Differential Effects of Visual Art Production and Cognitive Art Evaluation on Functional Brain Connectivity," *PLOS ONE* (July, 2014), http://dx.doi.org/10.1371/journal.pone.0101035.

26   T. D. Hoang et al., "Effect of Early Adult Patterns of Physical Activity and Television Viewing on Midlife Cognitive Function," *JAMA Psychiatry* 73, no. 1(January 2016): 73–79.

27   A. J. Xavier et al., "English Longitudinal Study of Aging: Can Internet/E-Mail Use Reduce Cognitive Disease?" *Journals of Gerontology, Series A, Biological Sciences and Medical Sciences* 69, no. 9(2014): 1117–21.

28   S. Alladi et al., "Bilingualism delays age at onset of dementia, independent of education and immigration status," *Neurology* (November, 2013): doi: http://dx.doi.org/10.1212 /01.wnl.0000436620.33155.a4.

29   E. Woumans et al., "Bilingualism delays clinical manifestation of Alzheimer's disease," *Bilingualism: Language and Cognition* 18, no. 3(July, 2015): 568–574.

30   S. Alladi et al., "Impact of Bilingualism on Cognitive Outcome After Stroke," *Stroke* (November 2015): http://dx.doi.org/10.1161/STROKEAHA.115.010418.

31   T. Särkämö et al., "Music listening enhances cognitive recovery and mood after middle cerebral artery stroke," *Brain*, 131(March 2008): 866–76.

32   B. Hanna-Pladdy, A. MacKay, "The relation between instrumental musical activity and cognitive aging," *Neuropsychology* 25, no. 3(May 2011): 378–86.

33   S. Seinfeld et al., "Effects of music learning and piano practice on cognitive function, mood and quality of life in older adults," *Frontiers in Psychology* 4(November 2013): 810.

34   T. Särkämö et al., "Cognitive, emotional, and social benefits of regular musical activities in early dementia: randomized controlled study," *Gerontologist* 54, no. 4(August 2014): 634–50.

35   J. François Dartigues et al., "Playing board games, cognitive decline and dementia: a French population-based cohort study," BMJ Open 3, no. 8(2013): e002998.

36   Verghese et al., "Leisure activities and the risk of dementia in the elderly."

37   J. A. Pilai et al., "Association of crossword puzzle participation with memory decline in persons who develop dementia," *Journal of the International Neuroscience Society* 17, no. 6(November, 2011): 1006–13, doi: 10.1017/S1355617711001111.

38   J. W. Grabbe, "Sudoku and Working Memory Performance for Older Adults," *Activities Adaptation & Aging* 35, no. 3(July 2011): 241–254.

39   S. A. Schultz et al., "Participation in cognitively-stimulation activities is associated with brain structure and cognitive function in preclinical Alzheimer's disease," *Brain Imaging Behavior* 9, no. 4(December 2015): 729–36.

40   J. A. Anguera et al., "Video game training enhances cognitive control in older adults," *Nature* 501(September 2013): 97–101.

41   Jason C. Allaire et al., "Successful aging through digital games: Socioemotional differences between older adult gamers and Non-gamers," *Computers in Human Behavior* 29, no. 4(July 2013): 1302–6.

42   R. Nouchi et al., "Brain Training Game Improves Executive Functions and Processing Speed in the Elderly: A Randomized Controlled Trial," *PLoS ONE* (January 11 2012): http://dx.doi.org/10.1371/journal.pone.0029676.

43   S. Kühn et al., "Playing Super Mario induces structural brain plasticity: gray matter changes resulting from training with a commercial video game," *Molecular Psychiatry* 19(February 2014): 265–71.

44   G. D. Clemenson, C. E. L. Stark, "Virtual Environmental Enrichment through Video Games Improves Hippocampal-Associated Memory," *Journal of Neuroscience* 35, no. 49(December 9, 2015): 16116–25.

45   C. Basak et al., "Can training in a real-time strategy videogame attenuate cognitive decline in older adults?" *Psychology and Aging* 23, no. 4(December 2008): 765–77.

46   Ibid.

47   L. A. Whitlock et al., "Individual differences in response to cognitive training: Using a multi-model, attentionally demanding game-based intervention for older adults," *Computers in Human Behavior* 28, no. 4(July 2012): 1091–96.

48   K. L. Blacker et al., "Effects of action video games on visual working memory," *The Journal of Experimental Psychology* 40, no. 5(October 2014): 1992–2004.

49   F. Zhang, D. Kaufman, "Older adults' social interactions in massively multiplayer online role-playing games (MMORPGs)," *Games and Culture* (August, 2015): 10.1177/1555412015601757.

INDEX

Underscored page references indicate sidebars and tables. **Boldface** references indicate photographs.

A

Abdominal fat, 68, 70–71, 120
Acetylcholine, 26, 89, 128
Acting classes, 211
AF (atrial fibrillation), 77
Age, as dementia risk factor, 4, 15, 38, 43
Ageless Brain notebook, 39
Ageless Brain quiz, 39, 41–42
    brain-health assessment in, 43–44
    lifestyle assessments in
        attitude, 51–53
        diet, 45–47
        mental stimulation, 56–58
        physical activity, 48–51
        stress burden, 54–56
    scoring guide for, 59
Aging, attitudes about, 52, 160–61
Agreeableness, as personality trait, 157
Alcohol use. *See also* Wine
    health risks from, 74
    in MIND diet, 131–32
    quiz assessing, 43, 48
    sleep disruption from, 197
Almond meal
    Flax-Almond Pancakes, 226
Almond milk
    Almond, Blueberry, and Banana Smoothie,
        234
Almonds
    Almond, Blueberry, and Banana Smoothie,
        234
    Baked Apples with Almonds and Maple Syrup,
        271
    Candied Spiced Nuts, 273
    Spicy Vegetarian Stir-Fry with Toasted
        Almonds, 254
    Spinach Salad with Almond-Encrusted
        Chicken Breast, 236
Alzheimer's disease. *See also* Dementia
    asymptomatic, 168
    as cause of dementia, 33–34
    diagnosis of, 35–36
    early-onset vs. late-onset, 14
    fear of, 3
    myths about, 7–9
    physical characteristics of, 7–8, 35, 65–66
    preventing, with
        ageless brain commandments (*see* 10
            commandments of ageless brain)
        antihypertensive drugs, 75
        attitude adjustments (*see* Attitude)
        coffee and tea drinking, 118–19
        exercise (*see* Exercise)
        lifestyle changes, 3–4, 6
        mental stimulation, 9–12, 23–24 (*see also*
            Play)
        nutrition (*see* Brain-boosting foods; Diet)
        SHARP pillars, 12–16, 39
        side sleep position, 193
        social interaction, 23, 30, 33
        stress reduction (*see* Stress management)
    progressive nature of, 3, 7
    risk factors for
        age, 4, 15, 43
        assessing (*see* Ageless Brain quiz)
        brain injuries, 36
        cardiovascular disease, 75–77
        carotid artery disease, 76
        chronic inflammation, 65–66
        depression, 134, 162
        diabetes, 78–80
        family history, 5, 15, 43
        genetics, 5, 10, 15
        gum disease, 83
        heart disease, 64
        high blood pressure, 44, 71

Alzheimer's disease. (*cont.*)
  risk factors for (*cont.*)
    high BMI, 70
    medications, 93–94
    mild cognitive impairment, 6
    oxidative stress, <u>107</u>
    personality traits, 157
    pesticide exposure, 86–89
    saturated fat consumption, 108
    sleep apnea, 64
    sleep deprivation, 134, 176
    sleep-disordered breathing, 84–85
    smoking, 94
    stress, 134, <u>164</u>, 176, 179–82
  statistics on, 3, <u>10</u>, 35
  symptoms of, <u>31</u>, 37
  treating, 37
  as type 3 diabetes, <u>79</u>
  unusual triggers of, <u>5</u>
  varying degrees of, 23, 27
  in women, <u>10–11</u>
Amaranth, <u>114–15</u>
Americantaichi.net, 192
Amygdala, <u>28</u>, 176, 177, 182, 184, 194
Amyloid precursor protein, <u>14</u>
Amyloid proteins, <u>11</u>, 23, 27, 66, 70, 78, <u>79</u>, 85, 87,
      181. *See also* Beta-amyloid proteins
Anchovies
  Roasted Red Peppers with Anchovies,
      265
Animal protein, vs. plant foods, <u>65</u>
Anthocyanins, 106, 122, 124
Anti-Alzheimer's plan, designing, 38–39
Anticholinergic medications, 92–93
Antioxidant sources
  beans, 124
  berries, 122, 123
  coffee, <u>118</u>
  organic poultry, 129
  red wine, 132
  vitamins A, C, and E, 106, <u>107</u>
  whole grains, 110, <u>113</u>, <u>115</u>
Antispasmodic medications, 92–93
APOE-e4 gene
  Alzheimer's risk from, <u>10</u>, <u>15</u>, 87, 89
  testing for, 37–38
Apples
  Baked Apples with Almonds and Maple Syrup,
      271
  Warm and Creamy Fruit Dessert, 272
Applesauce
  Fruit 'n' Nut Muffins, 232

Apricots
  Greek Yogurt with Apricots, Honey, and
      Crunch, 275
  Quinoa with Raisins, Apricots, and Pecans,
      242
Arts and crafts activities, 212–13
Aspirin, benefits of, 67
Atherosclerosis, 75–76
Atrial fibrillation (AF), 77
Attention, effect of age on, <u>9</u>
Attitude
  about aging, <u>52</u>, <u>160–61</u>
  brain-healthy, 14, 39, 153
  personality influencing, 155–58
  quiz assessing, <u>51–53</u>
  strategies for improving
    conscientiousness, 165–67
    depression treatment, 162–65
    emotional resilience, 167–70
    pursuit of life's purpose, 171–74
    social interaction, 158–61
Avocados
  Green Machine Smoothie, 235

B

Balance exercises, <u>36</u>, 142, <u>151</u>
Balance test, <u>150</u>
Bananas
  Almond, Blueberry, and Banana Smoothie, 234
Barley, <u>112–13</u>
  Curried Barley Salad with Shrimp and Baby
      Greens, 240
BDNF protein, <u>32–33</u>, 136–37, 189
Beans
  Grilled Fish and White Bean Salad, 258
  Mediterranean Salad Wraps, 244
  in MIND diet, 123–24
  preparing, 124–25
  Simmered Chickpeas in Tomato Sauce, 248
  Tomatoes Stuffed with White Bean Salad, 237
Bedroom environment, for better sleep, 199–200
Belly fat, 68, 70–71, 120
Benzodiazepines (BZDs), 93, 94
Berries. *See also* Blueberries; Raspberries;
      Strawberries
  choosing and storing, 123
  in MIND diet, 122
  for reducing brain age, 16
Beta-amyloid proteins, 7–8, 35, 92, 108, 127, 132,
      165, 181, <u>193</u>, 196, 198. *See also* Amyloid
      proteins

Beta-carotene, in leafy greens, 116
Blood-brain barrier, 21, 102
Blood pressure. *See also* High blood pressure
  belly fat increasing, 70
  in metabolic syndrome, 69
Blood sugar
  belly fat increasing, 70
  diets improving, 100
  fiber stabilizing, 81
  in metabolic syndrome, 69
Blueberries
  Almond, Blueberry, and Banana Smoothie,
    234
  choosing and storing, 123
  health benefits of, 16, 122
  Honey-Berry Ice Pops, 270
  Love-Your-Brain Smoothie, 228
  Tabbouleh with Fruit, 243
  Yogurt-Blueberry Bites, 269
BMI, 44, 68, 70
Body fat, excess, 68
  losing, 70–71
Body mass index (BMI), 44, 68, 70
Body scan meditation, 188–89
Brain
  age-related changes in, 20–23
  cognitive reserve protecting, 27–30
  enlarging, 137–40
  older, activities protecting, 23–24, 25, 27
  plasticity of, 24–25, 27, 136, 189
  stimulating, 201–4 (*see also* Play)
  stress and, 177–79
  structure and functions of, 19, 20–21, 28
Brain age, habits reducing, 16–17
Brain-boosting foods, 12
  in DASH diet, 77–78, 99–100, 101
  in Mediterranean diet, 77–78, 99–100,
    100–101
  in MIND diet, 12, 65, 77–78, 100, 101, 108–32
  plant foods, 65, 100, 102–3, 106, 108
Brain-derived neurotrophic factor (BDNF),
    32–33, 136–37, 189
Brain injury, 36, 173
Brain insulin resistance, 79
Brain training, computer-based, 6, 13, 27, 205–6
Breakfasts, 223
  Almond, Blueberry, and Banana Smoothie,
    234
  Flax-Almond Pancakes, 226
  Fruit 'n' Nut Muffins, 232
  Green Machine Smoothie, 235
  Hearty Oatmeal and Greek Yogurt, 230

  Love-Your-Brain Smoothie, 228
  Mediterranean Scramble, 231
  Overtime Oats, 227
  Peanut Butter and Yogurt Smoothie, 233
  Persian Herb Omelet, 224–25
  Strawberry Pancakes, 229
Broccoli
  Pasta Primavera with Pine Nuts, 253
  Spicy Vegetarian Stir-Fry with Toasted
    Almonds, 254
Brown rice. *See* Rice, brown
Buckwheat groats, 114–15
Bulgur, 112–13
  Bulgur with Mushrooms and Roasted Red
    Peppers, 267
  Mediterranean Bulgur Salad, 246
  Tabbouleh with Fruit, 243
Burgers
  Mediterranean Turkey Burgers, 247
B vitamins, in whole grains, 110
BZDs (benzodiazepines), 93, 94

C

Caffeine
  health benefits of, 118–19
  sleep disruption from, 197
Cantaloupe
  Tabbouleh with Fruit, 243
Cardio exercise
  health benefits of, 134–35, 148–49
  recommended amount of, 141–42
Cardiovascular disease. *See also* Heart disease
  alcohol preventing, 132
  health risks from, 11, 75–77
  from high blood pressure, 71
Career, mental stimulation from, 11, 203, 205
Carotenoids, 106, 116, 120
Carotid artery disease, 76
Carrots
  Chicken with Seven-Vegetable Couscous, 252
  Quinoa Salad with Carrot Fries, 245
  Zucchini and Carrots with Toasted Walnuts,
    268
Catfish
  Roasted Catfish with Zesty Sweet Potatoes, 251
Cauliflower
  Lemon-Garlic Roasted Cauliflower with
    Fennel and Gremolata, 266
CBT (cognitive behavioral therapy), 164
Celexa, 165
Cerebral small vessel disease (SVD), 150

Cerebrum, 20
"Certified Humane" food label, 129
Chantix, for smoking cessation, 96
Chicken
    Chicken and Potato Salad Over Greens, 255
    Chicken with Seven-Vegetable Couscous,
        252
    Greek Lemon Chicken, 257
    Savory Sautéed Pepper and Chicken Sandwich,
        238
    Spinach Salad with Almond-Encrusted
        Chicken Breast, 236
Chickpeas
    Mediterranean Salad Wraps, 244
    Simmered Chickpeas in Tomato Sauce, 248
Cholesterol
    HDL, 69, 74, 78
    high, dementia risk and, 44, 75–76
    improving levels of, 100, 106
    LDL, 70, 74, 75, 78, 108
Choline, 128
Chutney
    Baked Eggplant with Nutty Tomato Chutney,
        250
Citalopram, 165
Cod
    Mediterranean Cod, 260
Coffee, health benefits of, 118–19
Cognitive aging, 7, 8–9
Cognitive behavioral therapy (CBT), 164
Cognitive reserve, building, 27–30, 33, 203,
        204–7
Cold-turkey smoking cessation, 96
Comfort zone, effect on brain, 202
Computer-based brain training, 6, 13, 27, 205–6
Computer use, 214, 215
Concussion, 36
Conscientiousness
    developing, 166–67
    reducing Alzheimer's risk, 165–66
    traits associated with, 156, 165
Continuous positive airway pressure (CPAP)
        machines, 85–86
Cortex, of brain, 20, 95, 137, 140, 145, 176, 179,
        182
Cortisol, 177–78, 194, 202
Couscous
    Chicken with Seven-Vegetable Couscous, 252
CPAP machines, 85–86
Cranberries, dried, 123
C-reactive protein (CRP), 66, 67, 132
Crossword puzzles, 219

CRP, 66, 67, 132
Curry powder
    Curried Barley Salad with Shrimp and Baby
        Greens, 240
    Seared Salmon Over Curried Lentils, 256

D

Dancing, 212
DASH diet
    foods in, 77–78, 99–100, 101
        servings of, 102, 104
    health benefits of, 74, 77–78, 100, 101, 108–9
DDT residue, as Alzheimer's trigger, 5, 63, 86–87
Decaffeinated coffee and tea, 118–19
Deep breathing, for stress reduction, 184–85, 199
Dementia. See also Alzheimer's disease
    characteristics of, 7
    preventing, with
        ageless brain commandments (see 10
            commandments of ageless brain)
        antihypertensive drugs, 74–75
        attitude adjustments (see Attitude)
        coffee and tea drinking, 118–19
        depression treatment, 5
        education, 11, 204–5
        exercise (see Exercise)
        high BDNF, 32–33
        nutrition (see Brain-boosting foods; Diet)
        plant foods, 65, 117
        play (see Play)
        SHARP pillars, 12–16, 39
        stress reduction (see Stress management)
    risk factors for
        abdominal fat, 68
        age, 38
        assessing (see Ageless Brain quiz)
        atherosclerosis, 75–76
        depression, 162
        family history, 38
        gum disease, 82–83
        high blood pressure, 44, 71, 73
        high cholesterol, 75–76
        inflammation, 66
        medications, 63–64, 91–94
        mild cognitive impairment, 32, 33, 43
        sleep apnea, 84–85
        smoking, 95
        stress, 179–82
    signs of, 31, 33
    statistics on, 10
    types of, 33–35

Dementia with Lewy bodies (DLB), 34
Dendrites, 203–4
Depression, 52
  cognitive decline from, 23
  dementia and, 5, 162–63
  effect on brain, 21
  self-compassion reducing, 194
  symptoms of, 163
  treatments for, 164, 183
Desserts
  Baked Apples with Almonds and Maple Syrup, 271
  Candied Spiced Nuts, 273
  Greek Yogurt with Apricots, Honey, and Crunch, 275
  Grilled Peaches, 276
  Honey-Berry Ice Pops, 270
  Warm and Creamy Fruit Dessert, 272
  Wine-Poached Ginger Pears, 274
  Yogurt-Blueberry Bites, 269
DHA, in fish, 129, 130
Diabetes
  from stress, 175
  type 2
    health risks from, 44, 78–80
    managing, 82
    preventing, 80–82, 99, 110, 120, 132
  type 3, 79, 136
Diet
  for Alzheimer's and dementia prevention, 4, 6, 9, 65
  for blood pressure reduction, 74
  brain-healthy, 12, 39, 77–78 (see also Brain-boosting foods)
  fiber-rich, 81
  heart-healthy, 77–78
  quiz assessing, 45–48
Digestive system, stress harming, 180
Dill
  Mustard Greens with Dill and Lemon, 264
Dinners, 223
  Baked Eggplant with Nutty Tomato Chutney, 250
  Baked Turkey Cutlets with Savory Mushrooms and Peppers, 249
  Chicken and Potato Salad Over Greens, 255
  Chicken with Seven-Vegetable Couscous, 252
  Greek Lemon Chicken, 257
  Grilled Fish and White Bean Salad, 258
  Grilled Salmon with Brown Rice, 261
  Mediterranean Cod, 260
  Pasta Primavera with Pine Nuts, 253
  Roasted Catfish with Zesty Sweet Potatoes, 251
  Salmon in Vegetable Broth with Potato Slices, 262–63
  Seared Salmon Over Curried Lentils, 256
  Spicy Vegetarian Stir-Fry with Toasted Almonds, 254
  Tilapia and Spinach in Spicy Tomato Sauce, 259
Diseases, chronic, diet preventing, 99
DLB (dementia with Lewy bodies), 34
Dopamine, 26
Dumbbells, 288

E

Education level, 56
  for cognitive reserve, 204–5
  effect on Alzheimer's and dementia risk, 11, 11, 43, 205
Eggplant
  Baked Eggplant with Nutty Tomato Chutney, 250
Eggs
  Mediterranean Scramble, 231
  Persian Herb Omelet, 224–25
Emotional problems, as Alzheimer's trigger, 5
Emotional resilience
  building, 168–70, 171, 194
  reducing Alzheimer's risk, 168
  traits associated with, 167, 170–71
Estrogen, Alzheimer's risk and, 10–11
Exercise. See also Physical activity
  for Alzheimer's disease prevention, 4, 6, 9, 12–13
  balance, 36, 142, 151
  cardio, 134–35, 141–42, 148–49
  everyday movements as, 143
  health benefits of, 33, 67, 74, 133–40, 148–49, 182
  increasing hippocampus size, 21
  maximum heart rate and, 144
  motivators for, 149–53
  quiz assessing, 48–51
  recommendations for, 141–42
  in retirement, 208
  for sleep improvement, 199
  strength-training, 142, 146–48 (see also Strength-training workouts)
  tweaking routines in, 211
  walking as (see Walking)
  workouts, 138–39, 140–41
Extraversion, as personality trait, 157

F

Falls, preventing, 36
Family history, as Alzheimer's and dementia risk
    factor, 5, 15, 38, 43
Fats, dietary
    good vs. bad, 106, 108
    for heart health, 77–78
    in walnuts, 121
Fennel
    Lemon-Garlic Roasted Cauliflower with
        Fennel and Gremolata, 266
Fiber
    health benefits of, 81, 103
    recommended intake of, 103
    in whole grains, 110
    whole grains vs., 111
Fight, flight, or freeze response, 177
Fish
    cooking methods for, 131
    Curried Barley Salad with Shrimp and Baby
        Greens, 240
    Grilled Fish and White Bean Salad, 258
    Grilled Salmon with Brown Rice, 261
    Mediterranean Cod, 260
    mercury in, 130, 131
    in MIND diet, 129–30
    Roasted Catfish with Zesty Sweet Potatoes,
        251
    Roasted Red Peppers with Anchovies, 265
    Salmon in Vegetable Broth with Potato Slices,
        262–63
    sardines, 131
    Seared Salmon Over Curried Lentils, 256
    selecting, 131
    Tilapia and Spinach in Spicy Tomato Sauce,
        259
Flavonoids, 106, 107, 122
Flaxseeds
    Flax-Almond Pancakes, 226
Folate, 106, 116, 124
Forebrain, 20, 26
Forgetfulness, in senior moments, 3, 30. *See also*
    Memory loss
Free radicals, 22, 107
Frontal lobes, of brain, 20–21
Frontotemporal dementia (FTD), 34
Fruits. *See also specific fruits*
    Fruit 'n' Nut Muffins, 232
    local and organic, 88–89
    Warm and Creamy Fruit Dessert, 272
FTD (frontotemporal dementia), 34

G

GABA, 26
Games
    computer-based brain training, 6, 13, 27,
        205–6
    for mental stimulation, 12, 218–19
    video, 219–21
Garlic
    Lemon-Garlic Roasted Cauliflower with
        Fennel and Gremolata, 266
Genetics, Alzheimer's risk and, 5, 10, 14–15,
    37–38
Ginger
    Wine-Poached Ginger Pears, 274
Gingivitis, 82
Glutamine, 26
Grape-Nuts cereal
    Greek Yogurt with Apricots, Honey, and
        Crunch, 275
Grapes
    Fruit 'n' Nut Muffins, 232
Gray matter, of brain, 20, 25, 73, 137–38, 179,
    184–85
Greens
    Chicken and Potato Salad Over Greens, 255
    choosing, 118–19
    Curried Barley Salad with Shrimp and Baby
        Greens, 240
    healthiest, 117
    Mediterranean Salad Wraps, 244
    in MIND diet, 116–17
    Mustard Greens with Dill and Lemon, 264
    preparing, 119–20
    vitamin K in, 106
Gremolata
    Lemon-Garlic Roasted Cauliflower with
        Fennel and Gremolata, 266
Gum disease, 82–84

H

Habits, effect on health, 41
HDL cholesterol
    desired level of, 78
    exercise increasing, 74
    with metabolic syndrome, 69
Head injuries, 36, 205
Heart attack risk factors, 69, 71, 75, 77, 180
Heart disease. *See also* Cardiovascular disease
    from chronic stress, 175
    CRP levels and, 66

from oxidative stress, 107
  preventing, 99, 106, 110, 120, 125
Heart failure, 77, 180
Heart health
  Alzheimer's risk and, 11, 75–77
  guidelines for, 77–78
  stress harming, 180
Heart monitor, 144
Hemorrhagic stroke, 72, 73
Herbs
  Persian Herb Omelet, 224–25
High blood pressure
  from belly fat, 70
  dementia risk and, 44, 71, 73
  health risks from, 71–73, 150, 180
  with metabolic syndrome, 69
  reducing or preventing, 74–75, 99, 100, 101,
    125
  from stress, 175, 180
Hindbrain, 20
Hippocampus
  Alzheimer's disease starting in, 35
  factors enlarging, 21, 29, 138, 139, 145,
    184, 185
  function of, 28, 80
  shrinkage of, 21, 79–80, 137, 139, 160–61
  stress damaging, 176, 177–78, 181
Hobbies, 160, 211–12
Homocysteine, 95, 106
Honey
  Greek Yogurt with Apricots, Honey, and
    Crunch, 275
  Honey-Berry Ice Pops, 270
Hula-hooping, 151–52
Humanely raised animals, 129
Hypertension. See High blood pressure
Hypothalamus, 28

I

Ice pops
  Honey-Berry Ice Pops, 270
IGF-1, 147
Immune system, stress weakening, 180
Inflammation
  acute, 64
  age-related, 22
  from belly fat, 68
  chronic, 64–66, 75, 80
  foods promoting, 111
  reducing, 66–67, 109, 121, 122, 132, 189
Ingredient lists, reading, 110–11

Insulin resistance, 78–79, 79, 136
Integrated pest management (IPM), 90–91
Intelligence, effect of age on, 9
Interleukin-6, 67, 194
Interval training, 138
IPM (integrated pest management), 90–91
Ischemic stroke, 69, 72, 73

J

Journaling, as resilience builder, 170
Juggling, 25, 212

K

Kale
  Green Machine Smoothie, 235
Kirtan Kriya meditation, 187, 189, 190–91
Kiwifruit
  Green Machine Smoothie, 235
Knitting, 211–12
Kundalini yoga, 187, 190

L

Language ability, effect of age on, 9
Language lessons, 215–16
LDL cholesterol
  Alzheimer's risk and, 75
  belly fat increasing, 70
  desired level of, 78
  exercise lowering, 74
  trans fats increasing, 108
Leafy greens. See Greens
Learning opportunities, for increasing cognitive
    reserve, 29–30
Legumes, 101. See also Beans; Lentils
Lemons
  Greek Lemon Chicken, 257
  Lemon-Garlic Roasted Cauliflower with
    Fennel and Gremolata, 266
  Mustard Greens with Dill and Lemon,
    264
Lentils, 125
  Long-Grain Rice and Lentil Soup, 239
  Seared Salmon Over Curried Lentils, 256
Lewy bodies, dementia with, 34, 130
Limbic system, of brain, 28
Lizard brain, 21, 28, 176
Local produce, 88–89
London cabbies, brain study on, 29
Loneliness, 23, 159

Lunches, 223
  Curried Barley Salad with Shrimp and Baby
    Greens, 240
  Long-Grain Rice and Lentil Soup, 239
  Mediterranean Bulgur Salad, 246
  Mediterranean Salad Wraps, 244
  Mediterranean Turkey Burgers, 247
  Quinoa Salad with Carrot Fries, 245
  Quinoa with Raisins, Apricots, and Pecans,
    242
  Savory Sautéed Pepper and Chicken Sandwich,
    238
  Simmered Chickpeas in Tomato Sauce, 248
  Spinach Salad with Almond-Encrusted
    Chicken Breast, 236
  Tabbouleh with Fruit, 243
  Tomatoes Stuffed with White Bean Salad,
    237
  Vegetable Stew with Quinoa, 241
Lutein, 106, 116

M

Magnesium, 106, 110
Maple syrup
  Baked Apples with Almonds and Maple Syrup,
    271
Marital status, dementia risk and, 44
Maximum heart rate, 144
MBSR (Mindfulness-Based Stress Reduction),
    176, 182–86, 188
MCI. See Mild cognitive impairment
Meals, brain-healthy, 12, 223
  breakfasts, 224–35
  desserts, 269–76
  dinners, 249–63
  lunches, 236–48
  side dishes, 264–68
Medications
  as Alzheimer's and dementia trigger, 5, 63–64,
    91–94
  antihypertensive, 74–75
  sleep disruption from, 200
Meditation
  body scan, 188–89
  guided, 186
  Kirtan Kriya, 187, 189, 190–91
  yoga and, 187–91
Mediterranean diet
  foods in, 77–78, 99–100, 100–101
    servings of, 105
  health benefits of, 77–78, 100, 101, 108–9

Memory
  brain's role in, 20, 21
  effect of age on, 8
  exercise improving, 145
  olive oil protecting, 126–27
  poor sleep harming, 196, 198
  scents linked to, 28
  spatial, 28
  yoga/meditation improving, 187–88
Memory loss
  causes of
    disease, 7
    high blood pressure, 71
    high cortisol, 178
    metabolic syndrome, 69
    mild cognitive impairment, 30–33, 183
  dementia risk and, 43
  dental health and, 82–83
  normal vs. abnormal, 31
Mental stimulation. See also Play
  for brain health, 9–12, 15–16, 39
  quiz assessing, 56–58
Mercury, in fish, 130, 131
Metabolic syndrome, 69, 70
Microglia, inflammation and, 66
Midbrain, 20
Mild cognitive impairment (MCI)
  APOE-e4 gene and, 10
  caffeine and, 118
  depression and, 162
  description of, 30–33
  diabetes and, 80
  gum disease and, 82
  predicting risk of, 43
  preventing or delaying, 6, 33, 185
  sleep-disordered breathing and, 84, 85
  stress and, 183
MIND diet
  foods avoided in, 109
  foods in, 12, 65, 77–78, 100, 101, 223
    alcohol/wine, 131–32
    beans, 123–25
    berries, 122–23
    fish, 129–31
    green leafy vegetables, 116–20
    nuts, 120–22
    olive oil, 125–28
    poultry, 128–29
    servings of, 102, 105
    whole grains, 109–11, 112–15, 116
  health benefits of, 77–78, 108–9
Mindfulness, 182, 186

Mindfulness-Based Stress Reduction (MBSR), 176, 182–86, <u>188</u>
Mindfulness meditation, 33, 67, <u>184–85</u>, 186
Minerals, in plant foods, 103, 106
Mixed dementia, 35
Monounsaturated fats, 78, 106, 127
Motivation, for exercise, 149–53
Motor neurons, <u>24–25</u>
Movements, everyday, <u>143</u>
Mp3 player, 152
Muffins
    Fruit 'n' Nut Muffins, 232
Mushrooms
    Baked Turkey Cutlets with Savory Mushrooms and Peppers, 249
    Bulgur with Mushrooms and Roasted Red Peppers, 267
    Vegetable Stew with Quinoa, 241
Music, as exercise motivator, 152
Music lessons, 217–18
Mustard greens
    Mustard Greens with Dill and Lemon, 264

N

Naps, <u>197</u>
Neurogenesis, 8, 24, 25
Neuron forest, <u>24–25</u>
Neurons
    in brain, 19
    death of, with Alzheimer's disease, 8, 35
    effect of dementia on, 33, 34
    growing new, 16, 24, 27, <u>32</u>, 38
    neurotransmitters and, <u>26</u>
    in older brain, 21–22
    protecting, with
        antioxidants, 106, <u>118</u>
        berries, 122
        exercise, 133, 135–36, <u>140</u>, 147
    types of, <u>24–25</u>
Neuroticism, 157, <u>164</u>, 168
Neurotransmitters, 21, <u>26</u>
Nicotine patch, for smoking cessation, 96
Nuts. *See also* specific nuts
    for brain health, 101
    Candied Spiced Nuts, 273
    choosing, 121
    Fruit 'n' Nut Muffins, 232
    in MIND diet, 120–21
    storing, 122
    uses for, 121

O

Oats, <u>112–13</u>
    Hearty Oatmeal and Greek Yogurt, 230
    Overtime Oats, 227
Obesity
    BMI indicating, 68
    dementia risk and, <u>44</u>
    diet preventing, 99
    from stress, 175
Occipital lobes, of brain, <u>21</u>
Olive oil
    buying and storing, 128
    extra-virgin vs. other types, <u>126</u>
    in MIND diet, 125–27
    uses for, <u>126</u>, 127
Olive tapenade
    Mediterranean Salad Wraps, 244
Omega-3 fats, 121, 129, 130, 131
Omelet
    Persian Herb Omelet, 224–25
Onions
    Chicken with Seven-Vegetable Couscous, 252
Openness to experience, as personality trait, 156
Oranges
    Warm and Creamy Fruit Dessert, 272
Organic foods
    poultry, 128–29
    produce, <u>88–89</u>, 90, 123
Overweight, BMI indicating, 68
Oxidative stress, 95, 106, <u>107</u>, 109, 121
Oxytocin, 194, 195

P

PAD (peripheral artery disease), 77
Pancakes
    Flax-Almond Pancakes, 226
    Strawberry Pancakes, 229
Parietal lobes, of brain, <u>21</u>
Parkinson's disease dementia, 34
Pasta
    Pasta Primavera with Pine Nuts, 253
Peaches
    Grilled Peaches, 276
Peanut butter
    Peanut Butter and Yogurt Smoothie, 233
Pears
    Wine-Poached Ginger Pears, 274
Pecans
    Quinoa with Raisins, Apricots, and Pecans, 242
Pedometer, 70–71

Peppers
  Baked Turkey Cutlets with Savory Mushrooms
    and Peppers, 249
  Bulgur with Mushrooms and Roasted Red
    Peppers, 267
  Chicken with Seven-Vegetable Couscous, 252
  Pasta Primavera with Pine Nuts, 253
  Roasted Red Peppers with Anchovies, 265
  Savory Sautéed Pepper and Chicken Sandwich,
    238
Periodontitis, 82, 83
Peripheral artery disease (PAD), 77
Personality traits
  Big Five, 156–57
  changing, 155–56
Pesticides
  as Alzheimer's trigger, 5, 63, 86–89
  avoiding, 88–89, 90–91
  berries treated with, 123
  cautions with, 91
Phenolic acid, 106, 110
Photography, 212
Physical activity. See also Exercise
  for Alzheimer's disease prevention, 23, 140–41
  for brain health, 16, 39
  quiz assessing, 48–51
  for stress reduction, 182
Phytonutrient sources
  beans, 124
  in MIND diet, 109
  plant foods, 106, 107
  tea, 118
  whole grains, 110
Pine nuts
  Pasta Primavera with Pine Nuts, 253
Plant-based diet
  for brain health, 100
  nutrients in, 102–3, 106, 108
Plaque, arterial, 75
Plaque, dental, 82
Plaques, brain, with Alzheimer's disease, 7–8, 23,
    27, 30, 32, 33, 35, 36, 65, 66, 92, 130, 161,
    168, 172, 181, 193, 193
Plasticity, brain, 24–25, 27, 136, 189
Play
  for brain health, 15–16, 203–4
  for building cognitive reserve, 206–7
  suggestions for
    arts and crafts, 212–13
    game playing, 218–19
    hobbies, 211–12
    language lessons, 215–16

    music lessons, 217–18
    retiring to something, 207–8
    smarter screen use, 214–15
    tweaking routines, 209–11
    video games, 219–21
Polyunsaturated fats, 77, 106
Popcorn, 112–13, 127
Potatoes
  Chicken and Potato Salad Over Greens, 255
  Salmon in Vegetable Broth with Potato Slices,
    262–63
Poultry. See also Chicken; Turkey
  cooking methods for, 129
  in MIND diet, 128
  organic, 128–29
  safe handling of, 129
PPIs (proton pump inhibitors), 92, 94
Prebiotics, 81, 103
Prediabetes, 80–81
Prefrontal cortex, 176, 179, 182
Presenilin 1 and presenilin 2 proteins, 14
Problem solving, effect of age on, 8
Processed foods, 99
Processing speed of brain
  age affecting, 8–9, 22
  lifestyle improving, 6
Produce, local or organic, 88–89, 90
Protein
  needed by brain, 102
  in poultry, 128
  recommended intake of, 102–3
Proton pump inhibitors (PPIs), 92, 94
Purpose in life
  as exercise motivator, 152–53
  health benefits of, 171–73
  identifying, 173–74
Puzzles, 12, 219

Q

Quilting, 211–12
Quinoa, 114–15
  Quinoa Salad with Carrot Fries, 245
  Quinoa with Raisins, Apricots, and Pecans, 242
  Vegetable Stew with Quinoa, 241
Quiz, on brain health. See Ageless Brain quiz

R

Raisins
  Quinoa with Raisins, Apricots, and Pecans,
    242

Raspberries
   Honey-Berry Ice Pops, 270
   Tabbouleh with Fruit, 243
Reasoning, effect of age on, 8
Recipes, trying new, 210
Religious Orders Study, 22, 23–24, 30, 32, 165, 179–80
Remote memory, 8
Resveratrol, in red wine, 132
Retirement, 205, 207–8
Rice, brown, 114–15
   Grilled Salmon with Brown Rice, 261
   Long-Grain Rice and Lentil Soup, 239

S

Salads
   Chicken and Potato Salad Over Greens, 255
   Curried Barley Salad with Shrimp and Baby Greens, 240
   Grilled Fish and White Bean Salad, 258
   Mediterranean Bulgur Salad, 246
   Mediterranean Salad Wraps, 244
   Quinoa Salad with Carrot Fries, 245
   Spinach Salad with Almond-Encrusted Chicken Breast, 236
   Tomatoes Stuffed with White Bean Salad, 237
Salmon
   Grilled Fish and White Bean Salad, 258
   Grilled Salmon with Brown Rice, 261
   Salmon in Vegetable Broth with Potato Slices, 262–63
   Seared Salmon Over Curried Lentils, 256
Sandwiches
   Mediterranean Turkey Burgers, 247
   Savory Sautéed Pepper and Chicken Sandwich, 238
Sardines, 131
Saturated fats, 77, 106, 109
SDB (sleep-disordered breathing), 84–85
Seeds, 121–22
Selective serotonin reuptake inhibitors (SSRIs), 164–65
Self-compassion, for stress management, 194–96
Senior moments, 3, 30
Sensory neurons, 24, 25
Serotonin, 26
Sewing, 211–12
SHARP pillars of brain health, 12–16, 39. See also Attitude; Brain-boosting foods; Exercise; Play; Stress management

Short-term memory, effect of age on, 8
Shrimp
   Curried Barley Salad with Shrimp and Baby Greens, 240
Side dishes
   Bulgur with Mushrooms and Roasted Red Peppers, 267
   Lemon-Garlic Roasted Cauliflower with Fennel and Gremolata, 266
   Mustard Greens with Dill and Lemon, 264
   Roasted Red Peppers with Anchovies, 265
   Zucchini and Carrots with Toasted Walnuts, 268
Side sleeping, 193
Singing, 217–18
Sleep
   for Alzheimer's disease prevention, 4, 9
   for brain health, 14–17
   improving, 198–200
   quiz assessing, 55
Sleep apnea, 55, 64, 82, 84–86, 196, 200
Sleep deprivation, 176
Sleep-disordered breathing (SDB), 84–85
Sleep position, 193
Sleep problems
   contributors to, 197
   effect on memory, 196, 198
   inflammation from, 66–67
Smoking
   dementia risk and, 44, 94–95
   quitting, 67, 95, 96
Smoothies
   Almond, Blueberry, and Banana Smoothie, 234
   Green Machine Smoothie, 235
   Love-Your-Brain Smoothie, 228
   Peanut Butter and Yogurt Smoothie, 233
Snacks, late-night, 197
Snoring, 55, 64, 82, 84, 85
Social interaction
   health benefits of, 10, 23, 30, 158
   quiz assessing, 51
   in retirement, 208
   sources of, 159–61
Social isolation, 158–59
Soda, belly fat from, 70
Soup
   Long-Grain Rice and Lentil Soup, 239
Spinach
   Chicken with Seven-Vegetable Couscous, 252
   Love-Your-Brain Smoothie, 228

Spinach (*cont.*)
　Mediterranean Scramble, 231
　Spinach Salad with Almond-Encrusted
　　　Chicken Breast, 236
　Tilapia and Spinach in Spicy Tomato Sauce, 259
SSRIs, 164–65
Stew
　Vegetable Stew with Quinoa, 241
Stir-fry
　Spicy Vegetarian Stir-Fry with Toasted
　　　Almonds, 254
Strawberries
　choosing and storing, 123
　health benefits of, 16, 122
　Strawberry Pancakes, 229
Strength training
　health benefits of, 146–48
　recommended amount of, 142
Strength-training workouts
　guidelines for, 148–49, 277
　seated routine, 277
　　abs rotation, 286, **286**
　　backward lean, 287, **287**
　　chest squeeze, 278, **278**
　　curl and press, 280, **280**
　　leg extensions, 283, **283**
　　leg taps, 282, **282**
　　repetitions and sets in, 278
　　shoulder retraction, 279, **279**
　　thigh push, 285, **285**
　　thigh squeeze, 284, **284**
　　triceps extension, 281, **281**
　standing routine, 277
　　back pull, 289, **289**
　　biceps curl to shoulder push, 291, **291**
　　dumbbells for, 288
　　elbow-to-knee crunch, 297, **297**
　　front arm raise, 290, **290**
　　knee lift, 292, **292**
　　leg pushback, 293, **293**
　　leg side press, 294, **294**
　　leg side pull, 295, **295**
　　repetitions and sets in, 288
　　side bends, 296, **296**
　　standing pushup, 288, **288**
Stress
　acute, 175
　bodily effects of, 180
　brain effects of, 21, 175–76
　chronic, 175–76, 177–78
　dementia risk from, 179–82
　sources of, 178–79

Stress burden, quiz assessing, 54–56
Stress management
　for brain health, 4, 14–15, 39
　for heart health, 78
　techniques, 176
　　body scan, 188–89
　　deep breathing, 184–85
　　exercise, 182
　　Mindfulness-Based Stress Reduction, 176,
　　　182–86
　　mindfulness meditation, 67
　　self-compassion, 194–96
　　sleep, 176, 196–200
　　tai chi, 191–93
　　yoga, 187–91
Stress response, 177, 178, 182, 194
Strokes
　alcohol and, 74
　diabetes and, 80
　from high blood pressure, 71, 73, 180
　preventing, 72, 106, 120, 125
　recovery from, 216
　silent, 73
　from small vessel disease, 150
　symptoms of, 72
Sunlight, effect on sleep, 199
Support groups, 161
SVD (small vessel disease), 150
Sweet potatoes
　Roasted Catfish with Zesty Sweet Potatoes, 251
　Vegetable Stew with Quinoa, 241
Synapses, 19, 24

T

Tabbouleh
　Tabbouleh with Fruit, 243
Tai chi, 151, 191–93
Tangles, with Alzheimer's disease, 8, 23, 27, 30,
　　32, 33, 35, 36, 65, 66, 92, 130, 149, 161,
　　168, 172, 181, 193
Tau proteins, 8, 27, 35, 92, 149, 181, 193
Tea, health benefits of, 118–19
Technology use, sleep disruption from, 197
Television viewing, 214, 215, 216
Temporal lobes, of brain, 21
10 commandments of ageless brain, 17
　blood pressure control, 71, 73–75
　cardiovascular health, 75–78
　dental health, 82–84
　diabetes prevention or management, 78–82
　inflammation reduction, 64–67

medication caution, 91–94
pesticide avoidance, 86–91
sleep apnea treatment, 84–86
smoking cessation, 94–96
weight loss, 68, 70–71
Text messages, for smoking cessation, 96
Thalamus, 28
TIA (transient ischemic attack), 72
Tilapia
Tilapia and Spinach in Spicy Tomato Sauce, 259
Tofu
Spicy Vegetarian Stir-Fry with Toasted Almonds, 254
Tomatoes
Baked Eggplant with Nutty Tomato Chutney, 250
Mediterranean Scramble, 231
Pasta Primavera with Pine Nuts, 253
Simmered Chickpeas in Tomato Sauce, 248
Tilapia and Spinach in Spicy Tomato Sauce, 259
Tomatoes Stuffed with White Bean Salad, 237
Tooth loss, 82–83
Trans fats, 106, 108, 109
Transient ischemic attack (TIA), 72
Triglycerides, high
from belly fat, 70
with metabolic syndrome, 69
reducing, 125
Tumor necrosis factor, 67
Tuna
Grilled Fish and White Bean Salad, 258
Turkey
Baked Turkey Cutlets with Savory Mushrooms and Peppers, 249
Mediterranean Turkey Burgers, 247
Turnips
Chicken with Seven-Vegetable Couscous, 252

V
Varenicline, for smoking cessation, 96
Vascular dementia, 34, 71, 75, 76, 78, 80, 162
Vegetables. *See also specific vegetables*
Chicken with Seven-Vegetable Couscous, 252
local and organic, 88–89
for reducing brain age, 16
Salmon in Vegetable Broth with Potato Slices, 262–63
Vegetable Stew with Quinoa, 241
Video games, 219–21

Vitamin A, 106, 107
Vitamin C, 106, 107
Vitamin E, 106, 107, 110, 120
Vitamin K, 106, 116
Vitamins, in plant foods, 103, 106
Volunteerism, 153, 158, 160, 169, 208

W
Waist size
with metabolic syndrome, 69
reducing, 71
Walking
brisk, 192, 197
health benefits of, 138, 139, 142–45, 149
pace for, 144
proper form for, 145–46
for reducing
belly fat, 70–71
inflammation, 67
stroke risk, 72
in retirement, 208
tweaking routine for, 138, 139, 211
Walnuts
Candied Spiced Nuts, 273
Fruit 'n' Nut Muffins, 232
health benefits of, 121
Zucchini and Carrots with Toasted Walnuts, 268
Weight loss
diets for, 100
for reducing
belly fat, 68, 70–71
blood pressure, 74
brain age, 16
diabetes risk, 81–82
Wheat berries, 112–13
White matter, of brain, 73, 128, 137, 138, 212
Whole foods, 66, 74, 77, 101, 103
Whole grains
health benefits of, 101, 111
identifying, 110–11
in MIND diet, 109–11
preparing and storing, 116
sources of, 112–16
Wild rice, 114–15
Wine. *See also* Alcohol use
health benefits of, 132
Wine-Poached Ginger Pears, 274
Winter squash
Chicken with Seven-Vegetable Couscous, 252
Women, Alzheimer's disease in, 10–11

Workouts
    increasing challenge of, 138–39
    for reducing Alzheimer's risk, 140–41
    strength-training (*see* Strength-training
        workouts)
Worry
    effect on brain health, 14–15
    quiz assessing, 53
Wraps
    Mediterranean Salad Wraps, 244

Y

Yoga, for stress management, 187–91
Yogurt
    Greek Yogurt with Apricots, Honey, and
        Crunch, 275
    Green Machine Smoothie, 235
    Hearty Oatmeal and Greek Yogurt, 230
    Love-Your-Brain Smoothie, 228
    Peanut Butter and Yogurt Smoothie, 233
    Yogurt-Blueberry Bites, 269

Z

Zucchini
    Chicken with Seven-Vegetable Couscous,
        252
    Zucchini and Carrots with Toasted Walnuts,
        268